D1569644

THE IMPORTANCE OF PSYCHOLOGICAL TRAITS
A CROSS-CULTURAL STUDY

THE PLENUM SERIES IN SOCIAL/CLINICAL PSYCHOLOGY

Series Editor: C. R. Snyder

University of Kansas
Lawrence, Kansas

Current Volumes in the Series:

ADVANCED PERSONALITY
Edited by David F. Barone, Michel Hersen, and
Vincent B. Van Hasselt

AGGRESSION
Biological, Developmental, and Social Perspectives
Edited by Seymour Feshbach and Jolanta Zagrodzka

AVERSIVE INTERPERSONAL BEHAVIORS
Edited by Robin M. Kowalski

COERCION AND AGGRESSIVE COMMUNITY TREATMENT
A New Frontier in Mental Health Law
Edited by Deborah L. Dennis and John Monahan

THE IMPORTANCE OF PSYCHOLOGICAL TRAITS
A Cross-Cultural Study
John E. Williams, Robert C. Satterwhite, and José L. Saiz

PERSONAL CONTROL IN ACTION
Cognitive and Motivational Mechanisms
Edited by Miroslaw Kofta, Gifford Weary, and Grzegorz Sedek

THE PSYCHOLOGY OF VANDALISM
Arnold P. Goldstein

THE REVISED NEO PERSONALITY INVENTORY
Clinical and Research Applications
Ralph L. Piedmont

SOCIAL COGNITIVE PSYCHOLOGY
History and Current Domains
David F. Barone, James E. Maddux, and C. R. Snyder

SOURCEBOOK OF SOCIAL SUPPORT AND PERSONALITY
Edited by Gregory R. Pierce, Brian Lakey, Irwin G. Sarason, and
Barbara R. Sarason

THE IMPORTANCE OF PSYCHOLOGICAL TRAITS
A CROSS-CULTURAL STUDY

JOHN E. WILLIAMS
Georgia State University
Atlanta, Georgia

ROBERT C. SATTERWHITE
Georgia Institute of Technology
Atlanta, Georgia

and

JOSÉ L. SAIZ
Universidäd de La Frontera
Temuco, Chile

PLENUM PRESS • NEW YORK AND LONDON

Library of Congress Cataloging-in-Publication Data

Williams, John E., 1928-
    The importance of psychological traits : a cross-cultural study /
John E. Williams, Robert C. Satterwhite, and José L. Saiz.
        p.   cm.
    Includes bibliographical references and index.
    ISBN 0-306-45889-6
    1. Personality and culture--Cross-cultural studies.
2. Ethnopsychology--Cross-cultural studies.   I. Satterwhite, Robert
C. II. Saiz, José L.   III. Title.
BF698.9.C8W55   1998
155.2'3--dc21   98-41543
                                                                CIP

ISBN 0-306-45889-6

© 1998 Plenum Press, New York
A Division of Plenum Publishing Corporation
233 Spring Street, New York, N.Y. 10013

http://www.plenum.com

Printed in the United States of America

COOPERATING RESEARCHERS

The authors are greatly indebted to the following persons for their assistance with this project:

Ahams N. Adom, Nigeria and Norway

Marja Ahokas, Finland

Hasan Bacanli, Turkey

Michael Harris Bond and Royce Lee, Hong Kong

María Martina Casullo, Argentina

Kai Sook Chung, Korea

Abdul Haque, Pakistan

Dennis McInerney, Australia

Félix Neto, Portugal

Murari Prasad Regmi, Nepal

Esteban Roa, Venezuela

Purnima Singh, India

Louis W. C. Tavecchio, Netherlands

Hsiao Ying Tsai, Japan

Hans-Georg Voss, Germany

Colleen Ward, Singapore

Jiayuan Yu, China

To
Jane, Charlotte, and Ginger
Cat and Aidan
and to
Eugenia and Thomás

PREFACE

All traits were not created equal.
—WORCHEL AND COOPER (1983, p. 180)

This book reports the findings from extensive cross-cultural studies of the relative importance of different psychological traits in 20 countries and the relative favorability of these traits in a subset of 10 countries. While the work is devoted primarily to professionals and advanced students in the social sciences, the relatively nontechnical style employed should make the book comprehensible to anyone with a general grasp of the concepts and strategies of empirical behavioral science.

The project grew out of discussions between the first author and third author while the latter was a graduate student at Wake Forest University, U.S.A., in 1990. The third author, a native of Chile, was studying person-descriptive adjectives composing the stereotypes associated with the Chilean aboriginal minority known as Mapuche (Saiz & Williams, 1992). As we examined the adjectives used in this study, it was clear that they differed in favorability, and also on another dimension which we later termed "psychological importance," i.e., the degree to which adjectives reflected more "central," as opposed to more "peripheral," personality characteristics. More important descriptors were those which seemed more informative or diagnostic of what a person "was really like" and, hence, might be of greater significance in understanding and predicting an individual's behavior.

This discussion led to a study in which Wake Forest undergraduates rated the 300 items of the Adjective Check List for psychological importance. This study demonstrated that this concept could be reliably rated and that the importance ratings showed only a modest positive correlation with previously obtained favorability ratings. After these

ix

findings were replicated in Chile, we decided to initiate a major project to examine the question of cross-cultural similarities and differences in the importance assigned to various psychological traits. To this end, we enlisted the cooperation of psychologists in 18 additional countries, as listed on the cooperating researchers page of this book.

The psychological characteristics studied are the 300 items of the Adjective Check List (Gough & Heilbrun, 1980), translated as necessary. This highly versatile item pool has been used in previous cross-cultural studies of gender stereotypes (Williams & Best, 1990a), self concepts (Williams & Best, 1990b), and age stereotypes (Best & Williams, 1996; Williams, 1993). This use of a common method enables one to compare the relative degree of cross-cultural agreement in the various concepts studied (see Chapter 9).

Unique to the book are the appendices that enable interested readers to test hypotheses of their own devising related to the psychological importance and/or favorability of selected sets of person descriptors in different cultural settings. Appendix D provides, for the first time, the individual item values for the Five Factor scoring system for the Adjective Check List described by FormyDuval, Williams, Patterson, and Fogle (1995).

The authors are greatly indebted to our cooperating researchers and to the approximately 2,000 university students who served as research subjects. We are grateful for the support given the project by the Department of Psychology at Wake Forest University, during the data collection and analysis stages, and the Department of Psychology of Georgia State University, during the manuscript preparation stage. We express our appreciation to Deborah FormyDuval and Stephen Davis for their assistance with scoring and statistical analysis and to Teresa Hill for her outstanding work with the word processor.

Viewed broadly, the voluntary participation by researchers from 20 countries provides a compelling illustration of international scientific cooperation. The successful completion of such a project holds a promise for the further advance of knowledge in the increasingly important area of cross-cultural psychology.

John E. Williams
Robert C. Satterwhite
José L. Saiz

CONTENTS

Chapter 8

Chapter 9

CONCEPTS AND ISSUES IN CROSS-CULTURAL PSYCHOLOGY

All persons are psychologists! Everyone, almost every day, is involved in trying to understand and predict the behavior of the people with whom he or she interacts. In this effort, one of the first things we learn is that behavior is not determined entirely by situational factors but that, for a given person, there are consistencies in behavior across situations and through time. Statements in which we confidently declare, "Joe is like this" and "Susy is like that" imply a stability of personality across time and situations. The investigation of such behavioral consistencies is known in psychology as the study of "individual differences." In the sphere of personality, individual differences are usually discussed in terms of psychological traits, which are major behavioral dimensions on which persons may differ, e.g., Joe might be characterized as "extraverted" and Susy as "conscientious." The tendency to characterize persons by the use of trait adjectives seems a common feature of "folk psychologies" the world over.

How many different psychological characteristics are there? The answer depends on the level of analysis one employs. Years ago, Allport and Odbert (1936) surveyed English language sources of their day and found 17,953 words that referred to psychological states and characteristics! At the other extreme, we have the recent work by proponents of the Five Factor Model (e.g., McCrae & Costa, 1989) who believe that personality variation can be adequately conceptualized by five "supertraits." An intermediate approach is provided by Gough and Heilbrun's (1980) Adjective Check List (ACL), which contains 300 person-descriptive English adjectives (e.g., aggressive, emotional, adventurous, gentle, etc.).

The present project employs the ACL to determine whether some characteristics are considered "more important" in the sense that they provide more information concerning a person's psychological makeup and, thus, are more useful in understanding and predicting behavior. In this context, important is synonymous with "informative" or "diagnostic." In this study, we are interested in whether the psychological importance of traits varies across cultural groups and, secondarily, across gender.

Worchel and Cooper (1983, p. 180), in discussing the role of traits in person perception, have noted:

> We can use many different terms to describe people. We can say that a person is generous and kind, or intelligent and benevolent, or cruel and vindictive. But it sounds strange to say that a person is vindictive and neat. It is not that one trait is negative and the other positive; rather, we would probably all agree that the former is more important—that is, more central—in describing the person than the latter trait.

Consider the following situation. A friend of yours describes a person you have not met as *dependable* and *honest* as well as *awkward* and *forgetful*. Do these two pairs of characteristics seem equally important to you, or do the first two adjectives seem to convey more useful information than the second two? If the latter is true, would this also be true for persons from other cultures, or does the degree of importance of different traits vary with cultural influences? Perhaps the characteristics *autonomous* and *self-denying* would be considered of different importance in the more individualistic cultures of the West versus the more collectivistic cultures of the East. There is also the question of possible gender differences in psychological importance. Do women and men assign more importance to characteristics stereotypically associated with their own gender where, for example, women are said to be more affectionate and emotional and men are said to be more adventurous and rational? And is there a relationship between the importance of traits and their favorability? Are favorable and unfavorable characteristics of equal importance in providing information about a person's psychological makeup?

The current project addresses the foregoing questions in a study employing the importance ratings assigned to the 300 ACL adjectives, translated as necessary, by university students from 20 countries around the world and a secondary study of the favorability of the adjectives in 10 countries. While we refer to the project as being "cross-cultural" it is, strictly speaking, "cross-national" and relies on the assumption that it is meaningful to consider persons from different nations (e.g., Norway and Nigeria) as "carriers" of their respective "national cultures." In making this assumption, we are ignoring the very real cultural differences which may exist between different subgroups *within* some nations. Before proceeding to the project proper, we need to set the stage by a consideration of some of the issues involved in cross-cultural research and a review of some previous studies which have direct relationships to the present project.

CROSS-CULTURAL PSYCHOLOGY

Cross-cultural psychology has been defined as "the study of similarities and differences in individual psychological functioning in various cultural and ethnic groups; of the relationship between psychological variables and sociocultural, ecological, and biological variables; and of current changes in these variables" (Berry, Poortinga, Segall, & Dasen, 1992, p. 2).

Cross-cultural psychology is a relative newcomer on the scientific scene. Although there were important early antecedents (e.g., Bartlett, 1932; Rivers, 1905), the field is, for the most part, only a few decades old. This is reflected in two related facts: the *Journal of Cross-Cultural Psychology* began publication in 1970, and the International Association for Cross-Cultural Psychology was first organized in 1972. Another milestone in the evolution of the field was the 1980 publication of the first *Handbook of Cross-Cultural Psychology* (Triandis & Berry, 1980). A demonstration of the further maturing of the field is seen in the recent appearance of new journals (e.g., *Culture and Psychology, World Psychology*) and new textbooks dealing with culture and behavior for use in university courses (e.g., Berry et al., 1992; Brislin, 1993; Lonner & Malpass, 1994; Matsumoto, 1996; Moghaddam, 1998; Moghaddam, Taylor, & Wright, 1993; Segall, Dasen, Berry, & Poortinga, 1990; Smith & Bond, 1994; Thomas, 1993; Triandis, 1994). Paraphrasing Ebbinghaus' (1908) famous comment about the psychology of his day, we can say that cross-cultural psychology has had a long past but only a recent history.

In the following sections, we provide an overview of this relatively new field and consider some of the issues and methodological problems which arise in the effort to conduct sound, cross-cultural, psychological science. This discussion draws heavily on our earlier, more detailed treatment of these matters in previous books (Williams & Best, 1990a,

1990b), particularly the latter (pp. 15–23). The interested reader is also referred to the discussions of issues and problems in the first and second editions of the *Handbook of Cross-Cultural Psychology* (Berry, Poortinga, & Pandey, 1997; Triandis & Berry, 1980).

SCOPE OF THE FIELD

Marshall Segall (1986, p. 425), in an *Annual Review of Psychology* article, noted that "while all behavior occurs in cultural contexts, only a small portion of behavioral research attends to this . . . the preponderance of contemporary psychological research is still designed, conducted, and interpreted as if culture did not matter." Having evolved to rectify this neglect of cultural variables, the field of cross-cultural psychology focuses on the degree to which psychological processes vary as a result of differing cultural influences; that is, to what degree does the manner in which people think and behave vary as a function of the culture in which they have been reared and/or currently live?

Questions in cross-cultural psychology are often conceived in terms of whether psychological principles that appear to be valid in one setting can be successfully generalized to other settings. Consider the following questions. Are the stages of cognitive development identified by Western psychologists observed in all cultural settings? Does the law of effect apply evenly in all groups or are there societies in which the usual effects of rewards and punishments are modified by cultural influences? Is the phenomenon of "social loafing" (lowered production in a group setting) as evident in the more collectivistic cultures of the East as it is in the more individualistic countries of the West? Is ethnocentrism a pancultural phenomenon? How much do the characteristics desired in a mate vary with culture? To what degree are the same gender stereotypes found in different societies? Do Western theories of organizational behavior apply equally well in Eastern countries?

Considering the foregoing, it is clear that the area of cross-cultural psychology is *not* defined by its content but by the comparative nature of the questions it poses. In addressing such questions, cross-cultural psychology is concerned with exploring the generality of psychological theories and empirical findings across a variety of human groups. If generality is found, fine! If not, attempts are made to identify the cultural variables responsible for the observed difference. Although virtually any question in psychological science can be phrased in a cross-cultural manner, the preponderance of cross-cultural research has been in the areas of social, developmental, and personality psychology rather than in such basic science areas as cognition, perception, and biological psychology because the impact of culture is generally greater on the former areas than on the latter (Poortinga, 1992).

THE MEANING OF CULTURE

Let us pause to consider the meaning of the term *culture*. Richard Brislin (1983, p. 367), in an *Annual Review of Psychology* article, noted that "like a number of concepts long studied by psychologists, such as personality, intelligence, and abnormal behavior, there is no one definition of culture which is widely accepted." We will not add to the confusion by attempting our own formal definition of culture, but we would like to share our frame of reference regarding the concept.

At a very general level, the term *culture* is often employed as a concept referring to the global ways human societies differ from one another. When used at this level, the concept of culture limits the depth of cross-cultural research. For example, to ask whether differences in the behavior of industrial workers in Japan and the United States may be related to differences in Japanese and American "cultures" is only useful in identifying a general area of investigation; the question cannot be answered at this level of generality. One must examine the two cultures analytically and attempt to determine the more specific *cultural variables* (e.g., family structure, attitudes toward authority, and so on) that may be related to the behavioral differences we wish to understand. In Whiting's (1976) phrase, we must learn to "unpackage" cultures.

To the authors there is a general parallel between the use of *culture* and *cultural variables* with reference to societies, and the use of the terms *personality* and *personality variables* with reference to individual persons. Psychologists find the term *personality* useful in identifying a general domain of interest (as distinguished, for example, from the domain of perception), but efforts to understand differences in the behavior of individuals require a consideration of more specific *personality variables* (e.g., traits). Just as it is impossible to derive a unique score that reflects *the* personality of a person, it is impossible to deal with *the* culture of a society; specific cultural variables must be considered.

Although the term *culture* may be useful in identifying the "ball-park," we share the views of Munroe and Munroe (1980) and Segall (1986) that the "game" must be played at the level of specific cultural variables in attempting to explain behavioral variations between persons from different human societies. Thus, in the present project, we examine between-country differences in the importance of psychological characteristics in relation to such variables as individualism/collectivism and socioeconomic development.

PROBLEMS IN CROSS-CULTURAL PSYCHOLOGY

In view of the significance of cross-cultural findings, why is the cross-cultural strategy not more widely used? The answer lies, in part, in the difficulty of conducting good cross-cultural research. There are, for example, the obvious logistical problems in arranging to gather data in a number of geographically dispersed settings—an effortful and time-consuming task.

Other reasons for the neglect of cultural variables in psychological research seem to lie in the mentality of some investigators. On the one hand, there are psychologists who seem to assign little importance to culture because of their view that they are studying basic psychological *processes*, which are largely invariant in all human beings, and that culture merely provides the psychological *contents*, in which they are not interested. On the other hand, there seems to be another group of psychological researchers who ignore culture because they fear, perhaps unconsciously, that culture is *very* important and that their pet theories and related findings will not hold in other cultural settings. In our view, such a fear is largely irrational since the weight of evidence from cross-cultural research, to date, indicates that, psychologically speaking, people from different cultural groups are much more similar than they are different (see, e.g., Buss, 1989). If one has a robust theory, it is likely that it will have some application in other cultural settings, and may actually work better "over there."

Let us consider an illustration of how a theoretical concept developed in the West can be enriched when cross-cultural studies are conducted. The concept of *social loafing* was developed by Bibb Latané and his colleagues (Latané, Williams, & Harkins, 1979) based on the finding that, in the United States, individual productivity often declines in larger work groups. When this idea was studied in Taiwan (Gabrenya, Wang, & Latané, 1985) and Japan (Shirikasi, 1985; Yamaguchi, Okamoto, & Oka, 1985), an opposite *social striving* effect was observed in which group participation enhanced individual performance. Considering the more individualistic culture of the United States and the more collectivistic culture of Japan, the general principle may be that persons are more productive in "culturally congruent" work settings than in "culturally incongruent" ones. In this instance, cross-cultural research served to expand an important theoretical concept. The original concept of social loafing wasn't "wrong," just incomplete.

There are a number of methodological problems that the aspiring cross-cultural researcher must address. Cross-cultural research is often viewed as *quasi-experimental* in nature (Campbell & Stanley, 1966; Cook

& Campbell, 1979; Malpass & Poortinga, 1986). In this type of research, one studies the behavior of groups of persons who have been naturally exposed to different "treatments"—in this case, exposure to different levels of some cultural variable(s), e.g., nuclear versus extended families. The research objective is to approximate, as closely as possible, the experimental method where the groups to be compared are considered equivalent on all variables except the treatment variable(s).

Research using the quasi-experimental method must attempt to achieve equivalence in: the characteristics of the subject groups (other than the treatment difference); the research instruments; and the circumstances under which the data are collected. Only when such equivalence is at least approximated can the researcher reasonably conclude that observed behavioral differences are attributable to naturally occurring treatment differences. Quasi-experimental research is difficult enough when conducted within a single cultural group; all of the equivalence issues become greatly magnified when the research involves people from different cultural groups. For example, consider only the question of equivalence in research questionnaires when different languages are involved!

In cross-cultural research, the achievement of "equivalent" groups is often opposed to the achievement of "representative" groups. This is a problem of external *vs* internal validity or, in other words, between control of variables and generalizability of results. In the present study, our effort to obtain equivalent subject groups (equal numbers of men and women university students) is a conservative approach because the subject groups were made equivalent on some variables which might be considered to reflect cultural differences, such as between-country variation in the proportion of young people attending university or the ratio of men and women students in the university population.

A serious issue in cross-cultural research is what might be termed "intellectual imperialism" whereby the originating researcher (usually from the West) treats cooperating researchers in other countries as research assistants rather than as professional equals. This problem, which characterized several early projects in cross-cultural psychology, can be avoided by treating cooperating researchers as peers, welcoming their inputs in the planning, design, and analyses of the research, and properly recognizing their participation in subsequent publications. A specific practice which we have followed in the present project and in our previous cross-cultural work has been to treat the data collected at each site as the property of the local researcher who is free to use them as he or she chooses, e.g., reading or publishing a paper. All that we have asked is that the data be shared with us for purposes of cross-cultural comparisons. With such an egalitarian arrangement, it has been relatively easy to enlist the cooperation of scholars in other countries who are interested in cross-cultural research.

INTRACULTURAL VERSUS INTERCULTURAL VALIDITY

There are a number of theoretical and methodological issues to be addressed before a cross-cultural study is begun. One such matter, the *emic–etic distinction*, applies both to theoretical constructs and to measurements. Brislin (1980, pp. 390–391) has commented as follows:

> Briefly, the distinction relates to two goals of cross-cultural research. The first goal is to document valid principles that describe behavior in any one culture by using constructs that the people themselves conceive as meaningful and important; this is an emic analysis. The second goal of cross-cultural research is to make generalizations across cultures that take into account all human behavior. The goal, then is theory building; that would be an etic analysis.

From the foregoing, it can be seen that the emic view is concerned with questions of intracultural validity, a culture-specific approach; the etic view is concerned with intercultural or pancultural validity, a universal view. Berry (1980, p. 12) elaborated these concepts further:

> The *etic* approach is characterized by the presence of universals in a system. When these variables are assumed, they have been termed *imposed etic* (Berry, 1969, p. 124) or *pseudo etic* (Triandis, Malpass, & Davidson, 1972, p. 6). In such cases, these etics are usually only Euro-American emics, imposed blindly and even ethnocentrically on a set of phenomena which occur in other cultural systems. . . . On the other hand, a true etic is one which emerges from the phenomena; it is empirically derived from the common features of the phenomena. Such an etic has been termed a *derived etic*.

The terms *emic* and *etic* provide a useful vocabulary for the discussion of cross-cultural concepts and methodologies in the context of the present investigation which has both emic and etic features. We will examine these further in the methodological critique in Chapter 4.

STUDIES COMPARING SMALL VERSUS LARGE NUMBERS OF CULTURAL GROUPS

The ideal study in cross-cultural psychology would involve the intensive study of relevant behaviors in each of a large number of cultures. For practical reasons, this ideal is rarely achieved. Because the demands of data collection and analysis increase in proportion to the number of cultures studied, most cross-cultural studies tend to fall into one of two categories: the relatively intensive study of persons from small numbers of cultural groups (perhaps two or three) or the relatively less intensive study of persons from large numbers of groups (perhaps 10 or more). The two approaches have different advantages and disadvantages associated with them.

Studies involving small numbers of cultures can be further grouped into two categories, depending on whether the research is theory-guided or purely empirical. In the former, the cultures have been selected a priori because they differ on some salient cultural variable that, theoretically, should lead to predictable differences in behavior. Illustrating this approach are the many recent studies dealing with the topic of individualism/collectivism (e.g., Bochner, 1994; Gudykunst et al., 1992; Yamaguchi, Kuhlman, & Sugimori, 1995). In such studies the researcher: develops hypotheses about behavioral differences that should be found in more individualistic versus more collectivistic cultures; selects two or more cultures that have been independently classified as differing in individualism/collectivism (perhaps using Hofstede's index); and proceeds to see if the hypotheses are confirmed.

In contrast, there is the purely empirical study involving small numbers of cultures in which the groups are not chosen on a systematic, theoretical basis but are "targets of opportunity" that happen to be available to the researcher (see Lonner & Berry, 1986). The results of this type of study may or may not prove fruitful, depending on the nature of the findings. Studies of this sort may be useful when no important differences are found in the behavior of the subjects from the different cultural groups. Such findings, particularly when they are complex or patterned, merely provide evidence of the generality of the psychological principles involved. Difficulties arise, however, when significant differences are found in the behaviors of interest between or among the two or three cultural groups. In this situation, it is rarely possible to identify the salient aspects of the different cultures that account for the findings. If behavioral differences are found between people from two different societies, and if the two groups differ in a variety of cultural aspects like religion, economic development, and family structure, then it is difficult to know to which variable(s) one should attribute the observed differences.

By contrast, the merit in studies involving large numbers of cultures is that it may be possible to determine which cultural variables are associated with the behavioral differences observed. For example, if one has obtained data from 10 or 15 countries, then it is possible to correlate differences in behavior with indices of "cultural comparison variables" like religion, economic development, and family structure, and to determine which of these variables are associated across countries with the behavioral variation and which are not.

Cultural comparison variables in the present study included the following demographic variables: economic-social development; cultural homogeneity; population density; urbanization; and percent Christian affiliation, this being the only religion for which worldwide statistics were available. These variables were chosen for several reasons: they appeared to index different types of cultural variation; reasonably accurate data were available from library sources; and they had been found useful in previous large-scale cross-cultural studies. In addition, eleven indices of cultural values from the previous research of Hofstede (1980) and Schwartz (e.g., 1994) also were employed as comparison variables. Our interest was to determine whether any observed differences among countries in psychological importance (PI) were systematically associated with any of the 16 variables. In these analyses, countries rather than individual subjects constituted the unit of study.

TWO MAJOR CULTURAL DIMENSIONS

While we examine a variety of cultural comparison variables in the present study, two dimensions deserve special attention because of previous research findings linking them to cross-cultural differences on psychological variables. Both dimensions are viewed as complex composites of many factors rather than as simple, unitary variables.

Socioeconomic Development

Countries vary widely in their general level of socioeconomic development (SED). Measures of this multifaceted dimension reflect relative wealth, as well as the relative development of educational and health care systems. Western European countries tend to rank relatively high on such measures while most Asian countries rank relatively low.

Of interest in the present context are previous research findings indicating that, across countries, differences in SED are associated with a surprising number of psychological variables. Taking some illustrations from our own research, we found in our cross-cultural study of gender stereotypes (Williams & Best, 1990a) that the differences in the male and female stereotypes were greater in lower SED countries. In a related finding, it was shown that the self concepts of women and men are more differentiated in lower SED countries (Williams & Best, 1990b). In the area of sex role ideology, we found that young adults in lower SED countries approve of male-dominant relationships between men and women while in higher SED countries the model is more egalitarian

(Williams & Best, 1990b). Regarding age stereotypes, it was found that, while older adults were viewed as more nurturing than young adults in all countries, the nurturance difference between old and young was greater in higher SED countries (Williams, 1993). Other researchers (e.g., Hofstede, 1980) have also found strong linkages between psychological variables and SED.

The observed relationships between psychological variables and SED are, undoubtedly, mediated by differences on some more specific cultural variables. For example, the gender-related differences noted above are probably related to the fact that the status of women is generally higher in high SED countries than in low SED countries.

Findings such as those reviewed above provide the justification for the careful attention paid to SED in the present project.

Individualism and Collectivism

A second important dimension along which cultures may be located is individualism versus collectivism. Countries vary widely in the degree to which their dominant cultures may be described as being "individualistic" or "collectivistic." While these characteristics are correlated with SED, with greater individualism tending to be found in more developed countries, the two variables are sufficiently independent to warrant their separate consideration. In the present study, for example, the indices of individualism/collectivism and of SED have only 37 percent common variance.

Individualism/collectivism (I/C) has been a "hot topic" in cross-cultural psychology in recent years, generating a great deal of theoretical discussion and related empirical research with a major international conference devoted to this concept (Kim, Triandis, Kagitcibasi, Choi, & Yoon, 1994). An excellent overview of the topic is provided by Harry Triandis in his book *Individualism and Collectivism* (1995), where he refers to individualism and collectivism as "cultural syndromes" which are composed of more basic components. Triandis (1995, pp. 43–44) identifies four universal dimensions of the constructs, as follows:

1. The definition of the self is interdependent in collectivism and independent in individualism. . . . This is reflected in various aspects of daily life, including the extent to which individuals share resources with group members and conform to the norms of the group. . . .
2. Personal and communal goals are closely aligned in collectivism and not at all aligned in individualism. One can identify collectivism when group goals have priority and individualism when personal goals have priority. . . .
3. Cognitions that focus on norms, obligations, and duties guide much of social behavior in collectivist cultures. Those that focus on attitudes,

personal needs, rights, and contracts guide social behavior in individualistic cultures. . . .

4. An emphasis on relationships, even when they are disadvantageous, is
    common in collectivist cultures. In individualist cultures, the emphasis
    is on rational analyses of the advantages and disadvantages of maintain-
    ing a relationship.

The notion that cultures can be meaningfully described by a
simple I/C dichotomy has been challenged by some scholars, particularly by Shalom Schwartz and his colleagues (e.g., Schwartz, 1990;
Schwartz & Roa, 1995). From his cultural values perspective, Schwartz
(1990, pp. 151–152) offered three criticisms:

> First, the dichotomy leads us to overlook values that inherently serve both
> individual and collective interests (e.g., maturity values). Second, the
> dichotomy ignores values that foster the goals of collectives other than
> the ingroup (e.g., universal prosocial values). Third, the dichotomy pro-
> motes the mistaken assumption that individualist and collectivist values
> each form coherent syndromes that are opposed to one another. It fails
> to recognize that the subtypes of individualist and of collectivist values
> sometimes do not vary together and are sometimes not opposed. . . . This
> is not to contend, however, that the individualism-collectivism dichotomy
> and its psychological counterpart of idiocentrism-allocentrism are without
> merit. . . . The dichotomy therefore remains useful for broad-brush analy-
> ses, and it can certainly suggest fruitful research hypotheses.

Schwartz (1994) has found it useful to distinguish between two
types of individualism, which he has termed Intellectual Autonomy and
Affective Autonomy. In the present project, we will employ Schwartz's
indices of these variables as well as Hofstede's (1980) measure of I/C
that has been widely used in recent cross-cultural studies. The development of the Schwartz and Hofstede measures is discussed later in this
chapter and again in Chapter 7.

Individualism/collectivism as ordinarily assessed is a psychological variable which has been found to be related to other psychological
variables across countries. For example, our cross-cultural study of self
concepts among university students in 14 countries revealed that in
countries with higher Hofstede (1980) individualism scores there was:
more diversity in self concepts; more similar self concepts for men and
women; and more egalitarian sex role concepts (Williams & Best, 1990b).
As another illustration, Diener, Diener, and Diener (1995) conducted a
study of Subjective Well-Being (SWB) (i.e., happiness, life satisfaction)
in 55 countries and found that SWB was generally higher in more
individualistic countries than in more collectivistic countries.

Despite some criticisms, individualism/collectivism is viewed by
many scholars as a *key* cross-cultural variable. When Smith and Bond

(1994) surveyed social psychology from a cross-cultural perspective, they chose to use individualism/collectivism as *the* basic organizing principle. A similar usage is evident in recent "mainstream" textbooks in social psychology (e.g., Franzoi, 1996; Myers, 1996).

REPRESENTATIVE LARGE-SCALE MULTICOUNTRY STUDIES

Here we will review the results of three major multicountry cross-cultural projects, conducted by other researchers, that are linked to the current project in significant ways.

Osgood's Cross-Cultural Universals of Affective Meaning

Working at the University of Illinois in the United States, Charles Osgood and his associates (Osgood, Suci, & Tannenbaum, 1957) became interested in the connotative or *affective meanings* associated with words (and other stimuli) as opposed to their denotative or dictionary meanings. After conducting numerous studies in the United States, these investigators concluded that the principal component of affective meaning is a pervasive *evaluation* (good–bad) factor that is usually accompanied by weaker, secondary factors of *potency* (strong–weak) and *activity* (active–passive).

Osgood later extended this work on a cross-cultural basis and studied the affective meaning structure in 23 language/culture groups in Europe, Asia, and the Americas (Osgood, May, & Miron, 1975). The results of these studies indicated that the three-factor affective meaning system was a general one found in all languages studied. Of particular interest in the present context is the finding that, in all groups, the predominant factor was evaluation indicating that the principal affective response to most words is one of relative "goodness" or "badness," i.e., evaluation or favorability. Relative to the present project, the pan-cultural significance of this evaluation dimension undergirds our rationale for studying the relationship between the favorability of ACL adjectives and their psychological importance.

Hofstede's Work-Related Values

Attitude survey data obtained from thousands of employees of a large multinational corporation allowed Hofstede (1979, 1980) to compare work-related values in 40 countries.

Employing factor-analytic techniques, Hofstede identified four dimensions of work-related values along which individual countries could be located. The first factor, called *Power Distance*, indicated the extent to which people within a society accept the idea that power in institutions and organizations is distributed unequally. The second dimension, called *Uncertainty Avoidance*, indicated a lack of tolerance for uncertainty and ambiguity. The third factor, *Individualism*, reflected the degree to which people are supposed to take care of only themselves and their immediate families (individualism), as opposed to situations in which persons can expect their relatives, clan, or organization to look after them (collectivism). The final dimension was named *Masculinity* and expresses the extent to which "masculine" values of assertiveness, money, and things prevail in a society rather than the "feminine" values of nurturance, quality of life, and people. (Although this is obviously an important dimension, one can question whether a different label—perhaps materialism—might have been more appropriate.) Hofstede noted that, although the Power Distance and Individualism scales were negatively correlated across the 40 countries ($r = -.67$), he felt that they were sufficiently distinct, conceptually, to use the scores separately in his analyses.

For every country in the study, Hofstede derived indices of the four work-related value variables. These scores were then correlated across countries with a variety of national comparison variables, including wealth, economic growth, latitude, population size, population growth, and population density. These analyses revealed a large number of intriguing relationships between the work-related values in different countries and the comparison variables. For example, countries with high Power Distance scores tended to be economically poorer countries, in the relatively low latitudes (closer to the equator), with relatively high population growth rates. An opposite set of findings was obtained for the Individualism scores: Countries with more individualistic values tended to be wealthier countries, in the higher latitudes, with relatively low population growth rates.

Hofstede's work has had a major impact in the field of cross-cultural psychology with his four value dimensions being employed by other investigators, particularly in the study of individualism/collectivism. Hofstede's country-level value scores were available for 16 of the 20 countries in the present project and were employed as cultural comparison variables in the analyses of the PI data.

Schwartz's Cultural Dimensions of Values

In an ongoing project based at the Hebrew University of Jerusalem, Shalom Schwartz has led an international team of cooperating researchers in a comprehensive study of the cultural dimensions of values (Schwartz, 1990, 1992, 1994; Schwartz & Bilsky, 1987, 1990). In his 1994 paper, Schwartz noted that data were gathered from 1988 to 1992 using 86 samples drawn from 41 cultural groups in 38 nations. The samples came from every inhabited continent and included speakers of 30 different languages and adherents of 12 religions as well as atheists. Subjects included 35 samples of university students, 38 samples of school teachers, 12 general samples of adults, and two samples of adolescents.

Asking participants to rate each value "as a guiding principle in my life," the survey used a scale from 7 (of *supreme importance*) to 0 (*not important*) and –1 (*opposed to my values*). Included were 56 single values selected to represent 11 potentially universal types of individual-level values employed in earlier research.

The analyses of the data led to the identification of seven value regions, as follows:

- *Conservatism.* Values important in societies with close-knit harmonious relations, where the interests of the person are not viewed as distinct from the group.
- *Intellectual and Affective Autonomy.* Values important in societies viewing the person as an autonomous entity. Two aspects of Autonomy are distinguishable—a more intellectual emphasis on self-direction and a more affective emphasis on stimulation and hedonism.
- *Hierarchy.* Values emphasizing the legitimacy of hierarchical role and resource allocation.
- *Mastery.* Values emphasizing active mastery of the social environment through self-assertion.
- *Egalitarian Commitment.* Values stressing voluntary commitment in promoting the welfare of others who are viewed as equals.
- *Harmony.* Values emphasizing harmony with nature as opposed to values promoting actively changing the world.

Schwartz found that some values were generally more important and others generally less important, as can be seen in the following median values for the 38 samples: Intellectual Autonomy (4.97); Egalitarian Commitment (4.94); Mastery (4.14.); Harmony (4.08); Conservatism (4.05); Affective Autonomy (3.45); and Hierarchy (2.48). Thus, for example, people generally assigned a higher value to Intellectual Autonomy than to Affective Autonomy, and Hiearchy was generally rated low relative to the other six values. While interesting, these pan-cultural differences between values are of no concern in the present project where the focus is on between-country differences on each of the seven values, e.g., which countries were *relatively higher* and *relatively lower* on Intellectual Autonomy, or on Hierarchy? In his report, Schwartz notes the relationship of his seven value types to Hofstede's four work-related values. For example, Hofstede's Individualism factor correlated positively with Egalitarian Commitment and both types of Autonomy, and correlated negatively with Conservatism and Hierarchy. On the other hand, Hofstede's Power Distance factor correlated positively with Conservatism and negatively with Affective Autonomy.

Schwartz's seven value types, available for 14 of the 20 countries in the present project, were included as cultural comparison variables in the analyses of the PI data.

THE ADJECTIVE CHECK LIST (ACL) METHOD

The method in the present project employs the item pool of the Adjective Check List (Gough & Heilbrun, 1965, 1980), which consists of 300 adjectives appropriate to the description of persons, listed in Appendix D. Originally designed to capture the characteristics of individual persons, the item pool has proved useful in a variety of other applications including the description of groups of persons (i.e., gender or age stereotypes). Here we describe the item pool and four theoretically based scoring systems for ACL data, three of which were used in the present project.

The groundwork for the ACL can be found in the work by Allport and Odbert (1936), who listed 17,953 English words referring to psychological characteristics. Harrison Gough, the developer of the ACL, traces the origin of the item pool to the work of R. B. Cattell (1943, 1946), who reduced Allport and Odbert's extensive list to 171 variables. Beginning with Cattell's list, Gough and Heilbrun (1965, p. 5) note that words were added which were thought to be useful for describing personality from different theoretical vantage points:

> This first list, totalling 279 words, was introduced into studies at the Institute of Personality Assessment and Research (at the University of California, Berkeley) in 1950. It soon became apparent that a number of important words had been omitted and in 1951 the list was increased to 284 words. After further experience and further consideration of comments of assessment participants, the present version of 300 words was prepared in 1952. This 300-word Adjective Check List is therefore an emergent from the language itself, past study, intuitive and subjective appraisal, empirical testing, and a three-year overall evaluation.

It is clear that the Adjective Check List was not a casually constructed procedure, but represented a careful attempt to identify adjectives that seemed useful in the description of human behavior. That the development of the ACL was accomplished by psychologists in the United States working within the context of the English language undoubtedly created some bias in the item pool. It is likely that psychologists from other cultures would have developed somewhat different item pools that would permit the study of traits not included in the present study. While we have no formal basis for assessing the appropriateness of the item pool in cultures other than the United States, several observations can be made. We note the large size of the item pool; with 300 adjectives, including many near synonyms, we are certainly on sounder ground than if a small number of characteristics had been employed. In addition, one can argue that, while desirable, it is not necessary that the item pool be equally appropriate in all cultures as long as it provides the subjects with a reasonable opportunity to describe persons from their own culture. Supporting the latter view is the observation that in our earlier cross-cultural studies of self-concepts (Williams & Best, 1990b), gender stereotypes (Williams & Best, 1990a), and age stereotypes (Williams, 1993), neither our cooperating researchers nor their student subjects have complained that the ACL item pool was inadequate for the description of persons from their cultural groups. While we find this reassuring, we recognize that had we employed an emic approach and developed trait lists within each culture, we would probably have discovered additional traits that are important in the description of persons in particular cultures.

In a subsequent section of this chapter, we will summarize the findings from several large-scale, cross-cultural studies employing the ACL methodology. Prior to this, we will describe the different types of analyses which may be conducted when the ACL is employed.

ITEM-LEVEL ANALYSES

Certain kinds of questions can be addressed employing item level data. For example, if we scale the degree to which each of the 300 individual items is associated, stereotypically, with women and men, we can compare the values obtained from two different cultural groups with a correlation coefficient serving as an index of similarity in the gender stereotypes across cultures. Likewise, as in the present study, if we obtain a rating of the psychological importance of each item in Country A, we can use the correlation coefficient to indicate how similar these ratings are to those obtained in Country B. Item level analyses can also be used in gender analyses and in identifying items that are responded to atypically in particular cultural groups.

While the results of item level analyses are useful in determining *quantitative* similarities and differences in one's data, the results are highly abstract and provide no indication of *qualitative* similarities and differences. For this, we employ theoretically based scoring systems which summarize the qualities associated with similarities and differences in our findings. It must be noted that all of the scoring systems were developed by American psychologists using American research subjects. Being American-based, it is possible that the scoring systems are American-biased.

THEORY-BASED SCORING SYSTEMS

Here we describe four alternative scoring systems for the ACL based, respectively, on: psychological needs, affective meanings, ego states, and the Five Factor Model.

Psychological Needs

The original and best-known ACL scoring system characterizes item sets in terms of relative loading on psychological needs. Based on the original work of Murray (1938), Edwards (1959) developed a list of 15 needs and their definitions. Gough and Heilbrun (1965, 1980) presented these definitions to American graduate students in psychology, who were asked to examine the 300 ACL items and to indicate which adjectives were either indicative or contraindicative of each of the 15 needs, e.g., Dominance, Deference, Nurturance, Achievement, Aggression, etc. In this manner, Gough and Heilbrun developed a scoring system which indicated the relative strength of each psychological need in a given set of ACL adjectives, e.g., those chosen by an individual as self-descriptive, those highly associated with a particular gender group, etc. While we used the Psychological Needs scoring system in our earlier work on gender stereotypes (Williams & Best, 1990a), we did not use it in the present project.

Affective Meanings

Patterned after Osgood's three-factor theory of affective meaning described earlier in the chapter, this scoring system enables one to determine the relative favorability, strength, and activity of ACL item sets. In developing the system, groups of American university students rated each of the 300 ACL adjectives for favorability, strength, and activity along five-point scales (Best, Williams, & Briggs, 1980; Williams & Best, 1977). The mean values obtained in this manner provided a score on each of the three factors for each of the 300 items. Using this system, one can determine the relative favorability, strength, and activity for any given set of ACL items, e.g., an individual's self description, or the characteristics stereotypically associated with women or with men. Alternatively, if one has scaled the 300 items for some characteristic such as psychological importance, one can correlate these scores with the affective meaning scores to study the interrelationships.

In Chapter 3, we report a study of the favorability of the 300 ACL adjectives, or their translated equivalents, in 10 countries. Subsequently, in Chapters 5 and 6, these emically derived favorability scores are used to study the relationship of the favorability of items to their psychological importance.

Transactional Analysis Ego States

Based on the theoretical system of Eric Berne (1961, 1966), this system provides scores for each ACL adjective that reflect its "loading" on each of the five functional ego states of Transactional Analysis (TA) theory: Critical Parent, Nurturing Parent, Adult, Free Child, and Adapted Child (Williams & Williams, 1980). The ego state scores were based on the mean ratings of the 300 items by 15 expert judges who were highly trained in TA theory. The system enables one to compute mean scores reflecting the relative loading on the five ego states for any given set of ACL items or, alternatively, if 300 ACL items have been scaled for some characteristic such as psychological importance, one can correlate these values with the 300 values for each ego state to see what relationships are found.

We make extensive use of the ego state scoring system in the present project, and we will return in Chapter 2 for a more extensive discussion of both Transactional Analysis theory and the scoring system per se.

The Five Factor Model

The most recently developed ACL scoring system provides, for each ACL adjective, a value for each of the dimensions of the Five Factor Model (FFM) of personality: Extraversion, Agreeableness, Conscientiousness, Emotional Stability, and Openness (FormyDuval, Williams, Patterson, & Fogle, 1995). In this project, we make extensive use of the five factor scoring system and we will defer further consideration to

Chapter 2 where both the model and the scoring system will be discussed in detail.

MULTICOUNTRY STUDIES EMPLOYING THE ACL

Having described the various ways in which ACL data can be scored, we now briefly review the findings of several large-scale, cross-cultural studies in which the ACL methodology has been employed, but which, until now, have not been summarized in one place. This review provides the reader with a further orientation as to the types of findings which might emerge in the present project where the ACL methodology is applied to the study of psychological importance.

Gender Stereotypes

Deborah Best and the first author conducted a study of gender stereotypes among young adults in 25 countries around the world (Williams & Best, 1990a). In each country approximately 100 university students were presented with the 300 ACL items or their translated equivalents. They were instructed to indicate whether, in their culture, the adjective was more frequently associated with men or with women, or not differentially associated by gender. These data were combined to develop a gender stereotype score for each item with high scores indicating that the adjective was strongly associated with men, and low scores indicating that the adjective was strongly associated with women.

In the item-level analyses, the correlation coefficients between the 300 stereotype scores in each pair of countries ranged from .94 (Australia versus England) to .35 (Pakistan versus Venezuela) with a median value of .65 among all pairs of the 25 countries. From this, it was clear that there was substantial pancultural agreement in the gender stereotypes.

The application of three theoretically based scoring systems also provided strong evidence of pancultural similarities. Regarding Affective Meaning, the male stereotype in all countries was stronger and more active than the female stereotype; relative favorability, however, varied from country to country with the male stereotype being more favorable in some countries (e.g., Japan, South Africa, and Nigeria) and the female stereotype being more favorable in other countries (e.g., Italy, Peru, and Australia).

When the TA ego state scoring system was applied to the gender stereotype data, the male stereotypes were found to be generally higher on Adult (all 25 countries) and Critical Parent (22 of 25 countries), while the female stereotypes were higher on Adapted Child (24 of 25 countries) and Nurturing Parent (all 25 countries). Panculturally, Free Child was not systematically associated with either gender.

The psychological needs analysis revealed five needs which were more male-associated in all countries—dominance, autonomy, aggression, exhibition, and achievement—and four needs which were more female-associated in all countries—abasement, deference, succorance, and nurturance.

The similarities disclosed by the foregoing analyses enabled us to propose a robust, pancultural model of gender stereotypes. There were, however, some observed differences which seemed attributable to cultural influences. For example, the strength and activity differences favoring the male stereotype were greater in countries characterized as socioeconomically less developed, as low in literacy, and as low in the percentage of women attending the university. As another example, the female stereotype appeared relatively more favorable and less weak in Catholic countries than in Protestant countries. Overall, this cross-cultural study of gender stereotypes in 25 countries provided evidence of many pancultural similarities and some interesting differences attributable to culture.

Self-Concepts

As an outgrowth of the gender stereotype study just described, we conducted a study of the self and ideal self concepts of women and men university students in a diverse group of 14 countries (Williams & Best, 1990b). The previously collected gender stereotype data were used to develop a culture-specific (emic) measure of *masculinity/femininity* in each country. Self descriptions that included more of the local male stereotype items were said to be masculine, while descriptions involving more of the local female stereotype items were said to be feminine.

The method involved first presenting the students with the 300 ACL items, translated as necessary, and asking each person to select those adjectives which were *"descriptive of you as you really are,* not as you would like to be." Following this, the ACL list was presented again with instructions to select those adjectives *"descriptive of the person you would like to be,* not the person you really are." In addition, each subject completed a sex-role ideology inventory that asked for his or her views of the proper role relationship between men and women. Responses were subsequently scored along a dimension ranging from "male dominant" to "egalitarian."

The findings of the study revealed some pancultural effects. As would be expected, the men's self descriptions were relatively more masculine, and the women's self descriptions were relatively more feminine, although the magnitude of the differences in the men's and women's self descriptions were relatively small. A more interesting finding was that among both men and women the ideal self description was more masculine than the self description, probably due to the association of strength and activity with masculinity.

Are men more masculine—or women more feminine—in some cultures than in others? While some between-country differences were observed, these were not systematically related to cultural comparison variables, and we concluded that there was no clear evidence of variations in masculinity/femininity attributable to culture. On the other hand, when the men's and women's self and ideal self descriptions were scored in terms of affective meaning, evidence of cultural variation was found. For example, the affective meaning *differences* in men's and women's self concepts were *greater* in less-developed countries, and smaller in countries where more women were employed outside the home, where women constituted a large percentage of the university population, and where the prevailing sex-role ideology was relatively egalitarian.

Having illustrated the use of the ACL method in the study of self-concepts, we turn to another application in the study of stereotypes.

Age Stereotypes

Deborah Best and the first author employed the ACL method in a study of age stereotypes in 19 countries (Best & Williams, 1996; Williams, 1993). Considering each of the 300 ACL items in their appropriate translations, university students indicated whether, in their culture, each adjective was more frequently associated with old adults, more frequently associated with young adults, or not differentially associated by age. These data were combined to produce an age stereotype index score for each item with high scores indicating items associated more strongly with old adults and low scores indicating items associated more strongly with young adults.

Correlations of the age stereotype scores computed across the 300 items for each pair of countries produced coefficients ranging from .89 (Canada versus New Zealand) to .47 (Great Britain versus Korea). The median value across all comparisons was .68, indicating substantial pancultural agreement in the psychological characteristics differentially ascribed to old and young adults.

The Affective Meaning analysis also revealed evidence of pancultural effects. Regarding activity, the items associated with old adults were significantly less active in all 19 countries. Regarding strength, the old adult items were significantly weaker in 12 countries and not different in the other seven. Regarding favorability, the old adult items were significantly more favorable in 14 countries and not different in the other five. These results suggest that references to the "negative image" of older people are based on the perception of their relative weakness and passivity rather than their unfavorability.

Further evidence of pancultural similarity was found by an examination of the age stereotype data in terms of the five TA ego states. This analysis indicated general tendencies for the items associated with old people to be higher on Critical Parent, Nurturing Parent, and Adult, and lower on Free Child.

In addition to the pancultural similarities just noted, there was some evidence of cross-cultural variation. In correlating cultural comparison variables with the *differences* between the old adult stereotype and the young adult stereotype, we found, for example, that in more developed countries the age stereotypes were more differentiated in terms of Nurturing Parent and less differentiated on Free Child.

The gender stereotype, self-concept, and age stereotype studies just reviewed illustrate the versatility of the ACL method which, in the present project, is applied to the study of the relative importance of various psychological characteristics in different societies.

SUMMARY

In this first introductory chapter, we discussed the field of cross-cultural psychology and noted some issues and problems associated with research in this area. We reviewed previous cross-cultural studies by Osgood, Hofstede, and Schwartz and noted their relationship to the present investigation. The Adjective Check List (ACL) method was described, as were the variety of available scoring systems. Also outlined were summaries of the results of earlier cross-cultural studies that employed the method in the study of gender stereotypes, self-concepts, and age stereotypes.

PSYCHOLOGICAL IMPORTANCE, THE FIVE FACTOR MODEL, AND TRANSACTIONAL ANALYSIS THEORY

In this second introductory chapter we first discuss the general concept of the importance of psychological traits and summarize some of our earlier research on this topic. To provide background for our two theoretically based analyses, we review the history of the Five Factor Model of personality and the development of the five factor scoring system for the Adjective Check List (ACL). We then present a brief overview of Transactional Analysis theory and a description of the ego state scoring system for the ACL. We close the chapter with an overview of the remaining chapters in the book.

PSYCHOLOGICAL IMPORTANCE

The concept of differential importance in psychological traits proposes that some descriptors may be "more diagnostic" in that they provide more information concerning the individual's psychological makeup and, hence, are more useful in understanding and predicting behavior. More important traits may tell us more about "what the person is really like."

The idea that traits differ in importance or significance is not new. Gordon Allport (1937, p. 338) discussed *central* and *secondary* traits, which were described as follows: "Central traits are those usually mentioned in careful letters of recommendation, in rating scales where the rater stars the outstanding characteristics of the individual, or in brief verbal descriptions of persons. One may speak on a still less important level, of *secondary traits*, less conspicuous, less generalized, less consistent and less often called into play than central traits." Allport's distinction between central and secondary traits has been echoed by other scholars including Cattell (general and specific traits; 1965), Kelly (broad and narrow constructs; 1955), Eysenck (types, traits, and habits; 1947, 1990), and John, Hampson, and Goldberg (superordinate, basic, and subordinate traits; 1991).

Although there is substantial similarity between the present concept of importance and the theoretical concepts noted, the notions may not be identical. Indeed, the theorists' focus has been on the relative importance of traits in governing behavior, which is not necessarily the same as the relative importance of traits to an outside observer. Perhaps more relevant here is the idea expressed by Asch (1946, p. 262) in his classic article on impression formation: "Observation suggests that not all qualities have the same weight in establishing the view of a person. Some are felt to be basic, others secondary."

Matsumoto (1996, p. 54) discusses possible cultural differences in the manner in which personality is viewed and understood:

> [I]t may be true that people, regardless of culture, share many characteristics of personality that American as well as other views of personality suggest are important. Culture may serve to verbally formalize what is important in that particular culture concerning an understanding of personality, highlighting some aspects . . . while ignoring others. These choices inform us about what these cultures deem to be important in their understanding of people.

This comment nicely brackets the purpose of the present investigation, which is to gain knowledge concerning the similarities and differences in the importance of various psychological characteristics in different cultural groups.

In the present project we deal with the judgments of university students as to the relative importance of characteristics represented by the 300 items of the Adjective Check List. Our first three studies dealing with the concept of psychological importance have been described in detail elsewhere (Williams, Munick, Saiz, & FormyDuval, 1995). Here we provide brief summaries of these studies, all of which were conducted at Wake Forest University.

PREVIOUS STUDIES IN THE UNITED STATES

Study 1

The purpose of this study was to determine whether the concept of psychological importance (PI) was a meaningful one to American university students and, if so, to determine whether the PI of the ACL item pool was reasonably diverse, i.e., that there were substantial numbers of items representing different degrees of PI from low to high.

In this study, 160 undergraduate students (80 women and 80 men) from Wake Forest University were presented with 300 ACL adjectives and were given the following instructions:

> In describing what a person is really like, some traits seem to be relatively important because they seem to refer to central or basic personality characteristics. For example, describing someone as being *truthful* or a *liar* seems to be saying something very important about the person.
>
> On the other hand, in describing what a person is really like, some traits seem to be of less importance because they seem to refer to more superficial or peripheral personality characteristics. For example, describing someone as being *neat* or *sloppy* seems to be saying something of less importance regarding what the person is really like. . . .
>
> On the following pages, you will find a list of 300 adjectives. For each adjective you are asked to consider its *importance* in describing what a person is really like. There are no right or wrong answers and it is your first impression that we want.

The instructions also noted that there was no necessary relationship between the importance of an adjective and its favorability.

Subjects then rated each of the 300 items on a five-point scale from 1, *little or no importance*, to 5, *critical or outstanding importance*.

PI rating data were analyzed first by sex of subject. Across all 300 items, the overall mean importance ratings were 3.15 (SD = .54) and 3.13 (SD = 0.46) for women and men respectively. A correlation of .93 between the mean ratings by women and men, indicated a high degree of agreement between the two gender groups. In view of this high correlation, and the highly similar means and standard deviations, it was judged appropriate to pool the women's and men's ratings and to obtain a single mean importance rating for each item. The mean of the pooled ratings across all 300 items was 3.14 (SD = 0.49). Thus, it was seen that the PI concept was meaningful (i.e., could be reliably rated) and that the PI of the ACL item pool was reasonably diverse.

An examination of the relationship of the 300 PI ratings to the 300 favorability scores from the affective meaning scoring system (see Chapter 1) revealed a "U" shaped curve with both highly favorable and highly unfavorable items being more important, and items of intermediate favorability being less important. Thus, to these American students, both "good" and "bad" characteristics could be psychologically important.

The PI scores of the items were then related to John's (1989) classification of groups of ACL items shown to be indicative of each of the "Big Five" personality factors, to be discussed in the following section. The mean PI scores for these item sets indicated that Agreeableness and Extraversion items were rated as most important, with Emotional Stability and Conscientiousness items rated as somewhat less important and Openness items as least important.

Study 2

This was an impression formation study designed to explore the impact of the Big Five factors on person perception. Based on the findings of Study 1, it was reasoned that information concerning the more important factors of Agreeableness (A) and Extraversion (E) should have more impact on impression formation than information on the less important factors of Conscientiousness (C), Emotional Stability (ES), and Openness (O).

The participants in this study were 69 members of the graduate faculty at Wake Forest University who rated hypothetical, prospective graduate students who were described with sets of adjectives representing different combinations of the five factors.

Contrary to expectations, it was found that adjective sets containing C and O adjectives created a more positive impression than sets containing E and A adjectives. Further, adjective sets containing examples of all five factors did not create a more positive impression than the C and O adjectives alone.

The finding that the judges placed greater weight on supposedly "less important" factors might be due to the effects of context on judgments of psychological importance. Perhaps the importance of the qualities ascribed to the hypothetical graduate students was being influenced by the nature of the situations in which the students would be expected to perform. To what degree would the general, noncontextual judgments of psychological importance found in Study 1 vary if the ratings were made in the context of a work relationship versus the context of a close personal relationship? Study 3 was designed to examine this question.

Study 3

The instructions and rating task were identical to those in Study 1 with the addition of instructions to make the importance ratings as if describing someone either in a "work situation" or a "close relationship." Subjects were university students, as in Study 1.

The product-moment correlation across the 300 items between the PI scores for the work and relationship contexts was .51, indicating considerable variability in the PI scores obtained in the two situations. The correlation between the general PI scores from Study 1 and the work context scores was .57, and for the general PI scores and the relationship context scores it was .64, indicating that the general scores seem to reflect both work and relationship settings. However, the general PI scores seemed to be slightly more similar to the relationship context scores (41 percent common variance) than to the work context scores (32 percent common variance). Regarding the Big Five, it was found that Agreeableness was significantly *less* important in the work context than in either the relationship context or the general context. Furthermore, Conscientiousness was significantly *more* important in the work context than in either the relationship or the general context. These findings suggest that the graduate faculty judges in Study 2 were looking for "good workers" not "good friends."

The juxtaposition of the findings from Studies 1 and 3 indicate that, while the importance assigned to psychological traits can be shown to vary substantially with context, the concept of general, context-unspecified PI is a meaningful one as shown by the high reliability of the general ratings.

PSYCHOLOGICAL IMPORTANCE VIEWED CROSS-CULTURALLY

The study to be summarized here was a preliminary report on findings from the first seven countries involved in the present project (Williams et al., 1995).

The purpose of this study was to replicate, insofar as possible, the original American rating study, described above as Study 1, in order to identify similarities and differences in the psychological importance of different traits in different cultural groups.

Subjects were undergraduate university students, equally divided by gender, from Chile, China, Nigeria, Norway, Pakistan, Portugal, and the United States. Employing, as necessary, previously developed translations of the 300 ACL items, each of the subjects was instructed to rate the psychological importance of each adjective along a five-point scale. The detailed instructions were the same as those employed in the original American study, translated as necessary, with some modifications in the illustrative adjectives used to provide more culturally appropriate examples. The data in each country were analyzed first by comparing the 300 item means obtained from the ratings made by the women and men subjects with the resulting correlation coefficients: Chile, .86; China, .86; Nigeria, .68; Norway, .80; Pakistan, .94; Portugal, .90; and the United States, .93; with an average correlation of .87. From these high values it was concluded that the concept of psychological importance was meaningful (reliable) in all countries, and the women's and men's ratings in each country were pooled to get overall country ratings for each of the 300 items.

When correlations were computed across the 300 item means for each pair of countries, the coefficients ranged from .23 for Nigeria versus Norway to .73 for Nigeria and Pakistan, with an average correlation of .49 for all pairs of countries. It can be seen that these between-country correlations were much lower than the within-country (men versus women) correlations noted above. Thus, there appeared to be substantial cross-cultural variation in PI.

When the distributions of PI ratings in each country were examined relative to the Favorability scores from the Affective Meaning scoring system, there was a general tendency toward a positive association in all countries; favorable items were more important than unfavorable items. However, the magnitude of this tendency varied widely, as indicated by the following linear, product-moment coefficients: United States, .24; Norway, .27; Chile, .28; China, .49; Portugal, .64; Nigeria, .68; and Pakistan, .79. Further analyses indicated that, in the latter four countries, there was no evidence of departure from linearity while, in each of the first three countries, there was evidence of significant non-linearity and a tendency for the plot of PI versus Favorability to be "U" or "J" shaped. In the United States, Norway and Chile, in addition to the general tendency for more favorable items to be judged more important, there was also a tendency for very unfavorable items to be at least moderately important. On the other hand, in China, Portugal, Nigeria, and Pakistan one observed only the general tendency for good traits to be important and bad traits to be unimportant.

In sum, the seven-country study provided evidence that PI could be reliably rated and suggested substantial between-country differences in the characteristics considered psychologically important. The analysis also suggested important differences among countries in the relationship of trait importance to trait favorability.

The foregoing findings regarding favorability were viewed cautiously because of a methodological limitation. The scores employed for all samples were the favorability ratings given to the 300 English-language adjectives by American university students; thus, the Pakistani students' PI ratings of the items in the Urdu language were being examined relative to American-English language favorability ratings. Obviously, it would be more methodologically sound to obtain favorability ratings of the Urdu items from Pakistani students which could then be related to the Pakistani ratings of psychological importance.

In 10 of the 20 countries in the present project, we obtained local favorability ratings of the ACL items in the same language in which the PI procedure was administered. These findings are described in Chapter 3. In addition to the 10-country analysis, we extended the analysis to 15 countries by using *language-specific* favorability scores, with the Spanish language favorability ratings obtained in Chile used in Spanish-speaking Argentina and Venezuela, and the English language ratings from the United States used in other countries where the PI study was conducted in English, i.e., Australia, India, and Nepal.

Having completed our review of the concept of Psychological Importance and summarized some earlier research, we turn now to a more detailed consideration of the two theoretically based scoring systems that we employ in our analyses of PI data in subsequent chapters.

THE FIVE FACTOR MODEL

EVOLUTION OF THE MODEL

There is a growing consensus among many personality psychologists that the basic dimensions of personality can be encompassed by five "supertraits" constituting what is termed the Five Factor Model (FFM). This is an empirically based conception, the origins of which are traced to the classic trait language searches of Allport and Odbert (1936; for a historical review, see John, Angleitner, & Ostendorf, 1988). Cattell (1943, 1947) narrowed the Allport and Odbert list of approximately 18,000 trait adjectives to about 4,500 and, ultimately, uncovered 12 to 16 primary factors through factor analysis. These factors were assessed by Cattell's 16 Personality Factors Questionnaire (Cattell, Eber, & Tatsuoka, 1970).

Later, in an obscure report, Tupes and Christal (1961/1992) reanalyzed part of the Cattell data as well as data from additional samples, and found only five recurring factors from all data sets. Although the original report escaped general notice, Norman (1963) brought it to the attention of other psychologists in a now often-cited study in which he replicated the five-factor structure and labeled the five dimensions Extraversion, Agreeableness, Conscientiousness, Emotional Stability (reversed as Neuroticism), and Culture (later called Openness).

The five-factor structure has been found in studies other than those using trait adjectives. John (1989) reported a free-description study in which more than 300 students generated desirable and undesirable personality characteristics. Among the 10 most frequent terms was at least one for each of the five factors. The 60 most frequently used terms were employed to obtain self-descriptions that were then factor-analyzed, yielding five factors conceptually similar to those obtained in the Norman (1963) and Tupes and Christal (1961/1992) studies. The five-factor structure has been replicated across a range of cultures (Bond, Nakazato, & Shiraishi, 1975; McCrae & Costa, 1997; Paunonen, Jackson, Trzebinski, & Forsterling, 1992), instruments (McCrae & Costa, 1987, 1989; Piedmont, McCrae, & Costa, 1991), and observers (McCrae & Costa, 1987).

The consistency with which the five dimensions have been recovered led Goldberg (1981) to dub this five-factor structure "the Big Five" and led many researchers to conclude that the model is an adequate representation of the basic dimensions of personality. Diaz-Guerrero (1992) suggests that the five factors could be differentially related to psychological importance as a function of language (culture). Due to the fact that the FFM is originally based on personality-descriptive terms in the English language (a lexical approach), he indicates that in non-English languages people may ascribe different degrees of importance to the same psychological attributes. Costa and McCrae (1992) developed instruments specifically designed to assess personality in terms of the FFM: the 240-item NEO Personality Inventory-Revised (NEO-PI-R) and the 60-item NEO Five Factor Inventory (NEO-FFI) for use when administration time is limited. These well-designed instruments seem more than adequate for the assessment of the personalities of individual persons on either a self-descriptive or an observational basis. However, the declarative-statement items of the NEO instruments are not as easily adapted to the study of target groups as are the single person-descriptive adjectives of the Adjective Check List (ACL).

There have been three lines of research relating ACL data to the FFM. Piedmont and colleagues (1991) had university students complete self-descriptive ACLs and then factor-analyzed the 35 ACL scale scores obtained from the standard scoring system. Six possible factors emerged, and the researchers examined both five-factor and six-factor solutions. The first five factors clearly reflected the FFM, and each of the ACL scales clearly loaded on at least one of each of the five factors. In a second study, using a separate sample of older adults, it was demonstrated that the same five-factor structure emerged when the same factor-analytic procedure was used. In another study relating the ACL to the Big Five, McCrae and Costa (1990) administered the NEO-PI-R and the ACL to older adults and demonstrated that certain ACL items are reliably associated with each of the different facet scales of the five factors as measured by the NEO instrument.

The most direct approach relating the ACL and the Big Five was taken by John (1989), who had graduate students with training in the FFM sort the ACL items into one of the five categories, with adjectives that seemed not to fit any of the five factors being placed in a sixth category. John observed a high degree of agreement between the judges and noted that more than half of the 300 items were sorted into at least one of the five factor categories. Whereas John's study allows one to identify certain ACL items as being indicative or counterindicative of given factors, the categorical sorting procedure has its shortcomings. It does not allow for differences in the degree of association of adjectives with given factors nor does it allow for the likelihood that some adjectives may be associated with more than one factor. It was thought that having each of the 300 adjectives rated as to its degree of association with each of the five factors might avoid these limitations and prove more useful in studies comparing the judgments of different groups of raters (e.g., persons from different language or culture groups).

The question can be raised as to whether the five factors are the esoteric abstractions of personality psychologists or whether they can be considered as meaningful folk psychology concepts. McCrae, Costa, and Piedmont (1993) directly addressed this issue in a study in which meaningful relations were found between the NEO-PI-R and the California Personality Inventory (Gough, 1987), a personality-assessment procedure specifically designed to measure folk concepts. Thus it seemed reasonable to assume that the five factors are a reflection of folk concepts that laypersons should be able to understand. If this assumption is correct, one should be able to show convergent validity between five-factor ratings obtained from laypersons and those previously obtained from John's (1989) trained graduate student judges.

DESCRIPTIONS OF THE FIVE FACTORS

FormyDuval (1993, pp. 5–6) has provided the following descriptions of the five factors:

> *Extraversion.* The core characteristic of Extraversion seems to be sociability. Individuals high in Extraversion prefer stimulating environments to relaxed ones, filled with social interaction (McCrae & Costa, 1990). This

dimension is characterized by an active, outgoing, assertive style. Traits which typically load on the Extraversion dimension include talkative, frank, adventurous, energetic, and enthusiastic (John, 1989; Norman, 1963).

Agreeableness. The Agreeableness dimension may best be characterized by the traits kind and loving. Agreeable persons are nice to be around because of their trusting nature, and their ability to believe the best of others (McCrae & Costa, 1990). Traits which usually load highly on this dimension are affectionate, cooperative, sensitive, good-natured, gentle, and warm.

Conscientiousness. The conscientiousness dimension is characterized by achievement motivation and organization. The conscientious individual is self-disciplined and competent, and is therefore likely to accomplish desired goals. This dimension is characterized by the following traits: deliberate, dependable, responsible, thorough, efficient, persevering, scrupulous, and reliable.

Emotional Stability. It is easiest to describe this dimension in terms of its negative pole, Neuroticism. The characteristics of Neuroticism are anxiety, hostility, and impulsiveness. Whereas emotionally stable individuals tend to be "calm, cool, and collected," individuals high in Neuroticism are more likely to display their emotions frequently. Traits describing the stable individual are likely to be calm, contented, and stable. However, the neurotic individual is more likely to be described as nervous, tense, high-strung, moody, temperamental, touchy, and emotional.

Openness to Experience. This dimension is characterized by curiosity, or a desire to explore the world, trying new things as opposed to the common-place. Individuals high in Openness are likely to be characterized by the traits artistic, imaginative, insightful, intelligent, original, clever, polished, inventive, sophisticated, and foresighted.

THE FIVE FACTOR ADJECTIVE CHECK LIST SCORING SYSTEM (ACL-FF)

The ACL-FF scoring system has been described in detail elsewhere (FormyDuval, 1993; FormyDuval et al., 1995). Here we provide a brief summary of the method employed and note some of the main charac-teristics of the scoring system.

The objective of the study was to obtain numerical values which reflected the weighting of each of the five factors on each of the 300 ACL items. The ratings were made by university students, with a separate group of approximately 100 persons (evenly divided by gender) rating each of the items for one of the five factors. Each group of subjects was provided with instructions describing the salient features of the factor to be rated, but the factor was not identified by name. Ratings were made along a five-point scale ranging from −2 (highly counterindica-tive) to +2 (highly indicative), with the ratings subsequently converted to a 1 to 5 scale for ease in analysis. After determining that the ratings made by the women and men were highly similar for each factor (median r = .98), a mean rating for each factor was computed across all subjects for each adjective (e.g., the adjective *aggressive* had the following values: Extraversion, 3.91; Agreeableness, 2.50; Conscientiousness, 3.90; Emotional Stability, 2.17; Openness, 3.86). The five factor scores for each of the 300 items are shown in Appendix D.

The ACL-FF scoring system is used in this project in two different ways. When we have ratings of all of the ACL items on psychological importance, we can compute correlation coefficients to determine which of the five factors are most closely associated with importance. If we have discrete groups of items, e.g., the 30 most important items and 30 least important items, we can compute mean five factor scores for each of the item sets and compare them.

THE FIVE FACTORS AND FAVORABILITY

An examination of the ACL-FF scores (see Appendix D) suggested that, for each factor, items with higher scores seemed to be more positive or favorable than items with lower scores. This observation led to a systematic examination of the relationship of favorability to each of the five factors. When each set of factor scores were correlated with the Favorability scores from the Affective Meaning scoring system (see Chapter 1), positive coefficients varying from .51 to .89 were obtained. These findings indicated that, as assessed by the ACL-FF system, extraversion was more favorable than introversion, agreeableness than disagreeableness, conscientiousness than undirectedness, emotional stability than neuroticism, and openness to experience than closemindedness. While it was not surprising to find that each of the five factors as assessed by the ACL-FF system had a favorability component, we were interested in whether similar results would be found using a more widely known method of assessing the five factors.

Goodman and Williams (1996) reported two studies conducted to determine whether favorability is associated with the five factors when they are assessed using Costa and McCrae's (1992) NEO-FFI questionnaire. This instrument was specifically designed to measure the five factors and is generally accepted as providing a definitive assessment relative to the FFM. The 60-item NEO-FFI contains 12 items representing each of the five factors, with some items phrased in an indicative manner and some in a counterindicative manner. For example, an indicative item for Extraversion is: "I like to have a lot of people around me." A counterindicative item for Extraversion is: "I usually prefer to do things alone." In the standard self-descriptive use of the instrument, a person uses a 1 to 5 scale to indicate the degree to which the statement applies to herself/himself, with responses to the counterindicative items being reverse-scored.

In the first study, we reasoned that if the five factors as assessed by the NEO-FFI are positively associated with favorability, then indicative items should be viewed as more favorable than counterindicative items. When 106 university students rated the NEO-PPI items for favorability on a five-point scale, the mean ratings shown in Table 2.1 were obtained. This analysis indicated that, for each of the five factors, the indicative items were significantly more favorable than the counterindicative items.

In the second study, we reasoned that, if the five factors assessed by the NEO-FFI are associated with favorability, then asking persons to "fake good" would tend to raise their factor scores and asking them to "fake bad" would tend to lower their factor scores. Employing university students who had previously taken the NEO-FFI under standard self-descriptive instructions, we divided them into two groups who were given the following instructions:

> Your goal is to project the best (worst) image that you can by giving only answers that are "good" ("bad"). In other words, your responses should create the most favorable (unfavorable) impression possible.

The findings of the second study are shown in Figure 2.1, where it can be seen that, on each factor, the "fake good" descriptions had a higher mean score than the self-descriptions, while the "fake bad" descriptions had a lower mean.

The findings from the two studies led to the conclusion that the five factors, as assessed by the NEO-FFI, were each associated with favorability in a manner similar to the five factors as assessed by the ACL-FF.

TABLE 2.1. Mean Favorability Ratings for Indicative and Counterindicative Items for Each Factor

	Indicative		Counterindicative			
	M	SD	M	SD	df	t
Extraversion	4.03	0.45	2.24	0.67	105	19.07*
Agreeableness	4.30	0.50	2.00	0.46	105	29.75*
Conscientiousness	4.54	0.45	2.25	0.41	105	31.49*
Emotional stability	4.03	0.45	2.24	0.67	105	19.07*
Openness	4.05	0.47	2.70	0.45	105	18.88*

*$p < .001$

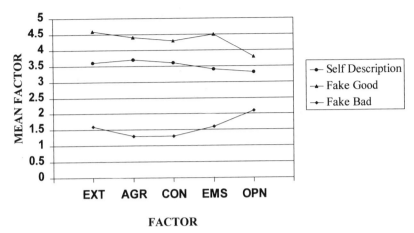

FIGURE 2.1. Mean five factor scores of self descriptions under standard, "fake good," and "fake bad" instructions.

The results of the studies just reviewed are consistent with the notion that each of the five factors is intrinsically evaluative. However, in subsequent analyses employing the ACL-FF, we will analyze the data in two ways: first, using the uncorrected five factor scores, and second, using the five factor scores with the influence of favorability controlled via partial correlation.

TRANSACTIONAL ANALYSIS EGO STATES

In the present project, in addition to examining the PI data in relation to the five factor theory, we also analyze the PI data in relation to the five ego states of Transactional Analysis theory: Critical Parent, Nurturing Parent, Adult, Free Child, and Adapted Child. Obviously, analysis of the same sets of PI ratings by two different scoring systems can be justified only if the ego state scoring system is reasonably independent of the five factor scoring system. We addressed this question by correlating, across all 300 items, the scoring system values for each of the five ego states with the scoring system values for each of the five factors. With item favorability controlled, some interesting relationships were observed, e.g., Extraversion was positively correlated with Free Child (.56) as was Openness (.58), while Conscientiousness was positively correlated with Adult (.45) and Critical Parent (.56). On the other hand, the median of the 25 partial correlations was only .18, indicating an average of only 3 percent common variance between the various pairs of TA and FF distributions. This finding led us to conclude that the TA scoring system was sufficiently independent of the FF system to warrant its use as a second way of examining the PI data from our 20 countries.

Transactional Analysis Theory

Transactional Analysis (TA), a theory of personality and interpersonal behavior developed by Eric Berne and his colleagues (Berne, 1961, 1966; Woolams & Brown, 1978), has been used extensively by applied psychologists in a variety of settings, particularly in the clinical area.

Berne's original intention was to conceptualize the nature of the interactions (transactions) between persons in terms of the psychological situation or "ego state" from which each of the persons was operating at a given point in time. The three primary ego states postulated by Berne were termed Child, Adult, and Parent. Although every person operates from each of the ego states at one time or another, Berne and his coworkers also recognized that some people used certain ego states more often than others. Consequently, the TA system could be used to describe relatively stable personological differences in the characteristic use of ego states. It is this latter conception of ego states which we employ in the present project.

An analysis commonly used in the functional analysis of ego states is to subdivide the Parent ego state into Critical Parent (CP) and Nurturing Parent (NP), and the Child ego state into Free Child (FC) and Adapted Child (AC), while the Adult (A) ego state remains undivided. It is this fivefold system that we use in our analyses. Berne's (1961) description of these five functional ego states has been summarized, as follows (Williams & Best, 1990a, p. 102–103):

> The Critical Parent (CP) ego state designates a set of feelings, attitudes, and behavior patterns that resemble those of parental figures and represents that part of the personality which criticizes, finds fault, and reflects the rules of society and the values of the individual. The Nurturing Parent (NP) ego state represents a parental figure that nurtures and promotes growth. The Adult (A) ego state represents patterns that are adapted to current reality and are used for logical reasoning and precise predictions. The Free Child (FC) ego state is a relic of an individual's own childhood and is characterized by fun, frivolity, self-indulgence, and natural spontaneous feelings. The Adapted Child (AC) ego state is also a relic of childhood and is manifested by behaviors that are inferentially under the domination of parental influence and are characterized by conforming and compromising behaviors.

THE EGO STATE SCORING SYSTEM

The ego state scoring system was developed in the United States by Kathryn B. Williams (Williams, 1978; Williams & Williams, 1980). The system was based on the ratings of 15 expert judges, each of whom was a certified member of the International Transactional Analysis Association. Provided with a set of instructions including brief descriptions of the five functional ego states similar to those above, each judge considered each of the 300 ACL items in turn and rated it on each of the five functional ego states. A rating scale of 0–4 was employed, a score of zero indicating that the adjective was not at all descriptive of the particular ego state and a score of 4 indicating that the adjective was highly descriptive of the ego state. The instructions were designed so that for each adjective, each ego state would be rated independently. Thus, any given adjective could receive a high rating on each ego state, a low rating on each, or a mixture of high and low ratings.

After determining that there was a high degree of agreement among the judges' ratings, a mean score was computed for each of the five ego states for each of the 300 ACL adjectives. These values will be found in Appendix D. A general impression of the nature of the judges' ratings can be obtained from Table 2.2, in which is listed a sample of adjectives that were highly associated with each of the five ego states.

In summary, the ego state scoring system provides a value for each of the five ego states for each of the 300 ACL adjectives. These scores can be correlated with other item ratings, such as for Psycho-

TABLE 2.2. Adjectives Strongly Associated with Particular Ego States

Critical parent	Nurturing parent	Adult	Free child	Adapted child
autocratic	affectionate	alert	adventurous	anxious
bossy	considerate	capable	affectionate	apathetic
demanding	forgiving	clear-thinking	artistic	argumentative
dominant	generous	efficient	energetic	arrogant
fault-finding	gentle	fair-minded	enthusiastic	awkward
forceful	helpful	logical	excitable	complaining
intolerant	kind	methodical	humorous	confused
nagging	praising	organized	imaginative	defensive
opinionated	sympathetic	precise	natural	dependent
prejudiced	tolerant	rational	pleasure-seeking	hurried
rigid	understanding	realistic	sexy	inhibited
severe	unselfish	reasonable	spontaneous	moody
stern	warm	unemotional	uninhibited	nervous

logical Importance, or can be used to compute mean ego state scores for any given subset of ACL items. In scoring a given subset of items (for example, those used in a self-description), the number of points accumulated for each factor is summed and expressed as a percent of all points accumulated. Thus, the scores for all five ego states always sum to 100.

EGO STATES AND FAVORABILITY

In our earlier discussion of the five factor scoring system, it was noted that the item values for each factor were positively correlated with item favorability. Item favorability is also correlated with the scores for each of the five ego states, as follows: Critical Parent (-.36), Nurturing Parent (.75), Adult (.65), Free Child (.31), and Adapted Child (-.73). Because of these associations with favorability, we will sometimes perform ego state analyses with the effects of favorability controlled by partial correlation.

The remainder of this book is organized in the following manner. In Chapter 3, we report the results of a 10-country study of the relative favorability of psychological characteristics, which are employed in subsequent analyses of psychological importance. In Chapter 4, we discuss the method of the study of psychological importance in 20 countries, followed by a critique of the method and analyses of the PI data by gender. In Chapter 5, we report item-level analyses of the PI data. In Chapter 6, the PI data are further analyzed in terms of our two theoretically based scoring systems: the Five Factor Model and Transactional Analysis Ego States. In Chapter 7, the PI findings from the preceding chapter are analyzed in relation to 16 cultural comparison variables. In Chapter 8, we summarize and synthesize our findings. In Chapter 9, we comment on the project from a broader perspective.

SUMMARY

In this second introductory chapter, we discussed the concept of psychological importance and reviewed the findings from earlier studies both in the United States and cross-culturally. We described two theoretical models—five factors and ego states—and the ACL scoring systems based on them. We discussed the matter of concept favorability as it relates to the various factors in the two theoretical models. We concluded the chapter with an overview of the remainder of the book.

THE RELATIVE FAVORABILITY OF PSYCHOLOGICAL TRAITS
A 10-COUNTRY STUDY

BACKGROUND

Charles Osgood and his associates (Osgood et al., 1957, 1975) have concluded that in many, if not all, of the world's languages the dominant affective (emotional) meaning component is evaluation or favorability. This means that beyond their denotative ("dictionary") meanings, words differ primarily in their connotations of goodness and badness. The fact that the world's languages have this pervasive characteristic does not, of course, mean that given adjectives are equally good or bad in all cultures. The degree to which given adjectives vary in favorability across cultures is a question for empirical investigation.

The reader of the two introductory chapters has already encountered the topic of trait favorability in several different contexts. In Chapter 1, favorability was identified as the primary factor in the affective meaning scoring system for the ACL. In Chapter 2, we described the relationship of favorability scores to PI scores in our first seven countries. Later in Chapter 2 we discussed the relationship of favorability to the five factor scoring system and the ego state scoring system. In each instance, the favorability scores employed were the mean ratings of the English language adjectives by American university students and it was likely that there was some degree of English/American bias in these ratings. Ideally, one would wish to have favorability ratings of the ACL items made in the local language by persons from the same cultural groups as those providing other ACL data, such as the ratings of PI. For example, the PI ratings made by Chileans of the 300 Spanish adjectives should be compared to favorability ratings of the Spanish adjectives also made by Chileans. When it is not possible to have favorability ratings from a given cultural group, a partial solution might be to use *language-specific* favorability scores. For example, the Spanish language favorability scores obtained in Chile might be also used in Spanish-speaking Argentina, and the English language scores developed in the United States might also be used in Australia. The study reported in this chapter was designed to examine similarities and differences in the favorability of psychological traits in 10 culture groups that constituted a reasonably representative subset of the 20 groups involved in the main study of psychological importance. The design also permitted an examination of the degree of agreement between women and men in their ratings of trait favorability. In addition to an interest in the comparative favorability findings per se we draw upon these findings in our subsequent analyses of PI, which is the reason for presenting the favorability findings in this early chapter.

There are several potential causes of differences in the favorability of translated item sets relative to the English language item set. The first concerns translation fidelity per se; if the denotative meanings of the two sets of adjectives differ somewhat then it would not be surprising that they might also differ in favorability. If, for example, the English word "aggressive" is translated by a foreign language word which is more like "assertive," we would not be surprised at differences in the favorability ratings of the two terms. However, even if the denotative translation is accurate, there is still the possibility of true cultural variation in the favorability of a given trait; i.e., "aggressive" may be viewed more negatively in some cultural contexts than in others. Another possible source of differences is "response sets" where the subjects in different groups may tend generally to rate the items in a more or less dispersed manner along the rating scale. These different kinds of effects will combine to produce whatever variations in favorability are found when the English language set and the foreign language sets are used with different cultural groups.

In the present study, seven translated versions of the ACL were rated for favorability by native language speakers. The translated versions were in the Chinese, Korean, Norwegian, Portuguese, Spanish, Turkish, and Urdu (Pakistan) languages. In addition, new sets of English language ratings were obtained from subjects in Nigeria and Singapore, and the original English language ratings made by the students in the United States were included for comparative purposes. These 10 sets of ratings were analyzed in terms of similarities and differences among the translated versions and between the translated and the English versions.

METHOD

The method in each country was patterned as closely as possible after the original English language favorability study (Williams & Best, 1977).

SUBJECTS

Subjects in each group were men and women students, evenly divided by gender, from universities in Chile (CHL), China (CHN), Korea (KOR), Nigeria (NIG), Norway (NOR), Pakistan (PAK), Portugal (POR), Singapore (SIN), Turkey (TUR), and the United States (USA). Group sizes ranged from 40 to 120.

MATERIALS AND PROCEDURE

Subjects in seven countries were given the appropriate foreign language translation of the standard list of ACL adjectives. Subjects in Nigeria and Singapore were given the original English language version since English is the standard university language in these countries.

Subjects were given the following instructions, translated as appropriate:

> The Adjective Check List is a group of 300 adjectives which are often used to describe people. In this study we wish to determine how favorable or unfavorable each of these adjectives seems to you. You will be asked to consider each adjective and decide whether the adjective says something favorable (positive) about a person, whether it says something unfavorable (negative) about a person, or whether it is neutral with regard to favorability.

Subjects then indicated their judgments of each adjective on a five-point scale ranging from very unfavorable (1), through neutral (3), to very favorable (5).

RESULTS

WITHIN-COUNTRY CORRELATIONS

In each country, the student ratings were averaged to produce a mean favorability rating for each of the 300 adjectives, separately for women and men students. The ratings given by men and women were then compared for possible gender effects and as an indication of the reliability of the rating procedure. The correlations in the different samples were, as follows: Chile .98, China .96, Korea .99, Nigeria .94,

Norway .99, Pakistan .94, Portugal .99, Singapore .98, Turkey .98, and the United States .96. These remarkably high values indicated that there were no appreciable gender differences. The finding of such high correlations between two independent groups in each country was taken to indicate that the favorability ratings in each country were highly reliable and the men's and women's data were merged in subsequent analyses. The mean favorability score for each of the 300 items in each of the 10 countries is displayed in Appendix B.

The means and standard deviations for the 300 favorability ratings in each country are shown in Table 3.1, where it can be seen that the means were all near 3.00, the scale midpoint. The standard deviations were all generally similar in magnitude, with the exception of Nigeria where the standard deviation appeared atypically small, indicating that the Nigerian PI ratings were less dispersed across the rating scale relative to the findings in other countries.

BETWEEN-COUNTRY CORRELATIONS

A product-moment correlation coefficient was computed between the favorability ratings in each pair of countries across all 300 items. These coefficients are presented in Table 3.2. Here it can be observed that the values ranged from a low of .68 between Korea and Nigeria to a high of .95 between the English language ratings in Singapore and the United States. It does not follow, however, that the use of a common language necessarily leads to relatively high correlations: the coefficients between the United States and Nigeria, and between Singapore and Nigeria, were both only .82.

TABLE 3.1. Means and Standard
Deviations (SD) of Favorability
Scores in Each Country

	Means	SD
Chile	3.04	1.07
China	3.05	.98
Korea	2.95	1.04
Nigeria	3.04	.77
Norway	2.91	1.08
Pakistan	3.07	1.16
Portugal	3.00	1.02
Singapore	3.00	1.03
Turkey	2.98	1.04
United States	3.02	1.08

TABLE 3.2. Correlation Coefficient and Percent Common Variance (in Parentheses) between Favorability Ratings of the 300 Adjectives for Each Pair of 10 Countries

	China	Korea	Nigeria	Norway	Pakistan	Portugal	Singapore	Turkey	United States
Chile	.84 (71)	.80 (64)	.77 (59)	.87 (76)	.82 (67)	.91 (83)	.87 (76)	.84 (71)	.89 (79)
China	—	.76 (58)	.72 (52)	.81 (67)	.80 (64)	.79 (62)	.85 (72)	.78 (61)	.85 (72)
Korea		—	.68 (46)	.80 (64)	.78 (61)	.77 (59)	.81 (66)	.77 (59)	.81 (66)
Nigeria			—	.74 (55)	.80 (64)	.77 (59)	.82 (67)	.77 (59)	.82 (67)
Norway				—	.79 (62)	.86 (74)	.86 (74)	.82 (67)	.89 (79)
Pakistan					—	.81 (67)	.85 (72)	.83 (69)	.84 (71)
Portugal						—	.85 (72)	.83 (69)	.87 (76)
Singapore							—	.85 (72)	.95 (90)
Turkey								—	.85 (72)

Shown in parentheses in Table 3.2, are the squares of the correlation coefficients. These provide an estimate of percent common variance between the favorability distributions in each pair of countries. Employing these values, it can be seen that the range of common variance was from 46 percent to 90 percent with a mean common variance across all comparisons of 68 percent. The mean common variance for each country versus the other nine countries is shown in Table 3.3. Here it can be seen that the United States had the highest overall agreement with the other countries, while Nigeria had the least.

MOST AND LEAST FAVORABLE ITEMS ACROSS ALL SAMPLES

For each item, a mean was computed for the 10 individual country means in order to determine the items considered most favorable and most unfavorable across all samples. The 15 most favorable and 15 least favorable items are shown in Table 3.4. The two item sets were then analyzed in terms of the Five Factor Model scoring system (FormyDuval et al., 1995) (see Chapter 2) to see whether the sets were different on qualities other than favorability. The results of this analysis revealed the following five factor scores for the sets of 15 favorable and 15 unfavorable adjectives, respectively: Extraversion, 3.94 and 1.99; Agreeableness, 4.18 and 1.62; Conscientiousness, 4.00 and 2.35; Emotional Stability, 3.66 and 2.33; and Openness, 3.60 and 2.36. Thus, the favorable items were found to be higher than the unfavorable items on each of the five personality factors. This conclusion is consistent with the findings of studies in the United States by FormyDuval et al. (1995) and Goodman and Williams (1996) (see Chapter 2) indicating that the high end of each of the five scales is intrinsically more favor-

TABLE 3.3. Mean Common Variance:
Each Country versus Nine Others

Chile	71.77
China	64.34
Korea	62.18
Nigeria	58.67
Norway	68.66
Pakistan	66.33
Portugal	69.00
Singapore	73.44
Turkey	66.56
United States	74.67
	$M = 67.56$

TABLE 3.4. Fifteen Most Favorable and 15 Most
Unfavorable Adjectives across All 10 Samples

Favorable characteristics (means = 4.30 to 4.59)	Unfavorable characteristics (means = 1.33 to 1.68)
capable	arrogant
cheerful	bitter
civilized	boastful
clear-thinking	cruel
friendly	deceitful
healthy	foolish
helpful	hostile
honest	irresponsible
industrious	nagging
intelligent	obnoxious
kind	quarrelsome
loyal	rude
responsible	selfish
sincere	thankless
understanding	unkind

able than the low end (e.g., extraversion is more favorable than introversion, etc.).

ITEMS WITH GREATEST AGREEMENT / DISAGREEMENT

For each of the 300 items, a standard deviation was computed among the ten country means. Relatively small standard deviations would indicate a high degree of agreement in the favorability values across all 10 countries; relatively large standard deviations would indicate items for which there was most disagreement regarding favorability. The 15 items on which there was greatest agreement and the 15 items on which there was greatest disagreement are presented in Table 3.5. While the low agreement on some adjectives may be due to translation difficulties—as with the English slang terms *spunky* and *zany*—disagreement on others may reflect cultural variations in what is considered favorable. For example, six of the countries in the present study were included in Hofstede's (1980) research on work-related values where the United States and Norway were classified as having individualistic cultures while Chile, Pakistan, Portugal, and Singapore were said to have collectivistic cultures. Two of the high disagreement items seem relevant here: *individualistic*, which might be more favorable in individualistic cultures, and *self-denying*, which might be more favorable in collectivistic cultures. Consistent with these expectations, the

TABLE 3.5. Fifteen Adjectives with Highest
Agreement and 15 Adjectives with Lowest
Agreement across All 10 Samples

Highest agreement (SD = .10 to .17)	Lowest agreement (SD = .75 to 1.08)
charming	aggressive
cheerful	artistic
clear-thinking	individualistic
confused	ingenious
distractible	interests wide
foolish	opportunistic
foresighted	outspoken
healthy	persistent
intelligent	self-denying
lazy	shrewd
pleasant	sophisticated
retiring	spunky
understanding	submissive
unstable	unselfish
weak	zany

mean favorability of *individualistic* was higher (3.79) in the two individualistic countries and lower (2.76) in the four collectivistic countries. Conversely, the mean favorability of the adjective *self-denying* was higher in the four collectivistic countries (3.11) than in the two individualistic countries (2.51). On the other hand, there was little evidence of pervasive differences in the two groups of countries; the mean common variance between the two individualistic countries was 79 percent, while the mean common variance among the four collectivistic countries was 73 percent.

In sum, the results of the 10-country favorability study revealed a rather remarkable degree of cross-cultural agreement in the relative "goodness" and "badness" of different psychological characteristics. The median cross-group correlation of .82 is similar in magnitude to the *reliability coefficients* obtained when personality/social assessment procedures are given to the *same* persons on two different occasions! While other culture/language groups remain to be studied, the present results are sufficiently robust to suggest a "derived etic" or pancultural model of trait favorability.

In addition to their intrinsic interest, the favorability ratings obtained in this study enabled us to study the relationship of psychological importance and favorability as reported in subsequent chapters. By using the Spanish language ratings obtained in Chile, in Argentina, and in Venezuela, and by using the English language ratings made in the United States, in Australia, in India, and in Nepal, we were able to employ language-specific favorability ratings in 15 of our 20 countries.

SUMMARY

In this chapter we examined the favorability of the 300 ACL adjectives in 10 countries employing eight different languages. The findings indicated a high degree of cross-cultural agreement in the relative favorability of psychological characteristics.

PSYCHOLOGICAL IMPORTANCE
METHOD AND GENDER ANALYSES

Having introduced the concept of psychological importance (PI) in Chapter 2, where we also described previous research on this topic, we turn now to the present study of psychological importance in 20 cultural groups.

In this chapter, we describe and critique the method employed in the PI study, followed by a report of findings from gender analyses. In Chapter 5, we summarize the results of PI analyses conducted at the level of individual items. In Chapter 6, we continue our examination of the PI data employing the five factor and ego state scoring systems described in Chapter 2. In Chapter 7, we focus on the degree to which observed PI differences among countries may be considered attributable to *cultural* factors through their relationship to independently assessed cultural comparison variables.

METHOD

SELECTION OF COOPERATING RESEARCHERS AND RESEARCH SITES

The first step in the identification of the research sites was to contact psychologists who had served as cooperating researchers in our previous cross-cultural projects dealing with gender stereotypes, age stereotypes, and self concepts. Each person was provided with a description of the general nature of the proposed project and was asked whether he or she would like to participate. In addition, we contacted several people who had expressed an interest in our earlier projects or who had been nominated by other cooperating researchers. These procedures led to the enlistment of persons from 18 countries, in addition to Chile and the United States, which were represented by the authors. The names of the participating psychologists are found on the cooperating researchers page of this book.

With the group of countries identified in the foregoing manner, it was possible that the group of 20 samples might be biased and not at all representative of the major cultures of the world. This did not prove to be a major problem. As can be seen in Table 4.1, the countries represented all inhabited continents and, generally, composed a heterogeneous group of cultures. While there are some obvious gaps in the sample (e.g., Eastern Europe), and some continents are underrepresented (e.g., Africa), the group of 20 countries seems sufficiently large and diverse to address the question of cultural variations in the importance assigned to different psychological characteristics.

SUBJECT CHARACTERISTICS

The persons participating as subjects in the project were male and female university students from 20 countries. Table 4.2 lists the countries in alphabetical order and indicates the university population which the subjects represent and the language of administration. The

TABLE 4.1. The 20 Countries in the Psychological Importance Study Grouped by Geographical Areas[a]

Europe	Asia
Finland (FIN)	China (CHN)
Germany (GER)	Hong Kong (HKG)
Netherlands (NET)	India (IND)
Norway (NOR)	Japan (JAP)
Portugal (POR)	Korea (KOR)
Turkey[b] (TUR)	Nepal (NEP)
	Pakistan (PAK)
South America	Singapore (SIN)
Argentina (ARG)	
Chile (CHL)	Africa
Venezuela (VEN)	Nigeria (NIG)
North America	Oceania
United States (USA)	Australia (AUS)

[a]Parentheses show abbreviations used in the study.
[b]Part of Turkey is in Europe, part in Asia.

TABLE 4.2. Sample Characteristics in
the Psychological Importance Study

Country	Institution	Language
Argentina	U. de Buenos Aires	Spanish
Australia	U. of Western Sidney	English
Chile	U. de La Frontera	Spanish
China	Nanjing Normal U.	Chinese
Finland	U. Helsinki	Finnish
Germany	Tech. Hochscule Darmstadt	German
Hong Kong	Chinese U. of H.K.	Chinese
India	U. Allahabad	English
Japan	Osaka U.	Japanese
Korea	Pusan National U.	Korean
Nepal	Tribhuvan U.	English
Netherlands	Leiden U.	Dutch
Nigeria	Abia State U.	English
Norway	U. Trondheim	Norwegian
Pakistan	U. of Sindh	Urdu
Portugal	U. of Porto	Portuguese
Singapore	National U.	English
Turkey	Gazi U.	Turkish
United States	Wake Forest U.	English
Venezuela	U.N.E. Fco. de Miranda	Spanish

plan of the study was to obtain data from approximately 100 students
in each country with an approximately equal division by gender. This
condition was reasonably well met with sample sizes ranging from 60
to 147 persons. In the third column it can be seen that the research
procedure was administered in English to six samples, in Spanish to
three samples, and in 11 additional languages to one sample each. The
student participants were chosen by the local cooperating researcher as
being reasonably representative of students at the local university
rather than being some highly selected group.

INSTRUMENT AND PROCEDURE

The English language version of the instructions for the psychological importance ratings was, as follows:

> When we are asked to describe a person we know, we frequently use
> adjectives that refer to certain characteristics that the person seems to have.
> Thus, we might describe one person as "inconsistent," another as "fun-lov-
> ing," and another as "careful." Psychologists refer to such behavioral char-
> acteristics as traits.

54   CHAPTER 4

The purpose of this study is to ask you to rate the importance of certain psychological traits in providing information as to what the person is really like.

In describing what a person is really like, some traits seem to be relatively important because they seem to refer to central or basic personality characteristics. For example, describing someone as being truthful or a liar seems to be saying something very important about the person.

On the other hand, in describing what a person is really like, some traits seem of less importance because they seem to refer to more superficial or peripheral personality characteristics. For example, describing someone as being neat or sloppy seems to be saying something of less importance regarding what the person is really like.

As can be seen in the examples given, there is no relationship between how favorable a trait is and how important it is. Some important traits are "good" and some are "bad"; some unimportant traits are "good" and some are "bad."

On the following pages, you will find a list of 300 adjectives. For each adjective you are asked to consider its importance in describing what a person is really like. There are no right or wrong answers and it is your first impression which we want. Do not spend a lot of time puzzling over individual adjectives. You are asked to record your impression using the following five-point scale:

1. Little or no importance
2. Minor importance
3. Moderate importance
4. Major importance
5. Critical or outstanding importance

Please record your age (nearest birthday) and gender (M or F).

For each of the following characteristics, please consider its *degree of importance* in describing what a person is really like. Please record your impressions by *circling one of the five numbers to* the right of each adjective.

With these instructions were presented the 300 items of the Adjective Check List which the subjects then rated along the five-point scale to record their impression of the psychological importance of the adjectives, as defined in the instructions. The items were presented to each group in the language shown in Table 4.2. The English language version of the 300 items is shown in Appendix D.

In countries where a language other than English was employed, the local researcher arranged for the translation of the rating instructions into the appropriate language. Each researcher was free to substitute culturally more appropriate adjectives for the English terms used as illustrations in the instructions (i.e., truthful, liar, neat, sloppy). For all of the languages employed, there was a previous translation of the 300 ACL items that had been used in earlier cross-cultural studies using the ACL methodology, as described in Chapter 1. However, a new

Chinese translation of the ACL items was made for use in Hong Kong by means of a cooperative effort among several persons familiar with both languages.

As a result of the foregoing procedures, the basic data for analysis were the ratings of psychological importance of each of the 300 adjectives obtained from the men and women subjects in each of the 20 countries.

CRITIQUE OF METHODS

The methods employed in the present project to gather and analyze data are not without criticism. Elsewhere, we have offered extensive critiques of the use of the ACL item pool in cross-cultural studies employing university student subjects (Williams & Best, 1990a, pp. 53–58; Williams & Best, 1990b, pp. 72–83). Here we will comment briefly on a few major concerns.

THE CONTENT OF THE ITEM POOL

The 300 items of the ACL do not begin to exhaust the person-descriptors in English or in any other language. We know that, had we employed a preliminary, emic procedure to identify person-descriptors in each country, we would have identified some characteristics not included in the ACL pool and that some ACL items would not have been included in the emic lists. On the other hand, the ACL item pool had been carefully developed over a period of years by Harrison Gough and his associates at the University of California (Berkeley) in an effort to develop a set of descriptors which was reasonably comprehensive of the variations in human personality. Included were items thought to be essential for describing personality from different theoretical vantage points—those of Freud, Jung, Mead, Murray, and so on (Gough & Heilbrun, 1965). Thus, instead of asking whether the ACL list is "complete," which it certainly is not, we might ask whether it is "adequate."

Perhaps the best evidence of adequacy comes from our previous cross-cultural studies in which the ACL pool has been used to study: gender stereotypes in 27 countries; age stereotypes in 19 countries; and self concepts in 14 countries. In these studies, there has never been a complaint—from cooperating researchers or their student subjects—that the ACL item pool as a whole was inadequate for the description of the indicated targets (i.e., men and women, young adults and old adults, self and ideal self). Apparently, the ACL item pool is broad enough to capture salient characteristics of persons in a great variety of cultural settings.

NATURE OF THE TASK

The instructions given above asked the participants to rate the items for their general importance with no attention to the possibility that importance judgments might vary depending on the social context in which behaviors occur. Brislin (1993, pp. 61–62) observes that the notion of describing persons with context-free trait labels may be more familiar to persons from more individualistic cultures than to persons from more collectivistic cultures. In the latter, more attention may be paid to traits in different social contexts (at home, at work, etc.) with less emphasis on situation-free traits. Brislin (1993, p. 77) writes: "If people in individualist societies make judgments about traits that supposedly generalize across situations. . . and if people in collectivist societies make judgments based on traits in situations, direct comparisons of the judgments will be difficult to make." On the other hand, Oerter, Oerter, Agostiani, Kim, and Wibowo (1996) studied views of human nature in the United States, Indonesia, Japan, and Korea and concluded that, in all four cultures, human beings are viewed as "owners" of psychological traits (also skills, competence, and values) that "explain" the persons' behavior and performance.

While the general point about the influence of context on judgments of trait importance is well taken (see Study 3, pp. 28–29), the question here is whether asking people to make judgments of psychological importance in a context-free situation is equally meaningful to persons from individualistic and collectivistic countries. If the task is less meaningful in collectivistic countries, we would expect less agreement in the ratings made by persons within a given country. Looking ahead, we found no evidence of such an effect in the data from the present project where the within-country agreement—as judged from the average correlation of men's and women's ratings—was not different in the clusters of countries subsequently classified as more individualistic (median $r = .885$) or more collectivistic (median $r = .865$). Thus, while context does have an influence on ratings of psychological importance, we conclude that the rating of general, context-free importance was a meaningful task in all of the countries studied.

TRANSLATION TO OTHER LANGUAGES

With one exception, all of the translations of the 300 items to languages other than English had been made for use in our earlier studies of gender stereotypes, age stereotypes, and self-concepts (Williams, 1993; Williams & Best, 1990a, 1990b). While we have no formal basis for judging the adequacy of the translations, we know that they were done with care using recommended methods such as the committee approach and back translation.

The relatively large size and nature of the ACL item pool provides a degree of "insurance" regarding translation difficulties. While each of the 300 English adjectives has a discriminably different meaning, there are many near-synonyms in the pool. Consider the following groups: steady, unemotional, unexcitable; or aggressive, assertive, forceful; or soft-hearted, sentimental, sensitive. There is obviously a substantial common meaning factor within each of these sets. If, for some reason, one of the items is not well translated, there is the hope that the others will be, and in this way the common-meaning factor will be represented in the translated item pool.

THE USE OF UNIVERSITY STUDENTS AS SUBJECTS

A question can be raised as to the use of university students as representatives of their respective cultural groups. University students are always selected samples and, in most countries, constitute elite, socially aware, and politically liberal groups which cannot be considered as "representative" of the general population. On the other hand, there are certain advantages in using students in psychological research due to: their intelligence, which enables them to comprehend abstract tasks; their intellectual orientation, which enables them to appreciate the value of research and be willing to cooperate in it; and, of course, their relative accessibility.

We have argued elsewhere (Williams & Best, 1990b, pp. 80–83) that, despite being atypical relative to the general population of their own countries, university students are still very much the product of their respective cultures: Indian students are "quite Indian," Japanese students are "quite Japanese," etc. While they may have been influenced by educational experiences which have brought them into contact with other cultures, this would seem likely to produce a "conservative error" in viewing them as cultural representatives, i.e., such experiences would tend to reduce differences between groups.

The use of atypical groups of persons from different cultures has been addressed by Hofstede (1979, 1980) in the context of his 40-country study of work-related values, which we examined in Chapter 1. Hofstede obtained his questionnaire data from the employees of one multinational business organization, coded as HERMES. The employees were primarily from the managerial, professional, and technical ranks of the company, with the great majority being male.

Hofstede (1979, p. 392) addresses the question of atypical samples, as follows:

> Valid comparisons of samples of individuals from countries should either be very broad (representative of entire populations) or narrow but very well matched (functionally equivalent in each country). The HERMES samples belong to the second category. Respondents from country to country are similar in many respects (education level, occupation, actual work done, company policies, and superstructure); they only differ in their nationality. An analysis comparing HERMES employees in one country to those in another should therefore reveal the effect of nationality quite clearly. Because the respondents have so much in common, the differences found within HERMES should in fact be a conservative estimate of the differences to be found elsewhere.

Another feature of the use of university students is that they may provide evidence of the direction of cultural change. Speaking of the use of students as subjects in research on values, Schwartz (1994, p. 91) notes that "undergraduate students, like HERMES employees, are more likely to show the influence of exposure to modernizing trends. Students are younger than the population in general, and their priorities may reflect directions in which the culture is changing."

In sum, we believe that, while university students may not be ideal subjects for cross-cultural studies, they can be meaningfully viewed as "cultural carriers" and as useful samples of persons from their respective cultural groups.

THE USE OF SCORING SYSTEMS DEVELOPED IN THE UNITED STATES

In the latter part of this chapter, and in Chapter 5, we analyze the data at the level of individual items without attempting to group them in any way. In these analyses there is no problem concerning "American bias," other than the possibility of such bias in the item pool itself, as discussed above. While the item-level PI analyses lead to some interesting findings, they are, generally, of a quantitative, atheoretical nature and not easily summarized as to their conceptual meaning.

In order to gain some sense of the qualitative differences in PI among our countries we turn, in Chapter 6, to an examination of the PI findings in relation to two theoretical systems which are American-based and, possibly, American-biased: the five factor system and the ego state system, both of which were described in some detail in Chapter 2.

The five factor ACL scoring system (FormyDuval et al., 1995) employed American judges to determine the degree to which each ACL item reflects each of five basic personality factors: Extraversion, Agreeableness, Conscientiousness, Emotional Stability, and Openness. The five factor Model on which this scoring system is based has received validation in several cross-cultural studies (e.g., Bond et al., 1975; Isaka, 1990; John, Goldberg, & Angleitner, 1984; McCrae & Costa, 1997; Paunonen et al., 1992). At present, it seems reasonable to assume that the model's five basic personality dimensions can be meaningfully employed in a great variety of—if not all—cultural settings.

The ego state scoring system (Williams & Williams, 1980) also employed American judges to determine the degree to which each ACL item reflects each of five ego states: Critical Parent, Nurturing Parent, Adult, Free Child, and Adapted Child. While there is no research bearing on the question of American bias in the system, impressionistically it seems that the nature of the concepts employed is such that they would be considered meaningful in almost any cultural setting. Further, it can be noted that this scoring system has been employed and found useful in previous cross-cultural studies (Williams, 1993; Williams & Best, 1990a).

Our study would have been strengthened by having emically derived five factor and ego state scoring systems developed in each cultural group but this ideal was far beyond the resources of the present project. Our defense of the use of the American-based systems lies in the compelling need to make summaries that go beyond the item level and the necessity of using the tools available to us. If one needed to measure the relative length of several physical objects, it would seem better to use a "biased" measuring stick, which was a bit too short or too long, than to use no measuring stick at all!

Having read our various comments concerning our methods, one can appreciate why cross-cultural psychologists spend so much time and effort on methodological concerns—sometimes it seems to the neglect of empirical research! Having given our opinions as to the strengths and weaknesses of our methods, we leave the final judgment of adequacy with our peers.

GENDER ANALYSES

This section deals with the intriguing question of whether women and men differ in what they consider to be psychologically important. While we had no a priori expectations regarding gender, it seemed important to examine the question empirically. To do this, we made separate studies of the ratings provided by the women and men subjects in each country to see whether there was evidence of substantial gender effects or whether the data in each country could be meaningfully pooled across gender in subsequent analyses.

The question of the similarity of the ratings given by men and women subjects was examined in several different ways. One type of similarity would involve the average ratings given by men and women across the entire item pool. This was explored by examining the values shown in Table 4.3, which revealed that the mean ratings given by the men and women subjects in each country were generally quite similar.

A different question regarding gender similarity concerned the degree of dispersion of the ratings around the item means, i.e., does one gender group tend to give more variable ratings to the adjectives than does the other? This question was addressed by examining the standard deviations (SD) for the men and women subjects across the entire item pool as presented in the middle column of Table 4.3. These values indicated that the degree of inter-item dispersion along the five-point rating scale was generally similar for men and women subjects, although there was the suggestion that the women's ratings were more variable than the men's ratings in Pakistan and Nigeria.

To what degree do the men and women subjects in each sample tend to agree on the level of psychological importance assigned to each of the rated characteristics? This question was addressed by computing, in each country, the product-moment correlation coefficient between the 300 mean ratings given by the women subjects and the 300 mean ratings made by the men subjects. These values are presented in the right-hand column of Table 4.3 where it can be seen that the degree of agreement for men and women subjects ranged from a high of .99 in Hong Kong to a low of .68 in Nigeria and Venezuela. The median correlation for the total group of 20 samples was .88, indicating that, in general, there was a high degree of agreement—77 percent common variance—between the ratings of psychological importance made by the men subjects and the women subjects in the project. It can be noted, however, that the cross-gender agreement on psychological importance was substantially less than the 94 percent common variance between men's and women's ratings of favorability as reported in Chapter 3.

The question of possible pancultural gender differences in the rating of psychological importance was pursued further. If there are pancultural gender differences in the importance assigned to certain traits, then the sets of correlation coefficients computed *among* the 20 men's groups and *among* the 20 women's groups should tend to be higher than the sets of correlations *between* the men's and women's groups. When these various types of correlations were computed, it was

TABLE 4.3. Descriptive Statistics (Total Item Pool: 20 Countries)

Country/gender	Mean	SD	Correlation (men vs. women)
ARG: M	3.33	.487	.91
ARG: W	3.48	.454	
AUS: M	3.22	.438	.78
AUS: W	2.91	.496	
CHL: M	3.33	.411	.86
CHL: W	3.48	.476	
CHN: M	3.12	.468	.86
CHN: W	2.84	.449	
FIN: M	2.88	.378	.86
FIN: W	2.84	.437	
GER: M	3.14	.637	.93
GER: W	2.91	.606	
HKG: M	3.03	.943	.99
HKG: W	3.02	1.026	
IND: M	3.01	.404	.77
IND: W	3.11	.322	
JAP: M	2.97	.571	.89
JAP: W	2.96	.538	
KOR: M	3.03	.460	.85
KOR: W	3.20	.505	
NEP: M	3.05	.514	.89
NEP: W	2.72	.657	
NET: M	3.30	.404	.89
NET: W	3.21	.438	
NIG: M	2.87	.293	.68
NIG: W	2.74	.457	
NOR: M	2.83	.475	.80
NOR: W	2.91	.482	
PAK: M	3.03	.738	.94
PAK: W	3.07	.988	
POR: M	3.11	.450	.90
POR: W	3.19	.482	
SIN: M	3.08	.427	.88
SIN: W	3.17	.471	
TUR: M	2.90	.458	.87
TUR: W	2.86	.527	
USA: M	3.13	.457	.93
USA: W	3.15	.543	
VEN: M	2.93	.613	.68
VEN: W	2.91	.582	

found that the median correlation among the male samples was .43, the median correlation among female samples was .45, and the median correlation between male and female samples was .45. This analysis indicated that the average correlation *between* men and women was not lower than the average correlations obtained *within* each of the gender groups and, therefore, no evidence was seen of pancultural gender differences in judgments of the psychological importance of traits.

Another gender analysis involving all 300 items was done by calculating, for each item, a grand mean of the 20 men's means and a grand mean of the 20 women's means. When the two sets of grand means were correlated across the items the resulting coefficient was a rather remarkable .968 which, when squared, yielded an estimated common variance of 93.7 percent. In view of the vicissitudes of language translations, this finding suggested virtual identity in the PI ratings made by the men and women subjects.

While the foregoing analyses provided no evidence of systematic gender differences in the total item pool, it seemed possible that some gender differences might appear if we focussed only on the items considered *relatively* more important in each of the two gender groups. This question was explored by computing, for each item, a difference score between the 20-country grand means for men and for women and identifying the 30 items which the women rated *relatively* more important (by .08 to .16 points), and the 30 items which the men rated as *relatively* more important (by .13 to .33 points). Such small difference scores might well have been due to chance, in which case one would not expect qualitative differences in the two item sets. But such was not the case.

The two 30 item sets are presented in Table 4.4. An examination of the tabled items suggested that the two item sets were qualitatively different. It appeared that the women's item set generally was composed of more favorable adjectives while the men's item set was composed of somewhat more unfavorable items. This observation was confirmed when the two item sets were scored for favorability using the United States scoring system (Mean = 500; SD = 100). This revealed that the items more important to women had a mean of 600.3 and the items more important to men had a mean of 459.1. This indicated that, if one sets aside the bulk of the items on which men and women agree as to their psychological importance, and focusses on the few items on which there was relative disagreement, we find women assigning relatively greater importance to a group of more favorable traits and men assigning more importance to a group of somewhat more unfavorable traits.

TABLE 4.4. The 30 Adjectives Rated as
More Important by Each Gender Group

More important to women	More important to men
clever	sexy
understanding	awkward
loyal	quick
poised	effeminate
mild	thankless
cheerful	lazy
helpful	argumentative
jolly	absent-minded
dependable	slipshod
initiative	disorderly
friendly	tense
responsible	serious
natural	superstitious
outspoken	thrifty
mannerly	unassuming
patient	rebellious
cooperative	unambitious
confident	pleasure-seeking
egotistical	fussy
intelligent	stolid
charming	severe
appreciative	unconventional
forgiving	immature
sincere	spendthrift
reliable	infantile
clear-thinking	sensitive
easy-going	selfish
interests wide	touchy
optimistic	hurried
warm	complicated

The qualitative differences between the two item sets in Table 4.4 were further examined by scoring each set using the five factor and ego state scoring systems described in Chapter 2. The results are presented in Table 4.5.

An examination of the five factor means indicated that the women's item set was higher than the men's item set on each factor. Since each factor is positively correlated with favorability, these effects may simply be another reflection of the differential favorability noted above.

The ego state findings were more interesting. A comparison of the two item sets indicated that the men's set was much higher on Critical

TABLE 4.5.　Five Factor and Ego State Analyses of the 30 Items
Rated as Relatively More Important by Men and by Women

	Five factor scores[a]				
	EXT	AGR	CON	EMS	OPN
Items more important to women	3.88	3.97	3.86	3.31	3.51
Items more important to men	2.74	2.68	2.73	2.31	2.91
	Ego state scores[b]				
	CP	NP	A	FC	AC
Items more important to women	13.1	32.1	24.9	18.9	11.0
Items more important to men	18.1	15.2	17.1	24.4	25.2

[a]EXT = Extraversion; AGR = Agreeableness; CON = Conscientiousness; EMS = Emotional Stability; OPN = Openness.
[b]CP = Critical Parent; NP = Nurturing Parent; A = Adult; FC = Free Child; AC = Adapted Child.

Parent and Adapted Child, suggesting that the men assigned more importance to qualities related to recognition of authority and conformity to it. By contrast, the women's item set was much higher on Nurturing Parent and Adult, suggesting that the women assigned more importance to qualities related to caretaking and problem solving. Further analyses revealed that the effects seen in Table 4.5 were equally evident in the 10 countries with the highest men versus women correlations and in the 10 countries with the lowest, as reported in Table 4.3.

The results just noted can be compared to the pancultural findings from studies of male and female gender stereotypes where, stereotypically, men are said to be higher in Critical Parent and Adult while women are higher in Nurturing Parent and Adapted Child (Williams & Best, 1990a). The results for Critical Parent and Nurturing Parent "match," with each gender group assigning more importance to the ego states stereotypically associated with their gender. On the other hand, the results for the Adult and Adapted Child ego states are reversed, with each group assigning greater importance to the qualities stereotypically assigned to the other gender group. Thus, there was little overall similarity between the importance judgments of women and men and the pancultural gender stereotypes.

Returning to the big picture, we conclude that, despite some interesting minor gender differences, the overall similarity in the ratings of psychological importance warranted the combining of the women's and men's data in each country to obtain a set of general ratings reflecting the psychological importance of each of the 300 items in each cultural group. It is these pooled gender ratings that were employed in all analyses reported in the following chapters.

SUMMARY

In this chapter, we first described and critiqued the method employed in the psychological importance study. We then examined the data for possible gender differences, concluding that, while there were some interesting minor differences in the ratings made by women and men, the high degree of overall similarity warranted the pooling of the gender data in subsequent analyses.

PSYCHOLOGICAL
IMPORTANCE
ITEM LEVEL ANALYSES

The preceding chapter ended with the conclusion that, while some interesting minor gender effects were observed, the overall similarity of the men's and women's ratings of psychological importance (PI) warranted their being pooled for subsequent analyses. In each country, this was done for each item by taking the mean of the men's mean and the women's mean to provide a single index of the psychological importance of each adjective in that country. The gender-pooled means for each of the 300 items in each country are displayed in Appendix A. These data are employed in all subsequent PI analyses. The means and standard deviations of the 300 items in each country are shown in Table 5.1.

Matsumoto (1996) and others have observed that researchers must be alert to the possibility of cross-cultural variation in "response sets" and there was some evidence of such in the ratings of psychological importance. For example, in Table 5.1, it appears that in Argentina and Chile there was a general tendency to rate all items somewhat higher than in other countries, while in Finland, Korea, Nigeria, and Norway, the average ratings across the entire item pool appear to be somewhat lower.

An examination of the standard deviations in Table 5.1 suggest some intercountry differences in the tendency to disperse the items along the rating scale. For example, the item ratings were more widely spread in Hong Kong than in Nigeria. In Hong Kong, there were 92 items with a mean value above 4.00 and 57 items with a mean value

TABLE 5.1. Means and Standard Deviations (SD)
of the Combined Gender Ratings for the Pool of
300 Items in Each Country

	Mean	SD
Argentina	3.41	.428
Australia	3.06	.440
Chile	3.41	.428
China	2.98	.441
Finland	2.86	.380
Germany	3.07	.548
Hong Kong	3.02	.982
India	3.06	.342
Japan	2.97	.539
Korea	3.12	.452
Nepal	2.90	.529
Netherlands	3.27	.384
Nigeria	2.80	.346
Norway	2.87	.453
Pakistan	3.05	.851
Portugal	3.15	.455
Singapore	3.13	.436
Turkey	2.88	.449
United States	3.14	.491
Venezuela	2.92	.548
Median (all groups)	3.05	.450

below 2.00, along the five-point scale. In Nigeria, there were no items above 4.00 and only 2 items below 2.00.

It is possible to control for the observed between-sample differences in means and standard deviations through the use of *standard scores*, and we employ these in some subsequent analyses. Generally, however, we used the PI ratings "as is" for two reasons: the response sets may, in fact, represent bonafide cultural/language differences; and the bulk of our analyses are correlational in nature and, thus, would not be affected by the transformation of the PI item means via standard scores.

COMMON VARIANCE BETWEEN PAIRS OF COUNTRIES

Our first interest was in studying the overall similarity among countries in the ratings of PI by comparing the distribution of 300 psychological importance scores in each country with the distribution in each of the other 19 countries. This was done by computing a product-moment correlation coefficient for each pair of the 20 countries, all of which were found to be positive in sign. Since correlation coefficients are somewhat difficult to manipulate statistically (e.g., means are misleading) and are easily misinterpreted regarding strength of relationship, we chose to present these findings in terms of "percent common variance," obtained by squaring the product-moment correlation coefficient and multiplying by 100. This transformation is appropriate when all coefficients have the same sign, as was true in this instance.

Table 5.2 presents the percent of common variance between the distributions of 300 psychological importance scores in each pair of countries. As can be seen, the common variance values ranged from a high of 64 percent between Australia and the United States to a low of 1 percent between Germany and Hong Kong. The median percent common variance for all values in Table 5.2 was approximately 25 percent. Earlier, it was noted that the median within-country correlation between the scores of men and women subjects was .88 which, when squared, led to an estimate of 77 percent common variance. Comparing these two percentages, one concludes that there are substantial differences in psychological importance among the various countries. Put another way, the relatively high reliability of the psychological scores *within* countries would have made possible a much larger degree of common variance *between* countries than was actually found.

We next addressed the question of whether there were certain countries where the PI ratings were more "typical" of the total group of countries than were others. This was done using the values presented in Table 5.2 to compute the mean percent common variance between each country and the 19 other countries. These values are given in Table 5.3, where it can be seen that relatively high means were found in India, Portugal, and Australia, while relatively low means were found in China, Germany, and Japan. These findings indicate that the PI scores in the former three countries were least distinctive relative to the total set of countries, while the PI scores in the latter three countries were most distinctive. Such typicality indices are obviously dependent upon the particular composition of the group of countries being studied. Since the sample of countries employed was a reasonably diverse one, the observed differences in mean common variance may be worthy of further study.

ATYPICAL ITEMS IN DIFFERENT COUNTRIES

We conducted an analysis to identify the items which were atypically high in psychological importance in each country. In making this

TABLE 5.2. Percent Common Variance ($r^2 \times 100$) between the PI Ratings in Each Pair of the 20 Countries

	AUS	CHL	CHN	FIN	GER	HK	IND	JAP	KOR	NEP	NET	NIG	NOR	PAK	POR	SIN	TUR	USA	VEN
ARG	32	53	14	25	21	15	27	12	18	18	34	18	22	21	30	28	14	26	14
AUS	—	30	14	30	21	17	53	14	28	34	51	21	30	27	44	52	23	64	19
CHL		—	15	36	26	5	23	12	20	12	30	10	34	13	38	34	12	39	8
CHN			—	15	17	22	25	7	17	24	9	25	11	23	26	15	15	10	15
FIN				—	29	4	27	11	13	11	43	9	36	9	31	34	12	41	6
GER					—	1	46	6	7	3	31	3	23	2	14	29	8	38	3
HK						—	37	7	35	50	6	41	3	55	30	4	20	2	37
IND							—	13	27	50	28	48	20	52	55	34	35	32	36
JAP								—	11	9	14	8	10	7	15	13	13	13	5
KOR									—	17	10	15	14	22	22	19	33	17	15
NEP										—	15	46	11	55	38	14	23	12	33
NET											—	7	27	9	29	39	11	39	9
NIG												—	5	54	39	12	29	8	26
NOR													—	8	29	10	31	41	8
PAK														—	45	13	33	10	36
POR															—	31	30	31	32
SIN																—	23	70	11
TUR																	—	12	17
USA																		—	8

TABLE 5.3. Mean Percent Common
Variance of Each Country versus
All 19 Others

IND	33.5	NIG	22.3
POR	32.1	FIN	22.2
AUS	31.8	HK	20.6
USA	27.0	NOR	19.5
SIN	26.6	KOR	19.0
PAK	26.0	TUR	18.8
NEP	25.0	VEN	17.8
CHL	23.7	CHN	16.3
ARG	23.3	GER	15.1
NET	23.2	JAP	10.5

analysis, we treated the observed differences in item pool means and standard deviations seen in Table 5.1 as "response biases" and employed standard scores as a control for these differences. This enabled us to identify items which were atypically high in PI in a given country relative to the other 19 countries.

We employed a standard score scale with a mean of 50 and a standard deviation of 10. In each country, each of the 300 PI scores was converted to the equivalent standard score, as follows: Item standard score = 50 + 10 [(item mean − item pool mean)/item pool standard deviation]. With this conversion, for example, an item with a mean two standard deviations above the item pool mean received a standard score of 70, while an item with a mean one standard deviation below the item pool mean received a standard score of 40.

Once these conversions were made, we identified items which were atypically high in each country, as follows. In Country X, for each item, the Country X standard score was compared with the mean of the standard scores in the 19 other countries with a difference score computed. Country X items with standard scores of 15 or more points above the 19 country mean were identified as "atypically high" in PI. The items reaching this criterion are identified with an asterisk in each country column in Appendix A. Examples of atypically high items were: *unassuming* in Argentina, *easy-going* in Australia; and *cynical* in Chile.

ITEM LEVEL COMPARISONS OF COUNTRIES

It was clear from the common variance analyses presented in Table 5.2 that there were substantial differences in the ratings of psychological importance in different countries. We believed that the best way to examine these differences was by correlating the 300 PI scores in each country with the different scales of our two theoretically derived scoring systems based on the five factor and ego state models of personality. We will describe these findings in the following chapter.

An alternative but inferior strategy is to compare the PI ratings in two countries—or two groups of countries—on an item by item level and to identify the items rated as more or less important. The interested reader can do this using the values presented in Appendix A, converted to standard scores by using the formula presented earlier, and the means and standard deviations presented in Table 5.1. Here we provide two illustrations of this approach, one involving a comparison of two individual countries and one involving a comparison of two sets of two countries each.

It was interesting to note, in Table 5.2, that the common variance between the two Chinese groups in the People's Republic of China (CHN) and in the former British Crown Colony of Hong Kong (HK) was only 22 percent—a bit below the average of 25 percent for all pairs of countries. From this, it would appear that there may be some identifiable differences in the characteristics considered psychologically important in the two Chinese groups. Interest in such a comparison is enhanced by the territorial integration of Hong Kong into the People's Republic in 1997.

In making this analysis, we employed the standard score for each of the 300 items in the two subject groups, and obtained a difference score for each item. These difference scores were used to identify the 25 items that were rated relatively more important in Hong Kong than in China (difference of 13 or more) and relatively more important in China than in Hong Kong (difference of 15 or more). These two sets of items are listed in Table 5.4.

An examination of the items in Table 5.4 indicated that the two item sets were qualitatively quite different. The items more important in Hong Kong than in China tended to be relatively favorable in nature, while the items more important in China than in Hong Kong tended to be relatively unfavorable. This suggests that the subjects in Hong Kong got more information about "what people are really like" from certain positive person descriptors, while the subjects in China got more information from certain negative descriptors. However, the relative nature of this finding must be stressed. We will see later in this chapter that the China group, like all others studied, generally places more importance on favorable than on unfavorable characteristics. The findings noted here merely indicate that persons in China appeared to get *relatively*

TABLE 5.4. Items Relatively Higher
in PI in Hong Kong and in China

HK > CHN	CHN > HK
strong	selfish
sharp-witted	snobbish
witty	self-pitying
appreciative	spineless
unassuming	egotistical
self-controlled	sensitive
unexcitable	weak
wholesome	cruel
tactful	affected
hurried	bossy
dignified	arrogant
sincere	vindictive
sexy	self-seeking
unselfish	superstitious
idealistic	masculine
initiative	deceitful
serious	rebellious
thoughtful	unscrupulous
distractible	tense
slow	suggestible
cheerful	greedy
cautious	sentimental
unemotional	show-off
handsome	autocratic
kind	frivolous

more information from negative characteristics than did persons from Hong Kong.

As a second illustration of the examination of differences in individual items, we compared combined PI data for the Australia (AUS) and United States (USA) with the combined data for Chile (CHL) and Argentina (ARG). This provided an examination of differences in PI in two English-speaking, predominantly Protestant Christian countries with two Spanish-speaking, predominantly Catholic Christian countries. A caution here is the possibility that some of the observed differences may be due to "slippage" in the original translation of the 300 items from English to Spanish.

The analysis was conducted by employing the standard scores for each of the 300 items in each of the four countries and averaging them in each of the two sets of countries. Difference scores were then computed for the mean AUS/USA standard scores versus the mean

CHL/ARG standard scores. Difference scores of 10+ were used to identify the items more important in each group (see Table 5.5). An "eyeball" examination of these sets of items did not reveal any obvious qualitative difference and we turned to our theory-based scoring systems (see Chapter 2) for assistance.

Mean Five Factor scores were obtained for the items of greater importance in AUS/US and in ARG/CHL, respectively, as follows: Extraversion, 3.24 and 3.01; Agreeableness, 3.09 and 3.03; Conscientiousness, 3.33 and 3.37; Emotional Stability, 3.11 and 3.19; and Openness, 3.19 and 3.04. These findings suggest that the principal qualitative differences in the two item sets are the tendencies for Extraversion and

TABLE 5.5. Items Relatively Higher
in PI in Australia/United States and
in Chile/Argentina

AUS/USA > CHL/ARG (10+ pts.)	CHL/ARG > AUS/USA (10+ pts.)
ambitious	blustery
artistic	deliberate
assertive	enterprising
attractive	fair minded
complaining	frank
considerate	industrious
dignified	painstaking
distrustful	persevering
forgiving	planful
good-looking	poised
good-natured	progressive
handsome	rattlebrained
headstrong	simple
individualistic	slipshod
opinionated	steady
praising	stingy
reflective	stolid
rude	suggestible
serious	unaffected
show-off	unassuming
shy	unexcitable
sly	wary
snobbish	wholesome
sophisticated	
thoughtful	
trusting	
unfriendly	
unselfish	

Openness to be more highly associated with PI in Australia and the United States than in Argentina and Chile. Thus, qualities of sociability and stimulation (E) and of curiosity and originality (O) appeared to be more important in the United States and Australia than in Argentina and Chile.

In order to examine the data another way, mean ego state scores were obtained for the items of greater importance in AUS/USA and CHL/ARG, respectively, as follows: Critical Parent, .19 and .19; Nurturing Parent, .24 and .19; Adult, .19 and .31; Free Child, .20 and .15; and Adapted Child, .17 and .15. The findings suggest that the principal difference in the two sets of countries is the greater importance assigned to the problem-solving characteristics of the Adult ego state in Argentina and Chile, relative to Australia and the United States.

While analyses of the type just illustrated may sometimes reveal interesting differences, the limited number of items employed restricts their usefulness. We believe that comparisons based on all 300 items are more useful and we report such analyses in Chapter 6.

PATTERNS OF SIMILARITY IN COMMON VARIANCE

Let us now return to an examination of the patterns of common variance scores in Table 5.2, which reveal some interesting and surprising relationships. As examples, consider the following:

- The three Northern European countries of Norway, Finland, and the Netherlands have relatively high common variance scores, as might be expected, but Germany is more similar to India than to the other three European countries.
- Considering the three Spanish-speaking countries, we find high common variance between Chile and Argentina but relatively low common variance between these countries and Venezuela. Actually, the PI findings in Venezuela are more similar to those in Pakistan, India, and Hong Kong than to those in the two other South American countries.
- There were three samples where the subjects were of predominantly Chinese extraction: China, Hong Kong, and Singapore. The common variances among pairs of these three samples were: China versus Hong Kong, 22 percent; China versus Singapore, 15 percent; and Singapore versus Hong Kong, 4 percent. Since all of these values are smaller than the all-country average of 25 percent, they provide no evidence of a "Chinese culture" factor in the ratings of psychological importance. It can

be noted that the Singapore ratings were more similar to the ratings from Australia (52 percent) and the Netherlands (39 percent) than to those from China and Hong Kong.

- The common variance among India, Nepal, and Pakistan was relatively high—in the 50 to 55 percent range, as might have been expected. On the other hand, the common variances between India and Australia and India and Portugal are equally high.
- For Portugal, the common variances with India and with Pakistan are higher than with other European countries.
- While the common variance between the two predominantly Muslim countries of Pakistan and Turkey was somewhat above average (33 percent), the similarity between these two countries and predominantly Hindu India was as high or higher.

The foregoing observations indicate that similarity in the PI ratings appeared to cut across conventional groupings of countries by geographic region, language, and religion. In view of this, we decided to attempt to group the countries on an empirical basis guided by the results of a factor analysis described in the following section.

FACTOR ANALYSIS

The PI correlation matrix that originated Table 5.2 was subjected to a factor analysis in an effort to combine the 20 counties into distinctly different groups or clusters. This was a "Q" factor analysis with the countries analyzed, rather than the more common "R" analysis in which items are analyzed.

The analysis led to the identification of two principal factors, with Factor 1 accounting for 51 percent of the variance and Factor 2 accounting for 14 percent of the variance. Presented in Table 5.6 are the country loadings on the two factors. It can be seen that the three countries loading highest on Factor 1 were the United States, the Netherlands, and Singapore, while the three countries loading lowest were Pakistan, Japan, and China. Regarding Factor 2, we note the highest loadings were obtained in Nepal, Pakistan, and India, with the lowest loadings found in Germany, Japan, Norway, and the United States.

TWO CLUSTERS OF COUNTRIES

An examination of the values presented in Table 5.6 suggested that the 20 countries might be meaningfully grouped into two major clus-

TABLE 5.6. Summary of Factor Analysis

Country	Loading on Factor 1	Loading on Factor 2
ARG	.73	.57
AUS	.79	.62
CHL	.78	.43
CHN	.44	.58
FIN	.77	.40
GER	.67	.22
HK	.25	.82
IND	.66	.85
JAP	.43	.36
KOR	.48	.74
NEP	.45	.89
NET	.83	.46
NIG	.37	.81
NOR	.74	.35
PAK	.41	.88
POR	.71	.77
SIN	.81	.44
TUR	.54	.60
USA	.90	.38
VEN	.37	.69

ters. Cluster 1 would be composed of countries which were higher on Factor 1 than Factor 2, while Cluster 2 would be countries with the opposite pattern of scores. The two clusters of countries are shown in Table 5.7. The meaningfulness of the two clusters was checked by returning to the data presented in Table 5.2, where we found that the mean common variance for pairs of countries *within* Cluster 1 was 29.9 percent and 32.4 percent *within* Cluster 2. On the other hand, the mean common variance for countries from different clusters was only 15.1 percent; thus, the similarity in judgments of psychological importance was greater within each of the two clusters than it was between the two clusters. In subsequent chapters, as we examine the similarities and differences in psychological importance in the individual countries, we will also examine similarities and differences in the two clusters of countries.

In Chapter 7, we will make a detailed examination of the differences between the Cluster 1 and Cluster 2 countries on our cultural comparison variables. It may be useful, however, to anticipate some of these findings at this point. For the Hofstede values, the Cluster 1 countries tended to be higher than Cluster 2 on Individualism and lower on Power Distance. For the Schwartz values, the Cluster 1

TABLE 5.7. The Two Clusters of Countries

Cluster 1 (N = 10)	Cluster 2 (N = 10)
Argentina (ARG)	China (CHN)
Australia (AUS)	Hong Kong (HK)
Chile (CHL)	India (IND)
Finland (FIN)	Korea (KOR)
Germany (GER)	Nepal (NEP)
Japan (JAP)	Nigeria (NIG)
Netherlands (NET)	Pakistan (PAK)
Norway (NOR)	Portugal (POR)
Singapore (SIN)	Turkey (TUR)
United States (USA)	Venezuela (VEN)

countries tend to be somewhat higher on both Autonomy measures and lower on Conservatism, Hierarchy, and Mastery. For the demographic variables, the Cluster 1 countries tend to be higher in socioeconomic development, urbanization, and Christian affiliation, and lower in population density.

As a convenience in exposition, we will sometimes refer to the Cluster 1 countries as "more developed and individualistic" and the Cluster 2 countries as "less developed and collectivistic." When this occurs, the reader should recall that the two clusters of countries differ on several other variables which may or may not be adequately subsumed by these labels.

Markus and Kitayama (1991) have proposed that the nature of the concept of self varies in different cultural settings. In more individualistic societies, there is said to be a more *independent construal of self* in which there is a focus on personal, internal attributes, such as personality traits, abilities, etc. Self is viewed as a bounded entity, clearly separated from other persons. In more collectivistic societies, there is a more *interdependent construal of self* in which the self is viewed as relatively unbounded, flexible, and inseparable from specific relationships and social contexts. In keeping with this view, one might expect that in the present study *all* of the trait characteristics might be rated as more important in the more individualistic Cluster 1 countries than in the more collectivistic Cluster 2 countries.

We tested this idea using the item pool data from Table 5.1 and found that the grand mean importance ratings of all items was 3.12 for the Cluster 1 countries and 3.01 for the Cluster 2 countries. This difference, while not dramatic, was consistent with the view that traits would generally be assigned less importance in more collectivistic countries. However, we will see in the following section that this effect was not distributed evenly through the item pool, but was confined to items of relative unfavorability.

PSYCHOLOGICAL IMPORTANCE AND FAVORABILITY

In Chapter 2, we described an early report from the present project in which we summarized the PI findings in our first seven countries (Williams, Saiz, et al., 1995). When the PI ratings in these countries were compared with the favorability ratings of the English language items made by university students in the United States, two effects were observed. First, the Pearson product-moment correlation was positive in all seven samples, indicating a general tendency for more important items to be more favorable and less important items to be less favorable. However, the magnitude of the coefficients varied greatly, ranging from +.24 in the United States to +.79 in Pakistan. Second, it appeared that, in some countries, the association between PI and favorability departed from a linear relationship and formed a "J" or "U" shaped function, indicating that some unfavorable items may be rated high in PI. In this paper we cautioned that all of the functions employed the English/American favorability scores, and it was suggested that it would be desirable to explore this matter further using more emically derived favorability ratings.

In Chapter 3, we reported a study of favorability ratings in 10 countries which provided us with *language-specific* favorability ratings for 15 of our 20 samples: six from Cluster 1 and nine from Cluster 2. Before proceeding, we examined the cultural comparison data (Appendix C) and satisfied ourselves that the six Cluster 1 countries with favorability data were reasonably representative of the total group of 10 Cluster 1 countries.

The nature of the relationship between PI and favorability in each of the 15 countries was first examined by dividing the appropriate favorability distribution into quintiles (fifths) and computing the mean PI score for the approximately 60 adjectives falling into each quintile.

The results of the foregoing analyses are shown in Table 5.8, which displays the mean PI scores for each quintile (Q) of favorability in each of the 15 countries. Here it can be seen that in some countries (e.g., Pakistan), the least favorable (Q_1) items were judged lowest in importance, with importance increasing regularly with the favorability quintiles and the most favorable items (Q_5) being judged most important. In this case, the relationship between favorability and importance appears rectilinear (straight-line). In other countries (e.g., Argentina), the mean favorability *decreased* from Q_1 to Q_2 or Q_3 and then increased to Q_4 and

TABLE 5.8. Mean Psychological Importance Scores by Quintiles (Q)
of Language Specific Favorability Scores in 15 Countries[a]

Country	Cluster	Q_1	Q_2	Q_3	Q_4	Q_5
Argentina	1	341	316	306	345	400
Australia	1	294	274	287	319	359
Chile	1	351	318	308	339	387
China	2	286	267	282	316	340
India	2	282	278	298	327	357
Korea	2	294	286	294	330	354
Nepal	2	239	251	282	329	350
Nigeria	2	241	258	277	303	323
Norway	1	304	259	258	283	332
Pakistan	2	224	230	280	375	414
Portugal	2	294	278	288	333	381
Singapore	1	320	294	285	311	352
Turkey	2	273	265	273	305	324
USA	1	337	278	288	312	356
Venezuela	2	238	254	291	329	349
Mean Cluster 1	(N = 6)	324.5	289.8	288.6	318.2	364.3
Mean Cluster 2	(N = 9)	263.4	263.0	285.0	327.4	354.7

[a]Two decimal places omitted.

Q_5. This effect reflects a curvilinear relationship in which both low and high favorability items were judged more important than items of intermediate favorability.

The different effects observed were examined systematically by determining, in each country, the degree to which the relationship between PI and the language-specific favorability scores departed from linearity. This was done by a comparison, in each sample, of the product-moment correlation coefficient (r), which indexes the rectilinear component of the relationship, and Eta, which reflects both linear and non-linear components.

The values of r^2 and Eta^2 computed in each sample are shown in Table 5.9 together with the $Eta^2 - r^2$ value, which provides an index of departure from linearity. Thus, it can be seen that the departure from linearity was greatest in Norway, Argentina, and Chile, and was least in Venezuela, Pakistan, Turkey, and Nepal.

An examination of the means of the $Eta^2 - r^2$ values in the six Cluster 1 countries and the nine Cluster 2 countries, shown at the bottom of Table 5.9, indicated that the departure from linearity was greater in the former group than in the latter. This effect is illustrated in Figure 5.1, which shows the mean PI scores for the five quintiles of favorability for the Cluster 1 and Cluster 2 countries. Here it can be seen

TABLE 5.9. Psychological Importance versus Favorability:
Departure from Linearity (Eta^2 – r^2) in 15 Countries with
Language-Specific Favorability Scores

Country	Cluster	Eta^2	r^2	Eta^2 – r^2
Norway	1	.360	.049	.311
Argentina	1	.445	.154	.291
Chile	1	.304	.044	.260
United States	1	.276	.035	.241
Portugal	2	.561	.361	.200
Australia	1	.410	.252	.158
Singapore	1	.259	.126	.133
China	2	.311	.183	.128
India	2	.589	.471	.118
Nigeria	2	.641	.543	.098
Korea	2	.301	.223	.078
Nepal	2	.585	.520	.065
Turkey	2	.218	.154	.064
Pakistan	2	.757	.711	.046
Venezuela	2	.508	.484	.024
Mean Cluster 1	(N = 6)	.296	.067	.229
Mean Cluster 2	(N = 9)	.742	.657	.085

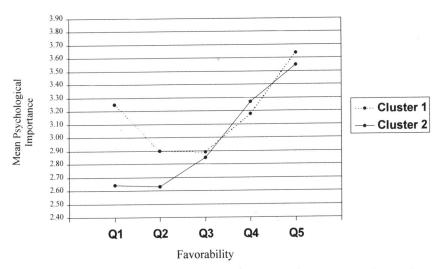

FIGURE 5.1. Mean psychological importance scores in Cluster 1 and Cluster 2 countries
for quintiles of language-specific favorability scores.

that the means in Cluster 1 decreased from a Q_1 value of 3.25 to a Q_3 value of 2.89 and then increased to a Q_5 value of 3.64, producing a "J" shaped curve. In the Cluster 2 countries, the mean PI scores increased regularly from Q_1 (2.64) to Q_3 (2.85) to Q_5 (3.55). These effects can be summarized as follows. In Cluster 1 countries, low favorability items are of moderate importance, middle favorability items are of less importance, and high favorability items are of the greatest importance. On the other hand, the mean PI scores for the Cluster 2 countries were lowest for the low favorability items, moderate for the intermediate favorability items, and highest for the most favorable items.

From this, we conclude that in Cluster 2 the relationship of PI and favorability is relatively straightforward—favorable items are important and unfavorable items are unimportant. The relationship in Cluster 1 is more complex. While in agreement that, overall, there is a tendency for PI and favorability to be positively associated, the Cluster 1 ratings indicate that at least some unfavorable items can be relatively important. In both clusters favorable adjectives provide more information about a person than do unfavorable adjectives. However, in the Cluster 1 countries, unfavorable adjectives may also provide useful information while in Cluster 2 countries they generally do not.

ITEM DIFFERENCES IN THE CLUSTERS

The point just made was illustrated by an examination of the items assigned *relatively* more importance in each cluster of countries. A grand mean was computed for each of the 300 items in the 10 Cluster 1 countries and a similar grand mean was computed in the 10 Cluster 2 countries. For each item a difference score was computed between the two grand means and used to identify the 25 items judged relatively more important in each cluster, as shown in Table 5.10. Here it can be seen that the items judged relatively more important in Cluster 1 were generally unfavorable in nature, while the items rated as relatively more important in Cluster 2 were generally favorable.

The foregoing analyses focussed only on the items where the ratings in two sets of countries *differed*. If we examine the grand item means in another way, a somewhat different picture emerges. In this case, we identified the 25 items with the highest grand means in each cluster. The two lists of 25 adjectives then were compared and divided into one of three categories: items high in PI in both clusters of countries (N = 11); items high in PI in Cluster 1 but not Cluster 2 (N = 14); and items high in PI in Cluster 2 but not Cluster 1 (N = 14). The individual items falling into the three categories are shown in Table 5.11.

TABLE 5.10. Items More Important in One
Cluster of Countries than in the Other

25 items Cluster 1 ≥ Cluster 2			25 items Cluster 2 ≥ Cluster 1		
Item #	1 – 2 Diff	Adjective	Item #	1 – 2 Diff	Adjective
70	.68	dominant	105	−.69	handsome
69	.69	distrustful	180	−.66	polished
175	.70	pessimistic	102	−.60	good-looking
286	.70	unscrupulous	110	−.59	healthy
289	.71	vindictive	91	−.57	foresighted
225	.71	shallow	64	−.57	dignified
23	.72	boastful	32	−.55	civilized
36	.72	cold	186	−.54	progressive
184	.73	prejudiced	150	−.54	methodological
76	.74	egotistical	30	−.53	charming
60	.76	dependable	176	−.52	playful
161	.77	obnoxious	153	−.52	moderate
211	.77	sarcastic	209	−.49	robust
138	.78	irritable	50	−.49	courageous
119	.80	immature	169	−.48	painstaking
114	.86	hostile	151	−.48	mild
284	.86	unkind	125	−.47	industrious
212	.88	self-centered	16	−.46	artistic
219	.91	selfish	251	−.45	strong
15	.94	arrogant	58	−.43	deliberate
56	.95	deceitful	154	−.43	modest
52	.97	cruel	160	−.38	obliging
277	1.03	undependable	204	−.38	resourceful
281	1.05	unfriendly	34	−.37	clever
137	1.14	irresponsible	165	−.36	organized

An examination of the item groups revealed that the items which were considered important in both clusters (column 1) were generally favorable in nature. The same observation can be made for the items considered important in Cluster 2 countries but not in Cluster 1 countries (column 3). The items considered important in Cluster 1 but not Cluster 2 (column 2) were more variable in nature, consisting of both favorable adjectives (e.g., *kind, sincere, sociable*) and unfavorable adjectives (e.g., *deceitful, irresponsible, selfish*). Note that both *dependable* and *undependable* are on the Cluster 1 list! Once again, the analyses indicated that in the less developed and more collectivistic countries of Cluster 2, only favorable adjectives are viewed as important, while in the more developed and individualistic countries of Cluster 1, both favorable and unfavorable adjectives may be important.

TABLE 5.11. High Importance Items in Cluster 1 and/or
Cluster 2 Countries (Top 25 Items in Each Cluster)

Items common to both	Unique to Cluster 1	Unique to Cluster 2
6. affectionate	7. aggressive	10. ambitious
31. cheerful	56. deceitful	26. capable
95. frank	60. dependable	32. civilized
96. friendly	137. irresponsible	33. clear-thinking
113. honest	140. kind	41. confident
132. intelligent	164. optimistic	43. conscientious
145. loyal	212. self-centered	49. cooperative
201. reliable	219. selfish	50. courageous
205. responsible	220. sensitive	63. determined
213. self-confident	223. sincere	79. enterprising
278. understanding	239. sociable	83. fair-minded
	272. trusting	111. helpful
	277. undependable	125. industrious
	291. warm	166. original

In addition to the favorability differences just noted, it seems that the two adjective lists in columns two and three may differ in other qualities. If we consider only the favorable adjectives in the two sets, we get the impression that the items more important in Cluster 2 (column 3) place more emphasis on qualities related to problem solving and achievement, while the items more important in Cluster 1 (column 2) seem more related to good interpersonal relationships.

We will explore the meaning of these differences later after we have examined other findings in the Cluster 1 and Cluster 2 countries.

PANCULTURAL ANALYSIS

While the earlier analyses indicated the existence of substantial differences in psychological importance across countries, the evidence of similarity was greater than the evidence of differences, i.e., all cross-country correlations were positive. Before leaving our analysis of psychological importance at the level of individual items, we examined the data for general, pancultural effects. In our earlier analyses, it was observed that there was an average of 25 percent common variance among all pairs of countries, which is equivalent to an average correlation coefficient of .50. This indicates the presence of some substantial cross-country similarities in the ratings of psychological importance and the following analysis was designed to examine this.

For each of the 300 ACL adjectives, a mean was computed of the psychological importance values across the 20 individual countries. These values are given in the right-hand column in Appendix A, where high mean scores indicate that the item was considered generally important across all samples and low mean scores indicate that the item was considered as relatively unimportant across all samples.

We then identified the 30 items with the highest overall mean scores (means of 3.54 to 4.19) and the 30 items with the overall lowest mean scores (means of 2.36 to 2.62). These items are displayed in Table 5.12. An

TABLE 5.12. Pancultural Analysis: 30 Most Important and 30 Least Important Items across All 20 Samples

30 most important items (means 3.54 to 4.19)		30 least important items (means 2.36 to 2.62)	
Item #	Adjective	Item #	Adjective
6	affectionate	1	absent-minded
26	capable	20	awkward
31	cheerful	21	bitter
33	clear-thinking	22	blustery
41	confident	37	commonplace
43	conscientious	62	despondent
49	cooperative	66	disorderly
60	dependable	67	dissatisfied
63	determined	68	distractible
83	fair-minded	72	dull
95	frank	81	evasive
96	friendly	85	fearful
100	gentle	89	foolish
111	helpful	92	forgetful
113	honest	94	formal
115	humorous	98	fussy
122	independent	108	hasty
132	intelligent	116	hurried
140	kind	144	loud
145	loyal	159	noisy
164	optimistic	189	queer
201	reliable	207	retiring
205	responsible	227	shiftless
213	self-confident	234	slipshod
233	sincere	235	slow
239	sociable	250	stolid
272	trusting	255	sulky
278	understanding	256	superstitious
291	warm	293	weak
296	wise	294	whiny

examination of the two sets of items suggests a clear difference in favorability, with the more important set being generally more favorable than the less important set. This is another indication of a general pancultural tendency to consider more favorable traits to be higher in importance than less favorable traits. In the authors' view, the more important item set also appears to contain more "central" traits, while the less important item set contains more seemingly "peripheral" traits, as would be expected if the concept of psychological importance, as defined here, is conceptually congruent with ideas of Allport, Cattell, and others as discussed in Chapter 2.

SUMMARY

In this chapter we studied the psychological importance data at the level of individual items. An examination of the degree of similarity in the ratings between pairs of countries indicated wide variation, with the greatest similarity found between the United States and Australia and the lowest similarity found between Hong Kong and Germany. The mean common variance across all pairs of comparisons was approximately 25 percent. Factor analysis was employed to compose two clusters of countries, with the first consisting of countries relatively high in socioeconomic development and individualism and the second cluster consisting of countries relatively low in socioeconomic development and high in collectivism. We examined the relationship between ratings of psychological importance and language-specific favorability ratings in 15 countries. By pooling the data across all 20 countries, we identified item sets which were high or low in psychological importance on a pancultural basis.

PSYCHOLOGICAL IMPORTANCE
THEORY LEVEL ANALYSES

In the previous chapter, we examined the findings regarding psychological importance at the level of the individual items. This led to a number of interesting observations but the findings were generally abstract, consisting mostly of statistical indices such as correlation coefficients. It was clear, for example, that there were differences in the psychological importance ratings in the Cluster 1 countries and the Cluster 2 countries but, beyond the favorability analyses, it was difficult to assign qualitative meaning to these observations.

In the present chapter, we will examine the findings regarding psychological importance in the 20 countries, and in the two clusters of countries, by means of two theoretically based scoring systems: the five factor Model and Transactional Analysis ego states, which were described in detail in Chapter 2.

The general plan of analysis in this chapter is as follows. In each country we used the product-moment correlation coefficient to index the degree to which the distribution of 300 PI scores was associated with the distribution of 300 score values for each of the concepts in the two scoring systems. For example, in Country X, was there an association between the 300 PI scores and the 300 Extraversion values from the five factor scoring system? If so, then we concluded that extraverted qualities were considered psychologically important in Country X. When a similar correlation was computed for Country Y, we were able to observe whether Extraversion was more important in one country or the other. Within a given country, we were able to determine the pattern of relationships, e.g., were the PI scores more highly correlated with Extraversion or with Conscientiousness, etc. In this way we examined the linkages between each country's or cluster's distribution of PI scores, each of the five factors and each of the five ego states.

For each of the two theoretically based analyses, we will first note for each country the uncorrected correlations of the 300 PI values and the 300 scoring system values, and examine these for pattern differences between countries. We will then report the mean scoring system values for the 60 most important and 60 least important items in each country. Following this, we will restrict our interest to the 15 countries where we have language-specific favorability ratings and examine the partial correlations obtained between the PI values and scoring system values when favorability is controlled.

PSYCHOLOGICAL IMPORTANCE AND THE FIVE FACTORS

CORRELATIONS OF PI SCORES AND THE FIVE FACTOR SCORES

In each country, the 300 PI scores from Appendix A were correlated, in turn, with each of the five factor score distributions from Appendix D. The results of this analysis are shown in Table 6.1.

Extraversion

The correlation coefficients between the distribution of psychological importance scores and the Extraversion scores are shown in the first (left-hand) column of Table 6.1. Here it can be seen that the strongest association between psychological importance and Extraversion was found in Venezuela, Nepal, and India, while the weakest association was found in Germany, Japan, and Chile. The median correlation for the 10 Cluster 1 countries was .28, while the median correlation for the 10 Cluster 2 countries was .61. Thus, there appeared to be a positive relationship between Extraversion and psychological importance in both clusters which was much stronger in Cluster 2.

Agreeableness

The correlations between the distribution of PI scores in each country and the Agreeableness scores are shown in the second column of Table 6.1. Here it can be seen that the strongest relationship between psychological importance and Agreeableness was found in Hong Kong,

TABLE 6.1. Product–Moment Correlations of PI Scores
with Five Factor Scores Presented in Rank Order[a,b]

EXT		AGR		CON		EMS		OPN	
VEN	73	HK	78	NEP	70	HK	66	VEN	60
NEP	69	NEP	76	HK	68	PAK	63	NEP	54
IND	67	PAK	74	IND	68	NEP	58	IND	53
HK	66	IND	68	PAK	68	KOR	53	HK	49
PAK	63	NIG	67	NIG	66	IND	52	PAK	48
NIG	58	KOR	62	KOR	64	NIG	50	POR	42
POR	55	VEN	60	POR	56	POR	47	NIG	41
AUS	53	POR	58	VEN	56	VEN	45	AUS	39
KOR	53	AUS	53	CHN	48	AUS	43	KOR	39
TUR	44	TUR	45	AUS	41	ARG	39	TUR	36
CHN	42	CHN	45	TUR	41	TUR	39	CHN	34
ARG	35	ARG	37	ARG	35	CHN	36	NET	25
SIN	34	NET	31	SIN	35	NET	25	SIN	25
NET	32	JAP	28	FIN	30	FIN	24	ARG	24
FIN	29	CHL	24	NET	28	JAP	24	FIN	24
NOR	27	SIN	24	CHL	26	CHL	23	NOR	21
USA	27	NOR	22	USA	23	NOR	19	CHL	20
CHL	25	FIN	21	NOR	21	SIN	18	USA	18
JAP	22	USA	18	JAP	15	USA	17	JAP	16
GER	09	GER	02	GER	08	GER	04	GER	10
Medians:									
Cluster 1	28		24		27		27		23
Cluster 2	61		64		65		51		48

[a]Decimal points omitted.
[b]EXT = Extraversion; AGR = Agreeableness; CON = Conscientiousness; EMS = Emotional Stability; OPN = Openness.

Nepal, and Pakistan, while the weakest relationships were found in Germany, the United States, and Finland. The median correlation for the Cluster 1 countries was .24, while the median correlation for the 10 Cluster 2 countries was .64. Thus, as with Extraversion, a positive relationship was seen between PI and Agreeableness in both clusters of countries that was substantially stronger in Cluster 2.

Conscientiousness

The correlations between the Conscientiousness scores and the PI scores in each country are shown in the third column of Table 6.1. Nepal, Hong Kong, and India showed the strongest relationship between PI and Conscientiousness, with Germany, Japan, and Norway showing the weakest. The median correlation for the Cluster 1 countries was .27, while the median correlation for the Cluster 2 countries was .65. As with the two previous traits, in all countries the items rated higher in psychological importance were higher in Conscientiousness, with the effect particularly strong in the Cluster 2 countries.

Emotional Stability

The association between Emotional Stability and the psychological importance scores are shown in the fourth column of the table. Psychological Importance was most closely linked to Emotional Stability in Hong Kong, Pakistan, and Nepal, with the weakest association found in Germany, the United States, and Singapore. The median correlation in the Cluster 1 countries was .27, while the comparable value in the Cluster 2 countries was .51. Again, as with the three prior traits, items reflecting Emotional Stability were higher in all countries but particularly so in the Cluster 2 countries.

Openness

On the right in the table are shown the correlation coefficients indexing the degree of association between psychological importance and Openness in the different countries. The association was strongest in Venezuela, Nepal, and India and weakest in Germany, Japan, and the United States. Continuing the trend, the median correlation in Cluster 1 was .23, while that in Cluster 2 was .48, indicating that the positive association of importance with Openness was stronger in Cluster 2.

Correlations across Dimensions

It can be seen in Table 6.1 that countries with relatively high correlations on one of the Five Factors tended to have relatively high correlations on the others as well. This observation was confirmed by computing a correlation coefficient between the 20 values in each column with the 20 values in each of the other columns (e.g., the 20 Extraversion correlations were correlated with the 20 Agreeableness correlations, etc.). This analysis revealed correlations ranging from .88 for Emotional Stability versus Openness to .99 for Extraversion versus Openness. This indicated a general tendency for the psychological importance scores in some countries to be more highly associated with *all* of the Big Five factors, whereas in other countries, there was a much weaker association with all of the five factors. The former countries are largely from Cluster 2 and the latter group largely from Cluster 1. Thus, the qualities associated with psychological importance are more closely aligned with the Five Factor Model in the less developed and more collectivistic countries of Cluster 2 than in the more developed and individualistic countries of Cluster 1. This finding might be viewed as somewhat paradoxical since the Five Factor Model was developed by Western (i.e., Cluster 1) psychologists.

Within-Country Patterns

Having observed the "big picture" regarding the relationships of the PI scores to the five factors, we reexamined the data from Table 6.1 to see if there were differences among countries in the *pattern* of association of the PI scores with the five factor scores. This was done by transforming the correlation indices (*r*) into common variance (*r*²) indices and regrouping the latter by country, as shown in Table 6.2. This enabled us to observe, in a given country, whether there were substantial differences in the relationships and, if so, to note those which were relatively high and relatively low. The results are summarized in Table 6.3.

TABLE 6.2. Percent Common Variance of PI Scores with the Five Factor Scores Grouped by Country[a]

	EXT	AGR	CON	EMS	OPN
ARG	12	14	12	15	06
AUS	28	28	17	18	15
CHL	06	06	07	05	04
CHN	17	20	23	13	12
FIN	08	04	09	06	06
GER	01	00	01	00	01
HK	44	61	46	44	24
IND	45	46	46	27	28
JAP	05	08	23	06	03
KOR	28	38	41	28	15
NEP	48	58	49	34	29
NET	10	10	08	06	06
NIG	34	45	44	25	17
NOR	07	05	04	04	04
PAK	40	55	46	40	23
POR	30	34	31	22	18
SIN	12	06	12	32	06
TUR	19	20	17	15	13
USA	07	03	05	03	03
VEN	53	36	31	20	36

[a]EXT = Extraversion; AGR = Agreeableness; CON = Conscientiousness; EMS = Emotional Stability; OPN = Openness.

TABLE 6.3. Relative Strength of the Relationship
of PI to the Five Factors within Each Country[a]

Country	Range of CVs[a]	Pattern[b]
ARG	12	S A E C > O
AUS	13	E A >> S C O
CHL	2	C E A S O
CHN	11	C A E > S O
FIN	5	C E S O A
GER	1	O E C S A
HK	37	A >>> C E S >>> O
IND	19	A C E >>> S O
JAP	20	C >>> A S E O
KOR	26	C A >> E S >> O
NEP	29	A > C E >> S > O
NET	4	E A C S O
NIG	28	A C >> E > S > O
NOR	3	E A C S O
PAK	32	A > C > E S >>> O
POR	16	A C E > S O
SIN	26	S >>> E C > A O
TUR	7	A E C S O
USA	4	E C A S O
VEN	33	E >>> A O > C >>> S

[a]Difference in common variance between adjoining factors.
[b]> = 5–9%; >> = 10–14%; >>> = 15% and up.
[b]E = Extraversion; A = Agreeableness; C = Conscientiousness;
S = Emotional Stability; O = Openness.

For each country, the five common variance estimates are listed in descending order, from left to right, using the letters E (Extraversion), A (Agreeableness), C (Conscientiousness), S (Emotional Stability), and O (Openness) to indicate the different factors. A "greater than" (>) symbol between the two letters indicate that the common variance difference between these two factors was five through nine percent; two symbols (>>) indicate a difference of 10 through 14 percent; and three signs (>>>) indicate a difference of 15 percent or more.

It can be seen that there were seven countries with no "greater than" symbols, i.e., Chile, Finland, Germany, the Netherlands, Norway, Turkey, and the United States. In these countries, no one trait was more important than the other four; all but Turkey belonged to Cluster 1.

Of the remaining countries, there were three—Argentina, China, and Portugal—with only one "greater than" symbol between adjoining factors which, conservatively, might have been attributable to chance. In the remaining 10 countries, there was at least one ">>" difference and we will comment on each of these, in turn.

- *Australia.* Extraversion and Agreeableness were more important than Emotional Stability, Conscientiousness, and Openness.
- *Hong Kong.* Agreeableness was much more important than Conscientiousness, Extraversion, and Emotional Stability, which, in turn, were much more important than Openness.
- *India.* Agreeableness, Conscientiousness, and Extraversion were much more important than Emotional Stability and Openness.
- *Japan.* Conscientiousness was much more important than the other four factors.
- *Korea.* Conscientiousness and Agreeableness were more important than Extraversion and Emotional Stability, which, in turn, were more important than Openness.
- *Nepal.* Agreeableness was somewhat more important than Conscientiousness and Extraversion, which were more important than Emotional Stability, which was somewhat more important than Openness.
- *Nigeria.* Agreeableness and Conscientiousness were more important than Extraversion, which was somewhat more important than Emotional Stability, which was somewhat more important than Openness.
- *Pakistan.* Agreeableness was somewhat more important than Conscientiousness, which was somewhat more important than Extraversion and Emotional Stability, which were much more important than Openness.
- *Singapore.* Emotional Stability was much more important than Extraversion and Conscientiousness, which were somewhat more important than Agreeableness and Openness.
- *Venezuela.* Extraversion was much more important than Agreeableness and Openness which were somewhat more important than Conscientiousness, which was much more important than Emotional Stability.

The foregoing summaries suggest that there are substantial differences among countries in the importance assigned to the different factors. The most highly contrasted patterns appear to have been in Hong Kong, with its emphasis on Agreeableness; Singapore, with its emphasis on Stability; and Venezuela, with its emphasis on Extraversion. The differences between the patterns in Hong Kong and Singapore are particularly interesting since in both countries the great majority of persons are of Chinese extraction.

Readers familiar with the 10 countries just noted should find food for thought—and perhaps ideas for future research!!—in the different patterns of importance assigned to the five factors. For example, does the rather distinctive pattern observed in Venezuela have any relationship to the concept of "simpatia," a cultural script among Latin Americans? This is a pattern of social interaction that emphasizes conformity, sharing others' feelings, respect toward others, and striving for harmony in interpersonal relations (Triandis, Marin, Lisansky, & Betancourt, 1984).

MEAN FIVE FACTOR SCORES OF HIGH IMPORTANCE AND LOW IMPORTANCE ITEM GROUPS

An alternate way to examine the relationship between psychological importance and the five factors was to identify a set of high importance items and a set of low importance items, compute the mean five factor scores for each item set, and examine the difference in the means. If there is a positive linear association between PI and a given factor, then the high PI item set should have a higher factor mean than the low PI item set. Further, the stronger the association, the greater should be the differences in the mean scores.

In each country, the distribution of PI scores for the 300 items was examined in order to identify the 60 items with the highest PI ratings and the 60 items with the lowest PI ratings. Each item set was then scored to obtain the mean scores for each of the five factors. Shown in Table 6.4 are the mean five factor scores for the high and low PI item sets in each country and the grand means obtained for the 10 Cluster 1 countries and the 10 Cluster 2 countries. Also shown, for all 20 countries, are the grand means for the high and low item sets and the high minus low differences between them.

Several observations can be made concerning the findings presented in Table 6.4. First it can be seen that in all countries the means for the high importance item set were higher than the means for the low importance item set for all five factors. This is the counterpart of the findings seen in Table 6.1, where all of the correlations of PI scores with five factor scores were positive in sign. Second, an examination of the findings for Clusters 1 and 2 indicate that the differences between the grand means for the high and low item sets were greater in Cluster 2 than in Cluster 1. This effect is summarized graphically in Figure 6.1, where it can be seen that, for Cluster 2, the high importance means were higher, and the low importance means were lower than for Cluster 1. This effect is the counterpart of the

TABLE 6.4. Mean Five Factor Scores for Sets of 60 Items Rated
as High (HI) or Low (LO) in Psychological Importance[a,b]

		EXT		AGR		CON		EMS		OPN	
		HI	LO	HI	LO	HI	LO	HI	LO	HI	LO
1	ARG	385	285	388	282	385	289	315	239	356	291
2	AUS	396	248	396	252	385	273	328	242	365	265
3	CHL	361	282	357	281	364	291	314	265	343	286
4	CHN	371	262	363	249	384	268	340	260	349	275
5	FIN	355	273	337	267	357	273	326	273	341	279
6	GER	316	294	297	284	322	291	313	305	312	296
7	HK	384	248	395	205	396	253	353	237	357	269
8	IND	399	230	397	228	395	240	340	241	367	252
9	JAP	350	289	347	272	346	311	323	275	328	288
10	KOR	380	248	397	246	392	254	348	238	349	267
11	NEP	388	224	396	209	391	238	360	244	359	251
12	NET	366	280	363	277	357	285	317	262	347	284
13	NIG	375	234	385	220	396	248	352	247	354	264
14	NOR	354	270	344	274	345	288	317	279	338	281
15	PAK	374	227	391	213	390	241	362	241	349	253
16	POR	389	257	395	256	392	265	332	245	361	274
17	SIN	355	273	341	275	365	276	316	274	335	282
18	TUR	367	248	365	247	382	264	343	257	351	263
19	USA	338	274	322	278	336	286	315	279	324	281
20	VEN	390	206	369	220	361	240	353	255	368	283
M Cluster 1		357.6	276.8	349.2	274.2	356.2	286.3	318.4	269.3	338.9	283.3
M Cluster 2		381.7	238.4	385.3	229.3	387.9	251.1	348.3	246.5	356.4	265.1
M totals		369.7	257.6	367.3	251.8	372.1	268.7	333.4	257.9	347.7	274.2
M HI–M LO:		112.1		115.5		103.4		75.5		73.5	

[a]Two decimal places omitted.
[b]EXT = Extraversion; AGR = Agreeableness; CON = Conscientiousness; EMS = Emotional Stability;
OPN = Openness.

earlier findings that the median correlations of PI and the five factor
scores were higher in Cluster 2 countries than in Cluster 1 countries.
The foregoing analysis provides another illustration of the finding
that each of the five factors is positively associated with psychological
importance, with this effect being more pronounced in the Cluster 2
countries.

The high minus low difference scores in the last row of Table 6.4
provided an opportunity to observe the relative importance assigned
to each factor, across all samples; the larger the difference score, the
greater the relative importance of the factor. Here it can be seen that
the factor of Agreeableness had the greatest importance (115.5), followed by Extraversion (112.1) and Conscientiousness (103.4). Substantially less importance was assigned to Emotional Stability (75.5) and

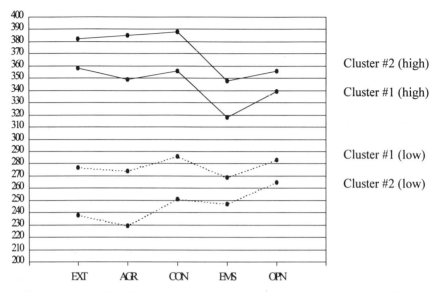

FIGURE 6.1. Mean Five Factor Scores for High and Low Importance Items in the Cluster 1 and Cluster 2 Countries.

Openness (73.5). Thus, in the view of all subjects, qualities associated with the Agreeableness and Extraversion factors were considered to provide more information about "what people are really like" than did the qualities associated with Emotional Stability and Openness. This pancultural finding will be of interest to psychologists exploring the utility of the Five Factor Model for the description of human personality.

PARTIAL CORRELATIONS OF PSYCHOLOGICAL IMPORTANCE AND THE FIVE FACTOR SCORES WITH FAVORABILITY CONTROLLED

We noted in earlier chapters that both the psychological importance scores and each of the five factor scores tend to correlate positively with favorability. Since variables which correlate with a common variable will tend to correlate with one another, this raises the question of the degree to which the values observed in Table 6.1 are influenced by their common link to favorability. The following analysis was designed to explore this question by examining the correlation between PI scores and each of the Big Five when the effects of favorability are controlled. Conducting such an analysis does not imply that favorability *should* be eliminated since, as discussed earlier, each of the five factors is intrinsically evaluative in nature.

In Chapter 3, we noted and summarized the findings from our study of the favorability of the 300 ACL adjectives in 10 countries. We also noted that there are five additional samples where we do not have local favorability ratings but we do have favorability ratings for the *language* in which the psychological importance measure was administered. We can use the English language favorability ratings obtained in the United States for the samples from Australia, India, and Nepal, and use the Spanish language favorability ratings obtained in Chile for the samples from Argentina and Venezuela. Thus, we have a total of 15 countries where *language-specific* favorability scores are available for use in this analysis.

The technique which we employ here, called partial correlation, provides an estimate of the linear relationship between variables X and Y (e.g., PI and Extraversion) after an adjustment for the linear relationships of variable Z (favorability) to variables X and Y. We observed in Chapter 5 (see Table 5.6 and Figure 5.1) that, while there was a significant, positive linear relationship of PI and favorability in all countries, there was also a non-linear component in the Cluster 1 countries. The partial-correlation technique adjusts only for the general linear component and ignores the non-linear component. Since the average (linear) correlation of PI and favorability was .81 in Cluster 2 countries and only .26 in Cluster 1 countries (see Table 5.8), the adjustment for favorability has a much greater impact on the Cluster 2 analyses than on the Cluster 1 analyses.

The partial correlations of the psychological importance values in each of the 15 countries with each of the Big Five score distributions with favorability controlled are shown in Table 6.5. There the 15 countries have been grouped in terms of their membership in either Cluster 1 or Cluster 2, with six of the Cluster 1 countries and nine of the Cluster 2 countries being represented.

Looking at the overall table, we see that, with favorability controlled, 33 of the 75 partial correlations remained statistically significant at the .05 level where only four would have been expected by chance. Thus, it is clear that substantial relationships between PI and the five factors remain after linear favorability is controlled. A second observation is that more significant correlations remain in Cluster 2 (28 out of 45, or 62 percent) than in Cluster 1 (5 out of 30, or 17 percent). A third observation is that, in Cluster 2, the significant residual positive correlations are particularly evident for Conscientiousness and Extraversion. In these less developed and more collectivistic countries, Conscien-

TABLE 6.5. Partial Correlations of PI and Five Factor Scores with
Language-Specific Favorability Controlled in 15 Countries[a,b]

	EXT	AGR	CON	EMS	OPN
Cluster 1 (N = 6)					
ARG	00	−04	02	10	−04
AUS	15**	04	−02	01	04
CHL	06	00	07	04	05
NOR	11*	00	04	02	06
SIN	21**	02	23***	02	12*
USA	13*	07	09	00	05
Cluster 2 (N = 9)					
CHI	15**	09	23***	04	11*
IND	17**	07	29***	−10	09
KOR	28***	35***	45***	24***	16**
NEP	11*	13*	25***	−10	03
NIG	01	−02	17**	−09	00
PAK	20***	16**	20***	13*	18**
POR	07	01	13**	−01	00
TUR	21***	16**	25***	14*	18**
VEN	39***	−07	05	−16**	33***

[a]Decimal points omitted.
[b]EXT = Extraversion; AGR = Agreeableness; CON = Conscientiousness; EMS =
Emotional Stability; OPN = Openness.
*$p < .05$; **$p < .01$; ***$p < .001$

tiousness and Extraversion emerge as psychologically important even
when the intrinsic favorability of each of the factors is controlled. The
finding for Conscientiousness may be related to Triandis' observation
that East Asian collectivists value "persistence" more than Western
samples (Triandis, Bontempo, Leung, & Hui, 1990).

PSYCHOLOGICAL IMPORTANCE
AND THE FIVE EGO STATES

We turn now to our second theory-based method for analyzing
psychological importance—the five functional ego states of Transactional Analysis.

CORRELATIONS OF PI SCORES AND THE FIVE EGO STATE SCALES

The distribution of 300 PI values in each country from Appendix
A were correlated, in turn, with each of the five ego state score distri-
butions from Appendix D. The results of these analyses are shown in
Table 6.6.

TABLE 6.6. Product–Moment Correlations of PI Scores with
the Five Ego State Scores Presented in Rank Order[a,b]

CP		NP		A		FC		AC	
HK	−29	HK	68	HK	67	VEN	48	HK	−64
VEN	−20	PAK	68	PAK	63	AUS	26	PAK	−57
NEP	−18	IND	63	NEP	57	IND	21	NEP	−56
PAK	−17	NEP	67	KOR	55	NEP	20	VEN	−53
NIG	−13	AUS	60	IND	53	POR	19	IND	−50
AUS	−12	NIG	58	NIG	52	NET	16	KOR	−46
IND	−11	POR	56	POR	49	SIN	16	POR	−43
CHN	−10	KOR	55	TUR	44	HK	15	NIG	−42
JAP	−08	VEN	50	VEN	41	FIN	14	TUR	−40
POR	−08	ARG	43	CHN	40	USA	14	AUS	−36
TUR	−08	NET	42	ARG	39	NOR	13	CHN	−34
KOR	−06	TUR	41	AUS	30	CHN	12	ARG	−33
ARG	−04	CHN	36	FIN	29	GER	11	FIN	−27
NET	−01	USA	36	CHL	26	PAK	11	NET	−26
CHL	04	JAP	35	SIN	23	TUR	11	CHL	−21
NOR	04	SIN	35	NET	22	JAP	10	JAP	−19
FIN	07	CHL	32	NOR	18	NIG	10	NOR	−18
GER	11	NOR	31	JAP	14	ARG	08	SIN	−15
SIN	13	FIN	28	USA	13	CHL	07	USA	−11
USA	13	GER	14	GER	04	KOR	06	GER	−05
Medians: Cluster 1									
	04		35		22		13		−20
Medians: Cluster 2									
	−12		57		53		14		−48

[a]Decimal points omitted.
[b]CP = Critical Parent; NP = Nurturing Parent; A = Adult; FC = Free Child; AC = Adapted Child.

Critical Parent

The correlation coefficients between the PI scores and Critical
Parent scores are shown in the first (left-hand) column of Table 6.6.
Here it can be seen that the correlations were modest in size, ranging
from slight negative correlations in such countries as Hong Kong and
Venezuela to slight positive correlations in Singapore and the United
States. The median correlation for the 10 Cluster 1 countries was .04,
while that for the 10 Cluster 2 countries was −.12. In general, there
appeared little consistent tendency to associate Critical Parent qualities
with psychological importance.

Nurturing Parent

An examination of the Nurturing Parent correlations, shown in
the second column of Table 6.6, indicates that in all countries there was

a tendency to associate Nurturing Parent qualities with PI. This relationship was strongest in Hong Kong and Pakistan and weakest in Finland and Germany. The median correlations were .35 in the Cluster 1 countries and .57 in the Cluster 2 countries. Thus, the general tendency to ascribe more importance to adjectives reflecting nurturing qualities was most evident in the less developed and more collectivistic countries of Cluster 2.

Adult

The correlations of PI with Adult are shown in the center column of Table 6.6, where it can be seen that the general tendency to associate Adult qualities with PI was strongest in Hong Kong and Pakistan and weakest in Japan, the United States, and Germany. The median correlations were .22 in Cluster 1 and .53 in Cluster 2; hence the rational, realistic qualities of the Adult ego state were more highly associated with PI in the less individualistic and less developed countries of Cluster 2.

Free Child

The distribution of correlations of Free Child and PI are shown in the fourth column of Table 6.6. While all coefficients were positive, most were relatively small, indicating, at most, a very modest positive association of Free Child qualities with PI. The median correlations for Cluster 1 and Cluster 2 were .13 and .14, respectively.

Adapted Child

The correlation coefficients between PI and Adapted Child, seen in the fifth column, were all negative in sign, indicating a tendency for items high in Adapted Child qualities to be rated low in PI, with this relationship being strongest in Hong Kong and Pakistan and weakest in Germany and the United States. The median correlations for Clusters 1 and 2 were −.20 and −.48, respectively, indicating that the tendency to assign less importance to Adapted Child qualities was stronger in the less developed countries of Cluster 2.

Correlations across Dimensions

The foregoing analyses indicated general tendencies for PI scores to be positively associated with Nurturing Parent and Adult characteristics and negatively associated with Adapted Child characteristics, with these tendencies being stronger in Cluster 2 countries. It was also observed that countries with high ranks on one of the three scales also tended to have high ranks on the other two scales as shown by the following correlations, computed between the columnar values in Table 6.6: NP versus A, .87; NP versus AC, −.89; and A versus AC, −.95. It was thought that a portion of these relationships might be attributable to the observation that NP and A are both positively correlated with favorability, while AC is negatively related (see Chapter 2).

Within-Country Patterns

Having reviewed the general relationships of the PI scores to the five ego states, we proceeded to examine the data from Table 6.6 for evidence of between-country differences in the patterns of association with the ego states. To do this we transformed the correlation indices into common variance indices and regrouped the latter by country, as shown in Table 6.7. This enabled us to observe which relationships were relatively stronger and relatively weaker in each country.

TABLE 6.7. Percent Common Variance of PI Scores
with the Five Ego State Scores in Each Country[a]

	NP	A	AC
ARG	18	15	11
AUS	36	09	13
CHL	10	07	04
CHN	13	16	12
FIN	08	08	07
GER	02	00	00
HK	46	45	41
IND	40	28	25
JAP	12	02	04
KOR	30	30	21
NEP	45	32	31
NET	18	05	07
NIG	34	27	18
NOR	10	03	03
PAK	46	40	32
POR	31	24	18
SIN	12	05	02
TUR	17	19	16
USA	13	02	01
VEN	25	17	28

[a]NP = Nurturing Parent; A = Adult; AC = Adapted Child.

Since the Critical Parent and Free Child ego states showed little relationship to PI across the 20 samples, and provided no evidence of Cluster 1 and Cluster 2 differences, we chose to focus on the three remaining ego states—Nurturing Parent (NP), Adult (A), and Adapted Child (AC). The results of this analysis are shown in Table 6.8. A "greater than" (>) sign indicates a difference of 5 to 9 percent in the common variance of the adjoining factors; two signs (>>) indicate a difference of 10 to 14 percent; and three signs (>>>) indicate that the difference was 15 percent or higher. In countries with no "greater than" signs, the common variance differences between adjoining values were all less than five percent. It can be seen that this was true in eight countries: Argentina, Chile, China, Finland, Germany, Hong Kong, Korea, and Turkey. In these countries, there was no clear evidence that PI was differentially associated with the ego states.

Of the remaining 12 countries, there were five—Japan, Pakistan, Singapore, the United States, and Venezuela—with only one single ">" sign between adjoining factors, which, conservatively, might be attributable to chance. In the remaining seven countries there were either two

TABLE 6.8. Relative Strength of the Relationship of PI to Three Ego States within Each Country[a,b]

Country	Range of CVs	Pattern
ARG	7	NP, A, AC
AUS	27	NP >>> AC, A
CHL	6	NP, A, AC
CHN	4	A, NP, AC
FIN	1	NP, A, AC
GER	2	NP, A, AC
HK	5	NP, A, AC
IND	15	NP >> A, AC
JAP	10	NP > AC, A
KOR	9	NP, A, AC
NEP	14	NP >> A, AC
NET	11	NP >> AC, A
NIG	16	NP > A > AC
NOR	7	NP > A > AC
PAK	14	NP, A > AC
POR	13	NP > A > AC
SIN	10	NP > A, AC
TUR	3	A, NP, AC
USA	12	NP > A, AC
VEN	11	AC, NP > A

[a]NP = Nurturing Parent; A = Adult; AC = Adapted Child.
[b]Difference in common variance between adjoining factors: > = 5–9%; >> = 10–14%; >>> = 15% and up.

">" signs or one ">>" or ">>>" sign, suggesting that certain ego states were more highly associated with PI than were others.

The seven countries displayed one of two patterns. The pattern NP > A > AC was seen in Nigeria, Norway, and Portugal, indicating that Nurturing Parent was somewhat more important than Adult, which was somewhat more important than Adapted Child. Thus, qualities associated with nurturance were more important than those associated with problem solving, which were more important than those associated with conformity.

The pattern NP >> A, AC was found in the four remaining countries—Australia, India, Nepal, and the Netherlands. In these countries, nurturance was much more important than problem solving and conformity, which themselves did not differ.

While the foregoing indicated some differences in patterning of the ego states in some countries, the patterns were not particularly distinctive, consisting mainly of differences in Nurturing Parent relative to the other two ego states. This relatively low degree of differentiation in ego states contrasts with the much higher degree of differentiation on the five factors, as noted earlier. From this, it appears that the five factor analysis is more effective than the ego state analysis in capturing between-country differences in the qualities associated with psychological importance.

MEAN EGO STATE SCORES OF HIGH IMPORTANCE AND LOW IMPORTANCE ITEM SETS

As an alternative way to examine the relation of ego states and psychological importance, we computed the mean ego state scores for the 60 item sets highest and lowest in PI in each country, as was done in the five factor analysis described earlier. The means for each country are shown in Table 6.9. Also shown are the grand means for the Cluster 1 and Cluster 2 countries.

An examination of the data in Table 6.9 leads to the following observations. Items of high psychological importance tend to be relatively high in Nurturing Parent and Adult qualities and low in Critical Parent, Free Child, and Adapted Child qualities. As would be expected, these findings are generally congruent with the results of the correlational analyses noted above (see Table 6.6). One exception was the modest tendency for Free Child qualities to be negatively associated with psychological importance in the present analyses and positively associated in the correlational analyses, although the degree of association in each case was modest.

TABLE 6.9. Mean Ego State Percents of Sets of 60 Items Rated
as High (HI) or Low (LO) in Psychological Importance[a,b]

		CP		NP		A		FC		AC	
		HI	LO	HI	LO	HI	LO	HI	LO	HI	LO
1	ARG	131	192	299	175	266	154	192	235	112	244
2	AUS	127	245	312	136	249	159	203	185	110	275
3	CHL	158	187	269	175	252	164	197	232	124	242
4	CHN	149	245	245	138	285	124	192	215	130	278
5	FIN	173	217	241	175	236	118	208	224	142	266
6	GER	206	188	221	185	176	174	209	214	188	239
7	HK	122	303	291	084	300	069	174	231	112	313
8	IND	132	261	292	107	276	105	195	207	105	320
9	JAP	157	238	278	173	210	170	208	187	150	231
10	KOR	129	213	302	140	290	110	164	224	115	313
11	NEP	129	283	304	086	275	068	185	219	108	345
12	NET	138	199	286	157	238	169	211	217	128	258
13	NIG	138	274	276	089	293	106	175	232	119	299
14	NOR	161	200	266	165	221	169	213	209	138	257
15	PAK	144	290	297	087	294	071	147	218	118	334
16	POR	134	220	292	168	277	131	186	212	112	269
17	SIN	185	198	261	174	235	169	178	218	142	241
18	TUR	141	249	252	130	308	127	183	197	116	297
19	USA	191	206	273	165	174	189	198	188	164	252
20	VEN	113	291	267	106	237	097	268	153	115	353
M Cluster 1		162.7	207.0	270.6	168.0	225.7	163.5	201.7	210.9	139.8	250.5
M Cluster 2		133.1	262.9	281.8	113.5	283.5	100.8	186.9	210.8	115.0	312.1
M totals		147.9	235.0	276.2	140.8	254.6	132.2	194.3	210.9	127.4	281.3
M HI–M LO		−87.1		135.4		122.5		−16.6		−153.9	

[a]Three decimal places omitted.
[b]CP = Critical Parent; NP = Nurturing Parent; A = Adult; FC = Free Child; AC = Adapted Child.

The grand mean ego state scores for the Cluster 1 and Cluster 2
countries are shown in Figure 6.2 where several effects can be noted.
In both clusters, the high importance item sets appeared higher on
Nurturing Parent and Adult characteristics and lower on Critical Parent and Adapted Child characteristics. A second observation is that
the effects just noted were more pronounced in the Cluster 2 countries
than in the Cluster 1 countries. These results generally parallel the
previously noted findings from the correlational analyses. Across the
countries, characteristics of a nurturant and problem-solving nature
are considered more important than characteristics related to stand-
ard-setting and adjustment to authority, with these effects being more
evident in the less developed and less individualistic countries of
Cluster 2.

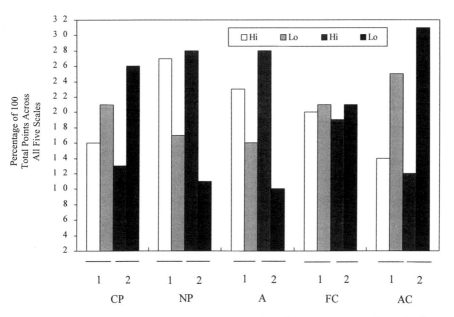

FIGURE 6.2. Mean TA Ego State Percents for High and Low Importance Items in the Cluster 1 and Cluster 2 Countries.

PARTIAL CORRELATIONS OF PSYCHOLOGICAL IMPORTANCE AND THE FIVE EGO STATE SCORES WITH FAVORABILITY CONTROLLED

We noted in Chapter 2 that the five ego states have substantial correlations with favorability; Nurturing Parent, Adult, and Free Child are positively associated and Critical Parent and Adapted Child are negatively associated. While we view favorability as an intrinsic component of the ego states, it was considered of interest to examine the relationship of the PI scores to the five ego states when favorability was controlled. For this analysis, we employ the PI data from the 15 countries for which we have language-specific favorability scores. As in previous analyses, six of the 15 countries are from the Cluster 1 group and nine from the Cluster 2 group. The partial correlations between the 300 PI scores and the five ego state distributions with favorability controlled are presented in Table 6.10.

An overview of the table indicates that 40 of the 75 coefficients remained statistically significant at the .05 level where perhaps four might have been expected by chance. As was the case for the five factors, it is clear that there are relationships between the ego states and psy-

TABLE 6.10. Partial Correlations of PI and Ego State Scores with
Language-Specific Favorability Controlled in 15 Countries[a,b]

	CP	NP	A	FC	AC
Cluster 1 (N = 6)					
ARG	11*	17**	12*	−05	−02
AUS	12*	31***	−12*	09*	11*
CHL	13**	16**	10*	−01	−03
NOR	14**	18**	02	06	−01
SIN	25***	24***	07	10*	06
USA	23***	28***	−03	07	08
Cluster 2 (N = 9)					
CHI	07	05	09	03	03
IND	26***	17**	06	−03	08
KOR	12*	27***	32***	−03	−16**
NEP	21***	16**	07	−10*	10*
NIG	17**	01	07	−05	10*
PAK	11*	18***	09	06	−11*
POR	20***	14**	07	00	03
TUR	05	15**	22***	05	−18***
VEN	03	01	−16*	47**	−07
Median Cluster 1:	14	21	05	07	03
Median Cluster 2:	12	15	07	00	03

[a]Decimal points omitted.
[b]CP = Critical Parent; NP = Nurturing Parent; A = Adult; FC = Free Child; AC = Adapted Child.
*$p < .05$; **$p < .01$; ***$p < .001$

chological importance that remain when favorability is controlled. A
second observation is that the significant partial correlations are con-
centrated on two ego states—Critical Parent and Nurturing Parent. It
seems clear that in both clusters of countries, there is a link between
parental qualities and psychological importance even when the intrinsic favorability of both parent ego states is controlled.

When the partial correlations for CP and NP in Table 6.10 are
compared with the corresponding uncorrected correlations in Table 6.6,
an interesting difference emerges. The relationships reflected in the
uncorrected correlations of NP and PI were all positive and relatively
strong and the effect of the partial correlation technique was to reduce
the magnitude of the positive relationship. The uncorrected correlations
of CP and PI suggested little overall relationship. However, with favorability controlled, a positive relationship emerged in most countries.
Thus, with favorability controlled, both types of parental qualities—rule-enforcing and nurturing—were found to be psychologically
important. Methodologically speaking, it appears that the somewhat
negative nature of CP was suppressing an underlying positive relationship of CP and PI in most countries.

NON-LINEARITY ANALYSES

In the main five factor and ego state correlational analyses, reported in Tables 6.1 and 6.6, it was observed that the coefficients tended to be substantially lower in the Cluster 1 countries than in the Cluster 2 countries for all of the five factors and for three of the ego states—Nurturing Parent, Adult, and Adapted Child. It should be noted that the correlations reported were the common, product-moment correlation coefficients which estimate the degree of rectilinear (straight-line) relationship between the variables. It seemed possible that the lower linear relationships observed in the Cluster 1 countries might be due to a tendency toward curvilinear relationships between PI and the various scoring system factors similar to that found between PI and favorability (see Chapter 5).

To explore this possibility, the data were reanalyzed to obtain an Eta coefficient between PI scores and each of the eight scoring system factors, separately for the pooled Cluster 1 data and the pooled Cluster 2 data. Evidence of non-linearity would be seen if the *Eta* value for a given scoring system factor was substantially larger than the corresponding r value, as reported in Tables 6.1 and 6.6. This analysis yielded negative results; the *Eta* values and the corresponding r values were comparable for all eight factors for both the Cluster 1 and Cluster 2 data. Thus, the lower correlations observed in the Cluster 1 countries were not artifacts of non-linearity, but appear to be bonafide evidence that the relationship between PI and the eight scoring system factors is weaker in the Cluster 1 countries than in the Cluster 2 countries, as shown graphically in Figures 6.1 and 6.2.

SUMMARY

In this chapter we employed two theoretically based analyses to assign conceptual meaning to the psychological importance ratings in each country. In the five factor analysis, it was found that in all countries the qualities associated with Extraversion, Agreeableness, Conscientiousness, Emotional Stability, and Openness were all considered psychologically important. In the ego state analysis, the qualities associated with Nurturing Parent and Adult were considered important, while Adapted Child qualities were considered unimportant. All of the effects just noted were stronger in the less developed and more collectivistic countries of Cluster 2. Subordinate analyses controlling for favorability generally reduced but did not eliminate the effects noted.

CHAPTER 7

PSYCHOLOGICAL IMPORTANCE

RELATIONS TO CULTURAL COMPARISON VARIABLES

A cautionary *dictum* in cross-cultural psychology is that observed variations in the behavior of different cultural groups are not necessarily due to cultural factors. The reason for this is that observed differences between groups, even when statistically significant, may merely be reflective of methodological difficulties (e.g., inaccuracy in language translations, or uncontrolled differences in subject characteristics). The most conservative approach to the interpretation of observed differences among groups is to assume that they do *not* reflect cultural differences unless they are correlated with independently assessed cultural indices. Thus, for example, if one observes differences in gender stereotypes among several cultural groups, and if the observed differences are found to be significantly correlated with an independent measure of the status of women in the groups, then one might conclude that at least some of the differences observed may be attributable to cultural differences.

In the present project, we employed a total of 16 indices, each of which seems to have some validity as a possible "cultural indicator" and all of which were obtained from sources independent of the present project. These indicators are value scores obtained from previous cross-cultural psychological research by Hofstede (1980) and Schwartz (personal communication), plus five general demographic indices obtained from library sources. While most of the demographic indices were available for all 20 countries, Hofstede values were available for only 16 countries and Schwartz values for only 14 countries. Furthermore, there were only 12 countries with *both* Hofstede and Schwartz data. Thus, the samples of countries shifted somewhat from one analysis to another, and caution in interpretation was indicated. The countries for which Hofstede and Schwartz data were available are shown in Table 7.1.

Appendix C contains two types of information related to the cultural comparison analysis. First, there is a listing of the individual country values for each of the 16 variables employed. Second, there is a matrix of correlations of each of the cultural comparison variables with each of the others, which indicates that, as one might expect, the 16 cultural variables are not all independent of one another.

In the following sections, we examine the relationship of the PI findings from Chapter 6 to the cultural comparison variables using the

TABLE 7.1. Overlap between Countries in the Present Project and in the Previous Studies by Hofstede and Schwartz

Countries in current project (N = 20)	Also in Hofstede (N = 16)	Also in Schwartz (N = 14)
Argentina*	+	
Australia*	+	+
Chile*	+	
China*		+
Finland	+	+
Germany	+	+
Hong Kong	+	+
India*	+	+
Japan	+	+
Korea*		
Nepal*		+
Netherlands	+	+
Nigeria*		
Norway*	+	
Pakistan*	+	
Portugal*	+	+
Singapore*	+	+
Turkey*	+	+
United States*	+	+
Venezuela*	+	+

*Indicates the 15 countries in the language-specific favorability analyses.

individual country as the unit of analysis. Because of the small numbers of cases involved in these cross-country analyses, we have chosen to indicate statistical significance at the .10 level as well as at the more conventional .05 and .01 levels. While we generally confine our attention to findings significant at at least the .05 level, we will sometimes note findings at the .10 level, particularly when such findings seem congruent with a meaningful pattern of findings on other variables.

In the final portion of the chapter, we return to our classification of countries into Cluster 1 and Cluster 2. Here we examine the average value of each of the cultural comparison variables in the two clusters of countries.

HOFSTEDE'S WORK-RELATED VALUES

In a project discussed in some detail in Chapter 1, Hofstede (1980) compared work-related values in 40 countries by obtaining access to attitude survey data obtained from thousands of employees of one large multinational business organization which manufactures and sells high-technology products. The company had conducted a survey of its employees in order to gain information about a variety of topics. Included within the 150-item questionnaire were a number of items concerning work-related values that Hofstede extracted and used in his investigation. Employing factor-analytic techniques, Hofstede identified four dimensions of work-related values:

- *Power Distance* (PDI). The extent to which people within a society accept the idea that power in institutions and organizations is distributed unequally.
- *Uncertainty Avoidance* (UAI). The degree to which persons have a lack of tolerance for uncertainty and ambiguity.
- *Individualism* (IDV). The degree to which people are supposed to take care of themselves and their immediate families only, as opposed to situations in which persons can expect their relatives, clan, or organization to look after them.
- *Masculinity* (MAS). The extent to which "masculine" values of assertiveness, money, and things prevail in the society rather than the "feminine" values of nurturance, quality of life, and people.

It should be noted that Hofstede found a substantial negative correlation between Power Distance and Individualism, i.e., countries high in Power Distance tend to be low in Individualism.

PSYCHOLOGICAL IMPORTANCE VERSUS HOFSTEDE SCORES

The 16 countries for which Hofstede values were available are noted in Table 7.1. The numerical scores for the individual countries are from Hofstede (1980) and are shown in Appendix C.

PI Scored for the Five Factors

In Chapter 6, we used the correlation coefficients between the PI scores in a given country and each of the five factors (FF) as indicators of the degree to which each factor was associated with PI in that country. The correlation coefficients obtained in each country were presented in Table 6.1. We next asked whether these indicators are systematically associated with the Hofstede values. For example, are the indicators (correlations) for PI versus Extraversion larger in countries which are higher in Hofstede's Power Distance? If so, one would expect a significant positive correlation across countries between the PI versus Extraversion indicators and the Power Distance scores.

Table 7.2 presents the correlation coefficients obtained when each of the five PI/FF indicators and each of Hofstede's four values are correlated across the 16 countries. An inspection of the values in Table 7.2 indicates some interesting relationships involving both Power Distance and Individualism. Countries where the psychological importance scores load heavily on the five factors tend to be countries high in Power Distance and low in Individualism; in countries high in Individualism and low in Power Distance, there is little association of psychological importance with the five factors. Thus, it appears that the importance assigned to traits reflecting each of the five factors decreases as a function of greater Individualism and lesser Power Distance. Un-

TABLE 7.2. Correlations between Each of the Four Hofstede Values and Each of the Five PI/FF Indicators in 16 Countries[a,b]

Hofstede values	PI/FF indicators				
	EXT	AGR	CON	EMS	OPN
Power distance	63***	57**	63***	51**	64***
Uncertainty avoidance	−08	01	−11	06	−05
Individualism	−47*	−48*	−54**	−48*	−49*
Masculinity	11	12	02	10	10

[a]Decimal points omitted.
[b]EXT = Extraversion; AGR = Agreeableness; CON = Conscientiousness; EMS = Emotional Stability; OPN = Openness.
*p < .10; **p < .05; ***p < .01

certainty Avoidance and Masculinity seemed uncorrelated with the degree of PI/FF association.

PI Scored for the Five TA Ego States

The analyses of the relationship of the Hofstede scores to PI scored for the five ego states (ES) parallels the five factor analysis in the preceding section. The PI/ES indicators were the correlation coefficients from Table 6.6, which, in turn, were correlated with the four Hofstede values with the results presented in Table 7.3.

An examination of the correlations in Table 7.3 reveals a number of interesting relationships. Power Distance was positively associated with Nurturing Parent and Adult qualities and negatively associated with Adapted Child qualities with some evidence of an opposite pattern seen for Individualism. Thus, it appears that qualities of nurturance, problem solving, and accommodation to authority are assigned greater importance in countries high in Power Distance values and low in Individualism values. Hofstede's Uncertainty Avoidance and Masculinity values appeared not to be related to the importance assigned to the ego states.

SCHWARTZ'S CULTURAL LEVEL VALUES

For over a decade, Shalom Schwartz and his coworkers have been developing a system for the classification of human values at the cultural level. This project was described in some detail in Chapter 1. After several revisions of his taxonomy, Schwartz (1994) proposed that there are seven basic cultural level values, as follows:

TABLE 7.3. Correlations between Each of the Four Hofstede Values and Each of the Five PI/ES Indicators in 16 Countries[a]

| Hofstede values | PI/ES indicators | | | | |
	Critical parent	Nurturing parent	Adult	Free child	Adapted child
Power distance	−21	45**	57***	37*	−55***
Uncertainty avoidance	05	−09	03	−06	−06
Individualism	26	−33	−59***	−13	53**
Masculinity	−21	10	−04	23	−06

[a]Decimal points omitted.
*$p < .10$; **$p < .05$; ***$p < .01$

- *Harmony* (HARM). Emphasizes harmony with nature. Stands in opposition to value types that promote actively changing the world and the exploitation of people and resources.
- *Conservatism* (CONS). Emphasizes close knit harmonious relations in which the interests of the person are not viewed as distinct from those of the group.
- *Hierarchy* (HIER). Emphasizes the legitimacy of hierarchical role and resource allocation.
- *Mastery* (MAST). Emphasizes active mastery of the social environment through self-assertion, including efforts to modify one's surroundings and get ahead of other people.
- *Affective Autonomy* (AFAU). Emphasizes autonomy related to an affective emphasis on stimulation and hedonism.
- *Intellectual Autonomy* (INAU). Emphasizes autonomy involving an intellectual emphasis on self direction.
- *Egalitarian Commitment* (EGCO). Emphasizes the transcendence of selfish interests and the promotion of the welfare of others.

PSYCHOLOGICAL IMPORTANCE (PI) VERSUS. SCHWARTZ SCORES

The 14 countries for which Schwartz values were available are noted in Table 7.1. The numbers used in this analysis were provided by Professor Schwartz and are shown in Appendix C.

PI Scored for the Five Factors

The PI/FF indicators in each country, taken from Table 6.1, were correlated with the seven Schwartz value scores with the results presented in Table 7.4.

An examination of Table 7.4 reveals that all five of the PI/FF indicators were positively correlated with Conservatism and negatively correlated with both Autonomy measures. Thus, in countries with high Conservatism and low Autonomy values, the psychological importance scores tend to be highly associated with each of the five factors. The other four values—Harmony, Hierarchy, Mastery, and Egalitarian Commitment—appeared not to be related to the PI/FF indicators.

PI Scored for the Five TA Ego States

The PI/ES indicators, the correlation coefficients from Table 6.6, were correlated with the seven Schwartz values. The results are presented in Table 7.5.

TABLE 7.4. Correlations between Each of the Seven Schwartz Values and Each of the Five PI/FF Indicators in 14 Countries[a,b]

Schwartz values	PI/FF indicators				
	EXT	AGR	CON	EMS	OPN
Harmony	−30	−32	−33	−31	−24
Conservatism	59**	55**	58**	51**	57**
Hierarchy	34	42	46*	39	35
Mastery	31	39	38	33	29
Affective autonomy	−62**	−57**	−59**	−55**	−60**
Intellectual autonomy	−62**	−56**	−66***	−52*	−57**
Egalitarian commitment	−20	−25	−26	−22	−17

[a]Decimal points omitted.
[b]EXT = Extraversion; AGR = Agreeableness; CON = Conscientiousness; EMS = Emotional Stability; OPN = Openness.
*p < .10; **p < .05; ***p < .001

An examination of the results in Table 7.5 indicates that in countries with high Conservatism values psychological importance was positively associated with Nurturing Parent and Adult qualities and negatively associated with Adapted Child qualities. This pattern was also observed, albeit in weaker form, in countries with high Hierarchy values. This pattern was reversed in countries high in both Autonomy values with less importance assigned to Nurturing Parent and Adult and more importance to Adapted Child. Egalitarian Commitment appeared not to be associated with the PI/ES indicators.

TABLE 7.5. Correlations between Each of the Seven Schwartz Values and Each of the Five PI/ES Indicators in 14 Countries[a]

Schwartz values	PI/ES indicators				
	Critical parent	Nurturing parent	Adult	Free child	Adapted child
Harmony	39*	−37*	−28	−04	25
Conservatism	−04	53**	53**	25	−49**
Hierarchy	−05	29	45**	−17	−36
Mastery	−47**	33	28	02	−25
Affective autonomy	24	−49**	−59**	−36	58**
Intellectual autonomy	08	−62***	−56**	−22	45*
Egalitarian commitment	24	−22	−18	09	−14

[a]Decimal points omitted.
*p < .10; ** p < .05; *** p < .01

DEMOGRAPHIC INDICATORS

Previous cross-cultural studies have indicated a surprising number of relationships between psychological variables (values, stereotypes, etc.) and demographic variables such as economic development, the status of women, and even latitude! (e.g., Hofstede, 1980; Williams & Best, 1990b). For these reasons, we have included five such variables in the present study. These are:

- *Economic/social standing (rank)* (SED). A composite of a variety of economic, educational, and health indices yielding an overall index of socioeconomic development in different countries. Since this is a rank measure, *low* scores indicate *more* developed countries.
- *Cultural homogeneity* (HOM). An index of the relative homogeneity/heterogeneity of the culture in a particular country with high scores indicative of relative homogeneity.
- *Percentage Christian* (CHR). Percent of the population having a Christian religious affiliation, the only religion for which worldwide statistics were available.
- *Population density* (DEN). An index of number of persons per unit of space with high scores indicative of lower density.
- *Percentage urban* (URB). The percent of a country's population living in urban areas.

The foregoing demographic indicators were available for between 18 and 20 of the countries in the psychological importance study. The individual country scores are from Kurian (1993) and Sivard (1993) and are shown in Appendix C.

PSYCHOLOGICAL IMPORTANCE VERSUS DEMOGRAPHIC VARIABLES

PI Scored for the Five Factors

The PI/FF indicators (correlations) from Table 6.1 were correlated with the five demographic indicators with the results presented in Table 7.6. An inspection of the values in Table 7.6 reveals that the relationship of PI to each of the five factors tended to be stronger in countries that were socioeconomically less developed, less urbanized, and less Christian. Conversely, the relationship of PI to the five factors appeared relatively weak in more developed, more urbanized, and more Christian countries. Cultural homogeneity and population density appeared not to be clearly related to the PI/FF indicators.

TABLE 7.6. Correlations between Each of the Five Demographic Variables and Each of the Five PI/FF Indicators in 18 to 20 Countries[a,b]

Demographic variables	PI/FF indicators				
	EXT	AGR	CON	EMS	OPN
Economic/social standing (rank) (N = 19)	68***	75***	78***	72***	68***
Cultural homogeneity (N = 18)	−28	−25	−29	−24	−25
Percentage Christian (N = 20)	−38*	−48**	−48**	−46**	−37*
Population density (N = 20)	02	−11	−14	−07	01
Percentage urban (N = 20)	−46**	−52***	−58***	−48**	−47**

[a]Decimal points omitted.
[b]EXT = Extraversion; AGR = Agreeableness; CON = Conscientiousness; EMS = Emotional Stability; OPN = Openness.
*$p < .10$; **$p < .05$; ***$p < .01$

PI Scored for the Five TA Ego State Scores

The sets of PI/ES indicators from Table 6.6 were each correlated with the five demographic variables with the results shown in Table 7.7. An examination of the tabled values indicates that in countries lower in socioeconomic development, there was a greater tendency for psychological importance to be associated with Nurturing Parent and Adult qualities and a lesser tendency for Adapted Child qualities to be viewed as important. This finding suggests that socioeconomic development leads to a decrease in the importance assigned to nurturing and problem-solving qualities and an increase in the importance assigned to qualities related to adjustment to authority. Similar patterns, in weaker form, are observed for the percent Christian and percentage urban

TABLE 7.7. Correlations between Each of the Five Demographic Variables and Each of the Five PI/ES Indicators in 18 to 20 Countries[a]

Demographic variables	PI/ES indicators				
	Critical parent	Nurturing parent	Adult	Free child	Adapted child
Economic/social standing (rank) (N = 19)	−34	64***	79***	00	−71***
Cultural homogeneity (N = 18)	−01	−36*	−21	−05	17
Percentage Christian (N = 20)	10	−41**	−49**	21	42**
Population density (N = 20)	04	−09	−12	25	06
Percentage urban (N = 20)	19	−41**	−54***	10	46**

[a]Decimal points omitted.
*$p < .10$; **$p < .05$; ***$p < .01$

indices. Thus, in more developed, more Christian, and more urbanized countries, psychological importance is less associated with nurturance and problem solving and more associated with adjustment to authority. The tabled values provide little evidence of linkages between the cultural homogeneity and population diversity variables and the qualities associated with different ego states.

INDIVIDUALISM, COLLECTIVISM, AND SOCIOECONOMIC DEVELOPMENT

Earlier in the chapter, we noted that some of our 16 cultural comparison variables are correlated with one another (see Appendix C). As an illustration, let us consider the relationships among seven of the variables with regard to the two major dimensions of cultural variation discussed in Chapter 1: individualism/collectivism and socioeconomic development. As shown in Figure 7.1, we included three variables which seemed related to individualism—Hofstede's Individualism (IDV) and Schwartz's Affective Autonomy (AFAU) and Intellectual Autonomy (INAU). If these three were all measuring aspects of individualism they should correlate with one another positively and they did (mean r = .57). We also selected three variables to represent collectivism—Hofstede's Power Distance (PDI) and Schwartz's Conservatism (CONS) and Hierarchy (HIER)—and found that they correlated positively with one another (mean r = .61). If individualism and collectivism were to be considered as two poles of a single dimension then

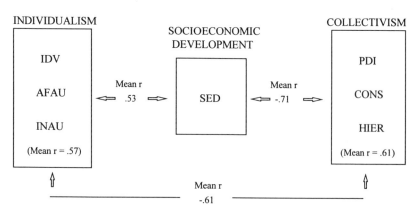

FIGURE 7.1. Relations among measures of individualism, collectivism, and socioeconomic development.

correlations between the three indices of individualism and the three indices of collectivism should be negative and, in fact, they were (mean $r = -.61$). Finally, if individualism is more characteristic of more developed countries and collectivism of less developed countries, then the measure of socioeconomic development (SED) should be positively related to the individualism measures and negatively related to the collectivism measures—and it was (mean r's of .53 and $-.71$, respectively). From the foregoing example it can be seen that the cultural comparison variables need not be viewed in isolation but, in many cases, are best understood as reflecting interrelated aspects of broader patterns of cultural variation.

CULTURAL CHARACTERISTICS OF THE CLUSTER 1 AND CLUSTER 2 COUNTRIES

IDENTIFICATION OF THE CLUSTERS

The rationale for the classification of the 20 countries into two clusters of 10 countries each was based on the findings from a factor analysis of the PI ratings in all countries which revealed two principal factors (see Chapter 5). Using the individual country loadings on the two factors, countries were assigned to Cluster 1 if their factor loadings were high on the first factor and low on the second factor, and to Cluster 2 if they were low on the first factor and high on the second factor. This rule led to the classification of the 20 countries, as follows: Cluster 1—Argentina, Australia, Chile, Finland, Germany, Japan, Netherlands, Norway, Singapore, and the United States; Cluster 2—China, Hong Kong, India, Korea, Nepal, Nigeria, Pakistan, Portugal, Turkey, and Venezuela. The meaningfulness of the two clusters was further demonstrated by the finding that the degree of similarity in PI ratings was greater *within* each of the two clusters than *between* the two clusters. From the foregoing it can be seen that the two clusters of countries were formed on the basis of their similarity in PI ratings rather than on some a priori basis. Thus, a comparison of the cultural variables for the two clusters provides another way to examine the relation of PI to culture.

CULTURAL CHARACTERISTICS OF THE TWO CLUSTERS

Because data were not available for all 20 countries, the following analyses are based on reduced clusters. The mean scores on each of the 16 comparison variables for each of the two reduced clusters are shown in Table 7.8.

Hofstede's Values

In Table 7.8 it can be seen that, relative to Cluster 2, the Cluster 1 countries were substantially higher on Individualism and lower on Power Distance. Although the observed differences were slight, the Cluster 2 countries appeared to be somewhat higher on Uncertainty Avoidance and Masculinity.

Schwartz's Values

The largest difference observed in Table 7.8 was on Hierarchy which was higher in Cluster 2 than in Cluster 1. Other apparent effects were higher scores for Cluster 1 on Affective Autonomy and Intellectual Autonomy and higher scores for Cluster 2 on Conservatism and Mas-

TABLE 7.8. Mean Values on 16 Cultural Comparison Variables for Countries in Reduced Cluster 1 (N = 6) and Reduced Cluster 2 (N = 9)[a]

	Cluster 1	Cluster 2
Hofstede values		
PDI	45.3	68.3
UAI	59.6	67.3
IDV	59.5	27.2
MAS	46.4	51.8
Schwartz values		
HARM	3.94	3.82
CONS	.3.75	3.97
HIER	2.30	2.90
MAST	3.92	4.16
AFAU	3.41	3.15
INAU	4.23	3.98
EGCO	4.92	4.81
Demographics		
SED*	19.7	83.5
HOM	79.7	76.8
CHR	74.3	29.8
DEN**	97.8	71.6
URB	78.2	39.4

[a]See text or Appendix C for variable names.
*Lower numbers indicate higher development.
**Lower numbers indicate greater density.

tery. The small differences observed for Harmony and Egalitarian Commitment suggest that the two clusters did not differ on these values.

Demographics

The tabled values indicate that Cluster 1 was substantially higher than Cluster 2 in socioeconomic rank, percent Christian, and percent urban, and somewhat lower in population density. Cultural homogeneity did not appear to differentiate the two clusters.

Summary of Cultural Characteristics Differences

In the authors' view, the cultural differences between Cluster 1 and 2 can be summarized in terms of two salient variables: individualism/collectivism and socioeconomic development. The higher scores for Cluster 1 on Individualism and the two Autonomy measures lead us to classify this group of countries as more individualistic. The higher scores for Cluster 2 on Hierarchy, Power Distance, and Conservatism lead us to classify this group as more collectivistic. The dramatic difference in socioeconomic rank justifies the characterization of Cluster 1 as more developed and Cluster 2 as less developed. Cluster 1's higher degree of urbanization and greater Christian affiliation seem congruent with this designation.

It should also be noted that the variables of individualism/collectivism and socioeconomic development are not independent of one another. As was shown in Figure 7.1, socioeconomic development tends to be positively associated with Individualism and the two Autonomy measures, and negatively associated with Power Distance, Conservatism, and Hierarchy. Thus, more developed countries tend to be more individualistic in values while less developed countries tend to be more collectivistic. Although something of an oversimplification, we consider it reasonable to characterize the principal cultural differences between the two groups of countries as follows: Cluster 1 is relatively more developed and individualistic, while Cluster 2 is less developed and collectivistic.

SUMMARY

In Chapter 6, we examined the degree to which the psychological importance ratings in each country were related to the variables from two theoretically based scoring systems based on the Five Factor Model and on Transactional Analysis ego states. This was done by correlating the PI ratings in each country with each of the 10 theoretical scales and considering each resulting correlation coefficient as an "indicator" of association. In the current chapter, these indicators were examined in relationship to 16 cultural comparison variables: Hofstede's four values, Schwartz's seven values, and five general demographic indices. It was found that variations in the Chapter 6 indicators were related to a number of the comparison variables and, hence, at least some of the variation in the indicators appeared to be reflective of cultural differences in the nature of psychological importance among the groups studied. When the Cluster 1 and Cluster 2 countries were compared, substantial differences were found on several of the cultural comparison variables leading to the designation of the Cluster 1 countries as more developed and individualistic and the Cluster 2 countries as less developed and collectivistic.

CHAPTER 8

SUMMARY AND INTEGRATION
OF FINDINGS

The concept of differential importance in psychological traits proposes that some characteristics may be of greater significance in that they provide more information concerning a person's psychological makeup and, hence, are more useful in understanding and predicting behavior. The basic idea behind the present project is that there may be cultural differences in what people consider to be psychologically important. For example, do persons in more collectivistic cultures assign greater weight to certain qualities than do persons from more individualistic cultures?

In the preceding chapters, we have examined in detail judgments of psychological importance made by women and men university students in 20 geographically dispersed and culturally diverse countries. In this chapter, we summarize and attempt to synthesize the major findings from the project, including the general findings concerning gender and those concerning differences observed in the more developed and individualistic countries versus the less developed and more collectivistic countries. Before proceeding to this we will comment briefly on the findings of our 10-country favorability study.

FAVORABILITY FINDINGS

We reported in Chapter 3 the results of a study in which university students in 10 countries rated the relative favorability of each of the 300 items of the Adjective Check List presented either in the original English language version (three countries) or in one of seven other language translations.

The extremely high correlations between the ratings given by the men and women subjects in each country indicate that the concept of favorability was highly reliable in each of the country/language groups; the median between-gender correlation of .98 indicates that the average within-country common variance was approximately 96 percent. By contrast, the average mean common variance for the between-country comparisons was estimated at 68 percent. As noted earlier, the lower between-country common variance is attributable to some unknown combination of "slippage" in the translation process, response sets, and true cultural differences in the favorability assigned to given personality traits.

The findings of this 10-country study indicate a remarkable degree of cross-cultural agreement in the relative "goodness" and "badness" of various psychological traits: capable, helpful, and industrious people are valued everywhere; foolish, selfish, and irresponsible people are valued nowhere. In this domain, the common "human nature" factor seems to loom much larger than the "cultural difference" factor. We also note that there is much more cross-cultural agreement as to what is favorable than as to what is psychologically important.

The results of the study indicate that, whenever possible, the favorability of sets of traits identified using translated versions of the ACL should be assessed via language-specific favorability ratings of the items in their translated form. On the other hand, the high degree of cross-cultural common variance observed suggests that, when language-specific favorability ratings are not available, one can obtain an estimate of findings relative to favorability by employing the grand mean favorability ratings shown in the right-hand column of Appendix B. The cross-country agreement in favorability is so high that, for example, the general picture regarding the relative favorability of male and female gender stereotypes in different countries, noted in Chapter 1 (Williams & Best, 1990a), would probably not be substantially altered by the use of culture-specific favorability data in each sample.

GENDER DIFFERENCES IN PI RATINGS

Before considering the observed gender differences in judgments of psychological importance, we must stress that the ratings made by the women and men students in each country were much more similar than they were different. The correlations between the men's and women's ratings across the 300 characteristics ranged from .68 in Nigeria and Venezuela to .99 in Hong Kong, with a median correlation of .88.

When all the men's data were pooled across the 20 countries and compared with the pooled women's data, a rather remarkable correlation of .968 was obtained. In many areas of psychological investigation, such correlations would be considered quite high and probably indicative of a theoretical identity in the variables being compared, with the relatively small departures from perfect correlations (1.00) being due to errors of measurement.

The numerical value of a correlation coefficient can be misleading by producing the impression that relationships between variables are stronger than, in fact, they are. For this reason, a useful procedure is to square the coefficient to obtain an estimate of the "common variance" between variables, i.e., the amount of the variation in one variable which can be accounted for by the variation in the other variable. When this procedure was applied to the correlations between men's and women's ratings, it was found that the common variance estimates ranged from 46 percent in Nigeria and Venezuela to 98 percent in Hong Kong with a median of 77 percent for the total group of 20 countries. The common variance for the pooled men's and women's data was 93.7 percent. Examined in this way, it appeared that, in most countries, there was still "room" for some systematic differences in the ratings made by women and men. And, in fact, this was what was found.

When we pooled all of the men's data and all of the women's data and identified items that each gender considered more important, the items more important to women were generally more favorable in nature than the items considered more important to men. Thus, it appeared that women considered favorable traits somewhat more informative about "what people were like" than did men. Additionally, when the ego state analysis was applied, women assigned more importance to Nurturing Parent and Adult, indicating that care-taking and problem-solving qualities were more informative. Men, on the other hand, assigned more importance to Critical Parent and Adapted Child, indicating that qualities associated with authority and conformity were considered of greater significance.

In relation to pancultural gender stereotypes, where male characteristics are higher on Critical Parent and Adult and female characteristics are higher on Nurturing Parent and Adapted Child (Williams & Best, 1990a), the two parent states "matched," with each gender assigning more importance to the parental state with which it is stereotypically associated. On the other hand, the findings for Adult and Adapted Child were "reversed" with each gender assigning greater significance to the characteristics stereotypically associated with the other gender. Thus, one cannot reach any general conclusion about similarities between gender stereotype and gender differences in judgment of psychological importance.

We caution the reader not to make too much of the gender differences which we have just described. These are very minor differences embedded in an overall picture of high similarity in the ratings of PI made by the men and women subjects. It must be remembered that the comparison of the pooled data for all men and all women, across all 300 items, revealed 94 percent common variance!

ITEM LEVEL FINDINGS

Having seen that the item level findings for men and women in each country were highly similar, we turned next to the question of item level similarities and differences among countries using the pooled PI data for women and men. Our first observation was that the similarities were greater than the differences, i.e., all between-country correlations were positive in sign. A second observation was to note the wide variations in similarity between pairs of countries where the common variance ranged from 1 percent to 64 percent, with a median of 25 percent. A third finding was that the 20 countries seemed to fall into two clusters—one consisting of more developed and individualistic countries and one consisting of less developed and more collectivistic countries. Later in this chapter, we will summarize the PI findings in these two clusters of countries.

COUNTRY LEVEL PATTERNS

It would have been most interesting had our theoretically based analyses revealed a culturally unique pattern of characteristics associated with psychological importance in each country—but such was not the case.

When the PI scores in each country were examined relative to the five factors (see Table 6.3), it was first observed that there were seven countries—mostly from Cluster 1—where the PI scores appeared to be equally associated with all five factors and generally at a low level. On the other hand, in half of the countries, it appeared that certain factors were more strongly associated with PI than were other factors. It was noted that the most highly contrasted patterns were in Hong Kong with its emphasis on Agreeableness, Singapore with its emphasis on Emotional Stability, and Venezuela with its emphasis on Extraversion. Thus, while cultural uniqueness was not always present, sufficient variability was observed to warrant the further exploration of between-country differences in the qualities associated with psychological importance.

DIFFERENTIAL FINDINGS IN THE TWO CLUSTERS OF COUNTRIES

We turn now to a topic of primary interest—namely, the qualities assigned greater or less psychological significance in our two clusters of countries. While we made a partial analysis of this at the level of individual items (see Table 5.8), we found it most useful to study the qualities associated with psychological importance by employing two theoretically based scoring systems—the five factor system and the ego state system, both of which were described in detail in Chapter 2. For each of the 300 ACL items, the five factor system provides values for Extraversion, Agreeableness, Conscientiousness, Emotional Stability, and Openness. For each of the items, the ego state system provides values for Critical Parent, Nurturing Parent, Adult, Free Child, and Adapted Child. Thus, across the 300 items, we correlated the PI scores in each country with the five factor and ego state scores to determine which theoretical factors were associated with psychological importance in that country.

THE FIVE FACTORS

In each country, there was a positive correlation between PI scores and each of the five factor scores. Thus, the more important items were higher in Extraversion, Agreeableness, Conscientiousness, Emotional Stability, and Openness than were the less important items. This pancultural finding will be of interest to advocates of the Five Factor Model, which they believe adequately comprehends the basic dimensions of human personality.

While the effects just described were evident in all countries, they were more dramatic in the Cluster 2 countries, where the median correlations ranged from .48 to .65, than in the Cluster 1 countries, where the median correlations ranged from .23 to .28 (see Table 6.1). A similar conclusion was reached when the means for sets of high importance and low importance items were compared with the finding that the differences in means were greater, for all five factors, in the Cluster 2 countries than in the Cluster 1 countries (see Table 6.4 and Figure 6.1). Earlier, in Chapter 2, we discussed the general tendency for PI ratings to be positively associated with favorability. We noted that each of the five factors has a favorable pole and an unfavorable pole, i.e., extraversion is more favorable than introversion, agreeableness than disagreeableness, conscientiousness than irresponsibility, emotional stability than neuroticism, and openness than closedness. While the authors believe that this evaluation must be considered an intrinsic component of each scale, one can inquire whether the factors are related to psychological importance when favorability is controlled by partial correlation.

Our partial correlation analysis revealed that, for all five factors, most of the previously significant correlations tended to disappear in the Cluster 1 countries, while over half of them remained significant in the Cluster 2 countries (see Table 6.3). In Cluster 2 countries, Extraversion and Conscientiousness continued to be associated with psychological importance when favorability was statistically controlled. While the Cluster 1 association of PI to the five factor scores *might* be attributed to a common association to favorability, the same cannot be said for Cluster 2, where important relationships continued when favorability was controlled.

Everything considered, we choose to retain our view that the five factors are intrinsically evaluative and that the findings regarding PI and the five factors are best interpreted by concluding that PI tends to be positively associated with each of the five factors, with these relationships being stronger in Cluster 2 countries than in Cluster 1 countries.

THE EGO STATES (ES)

When the PI ratings in each country were correlated with the ego state values, across the 300 items, some interesting results were obtained (see Table 6.6). PI was positively associated with Nurturing Parent in all countries, with the effect being larger in Cluster 2 (median $r = .57$) than in Cluster 1 (median $r = .35$). Similarly, PI was positively associated with Adult, with the relationship being higher in Cluster 2 (median $r = .53$) than in Cluster 1 (median $r = .22$). For Adapted Child, the relationship with PI was negative (Cluster 2, median $r = -.48$; Cluster 1, median $r = -.20$). For Free Child, there was a weak positive association with PI which did not appear to differ in the two clusters. For Critical Parent, the correlations with PI were generally negligible. Similar conclusions were reached when sets of high and low importance items were compared on Nurturing Parent, Adult, and Adapted Child, with the high–low differences found to be larger for Cluster 2 than for Cluster 1 (see Table 6.9 and Figure 6.2). Thus, there was a general tendency for items high in Nurturing Parent and Adult qualities and low in Adapted Child qualities to be considered relatively important, with this effect being more pronounced in the less developed and more collectivistic countries of Cluster 2 than in the more developed and individualistic countries of Cluster 1.

As was true for all of the five factors, at least four of the ego state scales appear to have an evaluative component, with favorability being positively associated with Nurturing Parent and Adult and negatively associated with Critical Parent and Adapted Child (see Chapter 2). When favorability was controlled via partial correlation (see Table 6.10), we found that the positive correlations of Nurturing Parent with PI generally were reduced, but remained significant in both clusters. Apparently, nurturing qualities are considered important apart from their favorable nature. While the uncorrected correlations of Critical Parent with PI implied little relationship, the generally positive partial correlations suggested that, in both clusters, Critical Parent qualities are considered of some importance, once their slightly unfavorable nature is set aside. Thus, with favorability controlled, the qualities associated with both Parent ego states were assigned more psychological importance. The previously noted positive correlation of PI to Adult and negative correlations of PI to Adapted Child were greatly reduced when corrected for favorability. Overall, the previously noted tendency for the uncorrected correlations of PI and Nurturing Parent, Adult, and Adapted Child to be higher in Cluster 2 than in Cluster 1 tended to disappear when favorability was controlled by partial correlation.

SUMMARY FOR FIVE FACTORS AND EGO STATES

The findings discussed reveal general, pancultural tendencies for greater psychological importance to be assigned to adjectives high in Extraversion, Agreeableness, Conscientiousness, Emotional Stability, Openness, Nurturing Parent, and Adult and less importance given to adjectives high in Adapted Child. In each instance, the relationships observed were stronger in the less developed and collectivistic countries of Cluster 2 than in the more developed and individualistic countries of Cluster 1. We will comment first on the general effects and then on the differences in the two groups of countries.

INTERPRETATIONS

In this project, persons from 20 culturally diverse countries rated the importance or "diagnostic value" of 300 different person descriptors in indicating what a person is "really like." In completing this task, there was no constraint on the raters as to which items they described as relatively important or unimportant. Subjects in Country X and Country Y were free to rate the adjectives in a similar, or unrelated, or even reversed manner; items rated important in Country X could have been rated as unimportant in Country Y and vice versa. In view of this, it was interesting to find that the item level analyses revealed that the PI ratings in all countries were more similar than different, i.e., there was substantial cross-cultural agreement in what was considered psychologically important. This agreement was reflected in the finding of an average correlation of approximately .50 (25 percent common variance) between individual pairs of countries.

We recognize that the underlying basis for this agreement could have been on dimensions other than those employed in the five factor and ego state scoring systems. After all, both of these systems are American-based and are possibly American-biased. It does not follow that, just because American psychologists consider these to be basic personality dimensions, they will be found to be related to what is considered psychologically important in different cultural groups. In view of this, it was interesting to find that the PI ratings were significantly correlated with all of the five factors and with three of the five ego states, suggesting that these theoretical formulations, and their assessment procedures, may have some cross-cultural utility.

Not only did the PI ratings in all countries correlate with the eight scoring system factors, they all correlated in the same direction. For the five factors, high psychological importance was associated with: extraversion rather than introversion; agreeableness rather than disagreeableness; conscientiousness rather than irresponsibility; emotional stability rather than neuroticism; and open-mindedness rather than close-mindedness. For the ego states, high psychological importance was associated with high Nurturing Parent and Adult and low Adapted Child. It can be observed that, for each dimension, it is the more positive end which is considered more psychologically important, a point to which we will return later in our discussion of psychological importance and favorability.

We turn now to the second major point about the relation of PI to the theoretically based scales—namely, that the relationships we have been examining were much stronger in the less developed/collectivistic countries of Cluster 2 than in the more developed/individualistic countries of Cluster 1. We note, in passing, that the direction of this difference was a bit surprising since the two theoretical systems had been developed in the West and, thus, might have been expected to have more relevance to the PI findings in the Cluster 1 countries than in the Cluster 2 countries. Had the obtained difference in results been reversed, this would almost certainly have been viewed by critics as a reflection of "Western bias" in the scoring systems and cited as another unfortunate example of an imposed etic strategy in cross-cultural research!

Returning to the main point, we can ask whether the lower correlations in the Cluster 1 countries can be attributed to some methodological problems or artifacts. One possibility was that the lower correlations in Cluster 1 might be indicative of some degree of nonlinearity in the relationships. This was examined and rejected (see Chapter 6): the relationships of PI and the scoring variables are as linear in Cluster 1 as in Cluster 2; they are just much weaker in Cluster 1. Another possible cause of lower correlations is restriction of range, but there was no evidence that the dispersion of PI scores was appreciably less in Cluster 1 countries than Cluster 2 countries (see Table 4.3). Perhaps there is more similarity in PI among the Cluster 2 countries than among the Cluster 1 countries? This idea was not supported when we obtained highly similar mean common variances among the countries in each cluster (see Chapter 5). Having found no evidence of artifactual causes, we must conclude that there is a bonafide effect in which the relationship of PI to the various theoretical variables is much stronger in Cluster 2 than in Cluster 1.

It was, of course, no surprise that the relationships between the PI scores and the theoretical variables were *different* in Clusters 1 and 2. The two clusters were originally composed on the basis of their differences on two factors derived from factor analyses, as described in Chapter 5. There it was shown that the common variance within Cluster 1 (29.95 percent) and within Cluster 2 (32.4 percent) was much greater than the common variance between the two clusters (15.1 percent). What was surprising was the nature of the observed differences—namely, the higher Cluster 2 correlations of PI with the five factor and ego state variables.

Early in the project, after the identification of the two clusters of countries, there was the implicit expectation that the theoretical variable analyses might indicate that PI in the two clusters might show different patterns of association with different variables, e.g., in Cluster 1, PI might be more highly associated with theoretical variables A and B, while in Cluster 2 PI might be more highly associated with C and D. Thus, we were not prepared for the findings which indicated a relatively uniform association of PI with all variables, with the degree of association being so much greater in the Cluster 2 countries.

The common variance among the Cluster 2 countries can be accounted for by stating that, in these countries, PI is highly associated with the positive pole of each of the eight theoretical variables. On the

other hand, the common variance among the Cluster 1 countries is not
adequately explained by the weak associations with the theoretical
variables—some other similarity among these countries is required to
account for the remainder of the common variance. We now believe that
the "missing factor" shared by Cluster 1 countries and not by Cluster 2
countries is the tendency to rate at least some unfavorable characteristics as being of moderate importance, which serves to attenuate
(weaken) the correlations between PI and the theoretical variables.
Consequently, we turn now to a consideration of the different relationships of PI and favorability in the two clusters of countries.

PI AND FAVORABILITY IN THE CLUSTER 1
AND CLUSTER 2 COUNTRIES

We reported in Chapter 3 a study of the favorability ratings of the
300 ACL items in 10 countries which enabled us to have *language-specific*
favorability scores for use in 15 of our 20 countries: six of the 10 Cluster
1 countries and nine of the 10 Cluster 2 countries.

When the language appropriate favorability scores were correlated with the PI scores, a significant positive product–moment correlation coefficient was obtained in each of the 15 countries, indicating a
general tendency for favorable adjectives to be rated as more important
than unfavorable adjectives. However, it was found that the strength of
this relationship was much higher in Cluster 2 (mean $r = .82$) than in
Cluster 1 (mean $r = .26$). Further analyses revealed that while the
relation of PI and favorability in Cluster 2 was essentially rectilinear
(straight-line), the relation in Cluster 1 tended to be curvilinear or "J"
shaped (see Figure 5.1 and Table 5.5). In Cluster 1, the most unfavorable
items were moderately important, the items of mid-range favorability
were of least importance, and the most favorable items were of the
greatest importance. Thus, both favorable and unfavorable characteristics were viewed as having some informational value. In Cluster 2,
by contrast, the importance of the items increased linearly with increasing favorability: the most unfavorable items were least important, the
mid-range favorability items were of moderate importance, and the
most favorable items were of the greatest importance. Thus, unfavorable characteristics were viewed as relatively less informative.

Two major findings require comment and an effort at explanation.
The first is the finding that, in all countries, favorable characteristics
were judged more important than unfavorable characteristics. The second is that this effect was less pronounced in the more developed and

individualistic countries of Cluster 1, where unfavorable characteristics were assigned moderate importance. We admit having no confident explanations for either of these effects. What follows are some speculative ideas, each of which would require further research to confirm its possible validity.

Regarding the general tendency for favorable traits to be more important, it may be that person descriptions employing favorable characteristics are more likely to be "accurate" and, hence, "more diagnostic" than descriptions involving unfavorable characteristics. While favorable descriptions may sometimes be influenced by ulterior motives (e.g., flattery), it may be that people believe that unfavorable descriptions are more frequently influenced by motives other than a desire for accuracy. One of our cooperating researchers (from a Cluster 2 country) suggested that negative descriptors may often be used by "enemies" and, hence, are of little value in providing information as to what the person "is really like." Thus, positive descriptors may be generally more believable while negative descriptors are more often suspect. This testable notion could be examined in a variety of ways, e.g., by comparing sets of favorable and unfavorable adjectives (mixed in different proportion) and having each set rated as to its "believability" as a description of a person.

Even if the foregoing speculation is accepted as reasonable, we must still attempt to account for the relative weakness of the general favorability effect in the Cluster 1 countries, where unfavorable traits can be of moderate importance and substantially more important than in the Cluster 2 countries. Our speculation here involves the differences in feelings and behaviors toward ingroups and outgroups in individualistic and collectivistic countries.

The ingroups/outgroups classification is one of the best established and most useful concepts in social psychology, being closely related to ethnocentrism, which is thought to be a universal human characteristic (Smith & Bond, 1994, p. 171; Triandis, 1995, p. 145). Relations within the ingroup are characterized by a feeling of familiarity, intimacy, and trust while outgroup relations lack such feelings and may involve negative feelings of aloofness, superiority, and even hostility. While the formulation applies, generally, in all societies, there seem to be variations in feelings and behavior toward ingroup and outgroup members in more individualistic and more collectivistic societies.

David Matsumoto, who has done extensive cross-cultural work on emotion, has provided an interesting analysis of differences in the expression of positive and negative emotions in individualistic and collectivistic countries (Matsumoto 1996, pp. 163–164):

Collectivistic cultures foster more positive and fewer negative emotions toward ingroups because ingroup harmony is more important to them. Positive emotions ensure maintenance of this harmony; negative emotions threaten it. Likewise, individualistic cultures foster more positive and less negative emotions toward outgroups. It is less important in individualistic cultures to differentiate between ingroups and outgroups, and thus they allow expression of positive feelings and suppression of negative ones toward outgroup members. Collectivistic cultures, however, foster more negative expressions toward outgroups to distinguish more clearly between ingroups and outgroups and to strengthen ingroup relations (via the collective expression of negative feelings toward outgroups).

Matsumoto's ideas are summarized in Table 8.1.

We believe that Matsumoto's formulation can be used as a starting point toward the understanding of the phenomenon of interest—namely, that in individualistic societies unfavorable adjectives are sometimes informative while in collectivistic societies they usually are not. Let us assume that all persons have some positive and some negative characteristics—hopefully, more of the former than the latter. In more individualistic societies, the focus is on the individual person, not on ingroups and outgroups, and realistic person descriptions should include positive and negative attributes, both of which may be informative as to what the person "is really like." Illustrative of this is the observation that, in individualistic countries, performance evaluations which include at least some negative descriptors usually are viewed as having greater verisimilitude than descriptions noting only positive characteristics. Thus, in individualistic societies, occasional negative descriptors are both expected and informative with regard to persons regardless of whether they belong to ingroups or outgroups.

In collectivistic societies, the focus is on the ingroup as a whole rather than on its individual members. In the interests of ingroup

TABLE 8.1. Consequences for Personal Emotions in Self–Ingroup and Self–Outgroup Relationships in Individualistic and Collectivistic Cultures

	Type of culture	
	Individualistic	Collectivistic
Self–ingroup relations	Okay to express negative feelings; less need to display positive feelings	Suppress expressions of negative feelings; more pressure to display positive feelings
Self–outgroup relations	Suppress negative feelings; okay to express positive feelings as would toward ingroups	Encouraged to express negative feelings; suppress display of positive feelings reserved for ingroups

Reproduced by permission from Matsumoto (1996, p. 164).

harmony and cohesion, the individual is likely to be described in terms of positive characteristics which contribute to ingroup goals rather than any negative characteristics which might detract (see Gudykunst, 1993). In the ingroup context, then, negative descriptors would occur infrequently and, when used, would be more likely to raise questions as to the motivation of the person providing the description (the "enemies," again) and, hence, less likely to provide valid information about the person so described. Negative person descriptors would most frequently be applied to outgroup members being used in a stereotypic manner which does not provide information about what individual persons "are really like." Thus in collectivistic societies negative descriptors are judged unimportant (uninformative, not diagnostic, etc.), while in individualistic societies negative traits are sometimes judged important (informative, diagnostic, etc.). In sum, the differential importance of unfavorable characteristics in the two types of societies may be related to the greater need for group cohesion and the greater ethnocentrism of collectivistic societies.

It is interesting to consider the foregoing ideas in the context of social evolution. It seems certain that earlier human societies were, of necessity, collectivistic in nature. The welfare of the individual was highly dependent on strong ingroup bonds of loyalty and cohesiveness; a negative view of outgroup members was highly adaptive. With the evolution toward more modern and individualistic societies, the dependency of the individual expands to involve outgroup as well as ingroup members. Under these latter conditions, the formerly critical ingroup/outgroup distinction tends to weaken and negative person descriptors begin to have some significance concerning the character of persons rather than being applied stereotypically only to outgroup members.

An even more speculative notion would attempt to relate the two favorability effects to general views of human nature, particularly as these are conditioned by traditional religious and philosophical orientations. The major world religions generally propose that human nature is intrinsically "bad" (sinful, incomplete, etc.) but, under the right circumstances, people have the potential for becoming "good." Persons holding such views would seem likely to expect a stranger to be "bad" until shown to be "good." Thus, person descriptors reflecting unfavorable characteristics (dishonest, irresponsible) would be expected and, hence, not very informative regarding individual differences. On the other hand, descriptors suggesting favorable characteristics are less expected and, hence, seem to be of more importance in providing information as to what a person is really like.

So far, the theory addresses only the general tendency in all countries for favorable traits to be viewed as more important than unfavorable traits. What about the secondary result where the favorability effect was less evident in the more individualistic and more developed countries? Here, our theory might propose that, in more individualistic and more developed countries, people hold a somewhat less negative view of human nature, perhaps because traditional religious views have been weakened by the impact of secular humanism. The result is that the expectations of strangers have moved a bit along the scale from "bad" to only "somewhat bad." Under these circumstances, while positive descriptors remain most informative, negative descriptors might also be important, i.e., the stranger might be worse than expected. Thus, negative characteristics would assume some psychological importance. The theory that persons from less developed countries may hold a more negative view of human nature finds some support in the results of a study conducted among graduate students at an American university (Sodowsky, Maguire, Johnson, Ngumba, & Kohles, 1994). Here it was found that students from Africa, Mainland China, and Taiwan found human nature to be "evil" significantly more than did White American students.

The theoretical notions just discussed are not mutually exclusive; there is possible merit in any or all of them. All are of the "cut and fit" variety and, at this point, none can be viewed as providing a confident explanation of the findings. This is not, for the moment, a criticism, since most new theories are circular in nature, serving only to account for the observations on which they are based. Theories become useful when they are able to predict additional empirical relationships. For example, the last described theory would predict that, in a cross-cultural study of views of human nature, the general view would be negative, but somewhat less negative in more developed countries than in less developed countries. If this prediction were confirmed, then the theory would receive support and would begin to have some utility in explaining the behaviors of interest.

SUMMARY

In this chapter we reviewed the favorability findings and the psychological importance findings related to gender and to the classification of countries as more developed and individualistic versus less developed and collectivistic. We discussed theoretical models which may explain the findings relating psychological importance and favorability.

RETROSPECT AND PROSPECT
A BROADER VIEW

This project has examined similarities and differences in the importance and favorability of various psychological characteristics in different cultural groups. Having summarized and attempted to integrate the findings in the preceding chapter, we turn now to a consideration of the broader implications of the project and directions for further investigation.

It is often said that one feature of a good research study is that it raises more questions than it answers. According to this criterion, the present project may qualify as a "good" one for there are many unanswered questions concerning the relative importance of psychological traits. We will organize our discussion around four topics: (1) further exploration of the nature of psychological importance; (2) questions concerning the possible role of psychological importance relative to various psychological processes and behaviors; (3) possible methodological and applied uses of the concept of psychological importance; and (4) further investigation of the Five Factor Model and the concept of "traitedness."

FURTHER EXPLORATION OF THE NATURE OF PI

In the present study, we focussed on the *general* psychological importance of various descriptors with importance defined as the diagnostic value of each characteristic in indicating what the person described was "really like." That general psychological importance was a meaningful concept was shown by the relatively high reliability of the

138

CHAPTER 9

importance ratings in each country. This finding does not, however, preclude the possibility of "context effects," where the significance of various person descriptors may vary across different types of situations or relationships.

The effects of context were examined in a study conducted with American university students which we described earlier in Chapter 2 (Williams, Munick, et al., 1995). In this study the general instructions for rating psychological importance were supplemented with instructions to one group to make the importance ratings as applied to someone in a "work situation"—that is, a fellow employee—and, to the second group, to make the ratings as applied to someone in a "close relationship"—that is, a close friend or spouse. The "diagnostic value" of the items was found to vary appreciably with the two situations in intuitively meaningful ways; for example, five factor Agreeableness was found to be higher in the relationship setting, while Conscientiousness was higher in the work setting. A further finding was that the relationship ratings appeared somewhat more similar to the general ratings than did the work situation ratings. Thus, it would appear that when rating the items for general psychological importance people may tend to think of them more in the context of personal relationships.

It would be interesting to explore context effects in different cultural settings, examining such factors as the degree to which the ratings differ by situation and the qualities associated with the differentiation (e.g., are there cultural differences in the importance assigned to Conscientiousness in the context of personal relationships?). Furthermore, one could further extend the situations employed, e.g., having one group rate "friend" and another rate "spouse" (or "potential spouse"), etc. An hypothesis for exploration is that the difference in importance ratings in work settings and close relationships would be greater in more individualistic countries than in more collectivistic countries, paralleling the general observation that work and leisure life are more highly differentiated in individualistic countries (Matsumoto, 1996, p. 108). Also worthy of further exploration is Brislin's (1993, pp. 61–62) theory that persons from individualistic societies are more comfortable dealing with context-free personality descriptors than are persons from collectivistic societies, who may find it more natural to describe personality in situation-specific terms.

Another substantive matter for further exploration concerns the different relationship between trait importance and trait favorability in less developed, collectivistic countries versus more developed, individualistic countries. In the former countries, the relationship is essentially linear, with favorability increasing with importance, and vice versa. In the latter countries, the relationship is curvilinear ("J" shaped), with low favorability items being moderately important, moderate favorability items being of less importance, and high favorability items being of greatest importance. The functions in the two groups of countries coincide at the upper end but diverge at the lower end (see Figure 5.1); what is to be explained is why items of low favorability are of moderate importance in individualistic countries and of low importance in collectivistic countries.

In the preceding chapter we offered some speculative thoughts about this finding. One theory related these findings to the greater need for group cohesion and harmony, and greater ethnocentrism, usually found in more collectivistic societies. A second theory proposed that the observed effects might be a result of cultural differences in the degree to which strangers are assumed to be "bad" until proven otherwise. This leads to the prediction that the general view of human nature would be found to be more negative in collectivistic than in individualistic countries, an idea which received modest support in the study by Sodowsky et al. (1994) discussed in Chapter 8. In this study, the instrument employed was Ibrahim and Kahn's (1987) Scale to Assess World Views which was based on the earlier work of Kluckhohn (1968). Perhaps this instrument might be adapted and employed to address the question of interest in a cross-cultural study with respondents from a variety of more and less developed countries.

Other questions concerning the nature of PI include the following: Are more important traits really more "diagnostic" in real life situations? Are there stable individual differences among persons in the tendency to describe themselves primarily with more important or less important traits? If so, is a self-description composed largely of unimportant, "peripheral" adjectives indicative of a poorly organized personality, or a tendency to avoid self-disclosure? Would longitudinal studies in developing countries reveal changes in PI consistent with the relative differences found between less and more developed countries in the present study? These and many other questions related to the nature of PI await future research efforts.

POSSIBLE ROLES OF PI IN PSYCHOLOGICAL PROCESSES

A second set of questions concerns the possible role of PI in the operation of various psychological processes. We mention only a few illustrative instances.

- *Person perception.* Psychologists have developed different theories concerning the way in which a set of person descriptors is combined to produce an overall impression of the person being described (Asch, 1946; Fiske, 1995). In elemental or "algebraic" theories (e.g., Anderson, 1981), the overall impression is viewed as the weighted average of the various descriptors, with the value assigned to each element being the product of its importance and its favorability. The importance and favorability ratings of the person-descriptive adjectives in the present project may be useful to researchers interested in testing this model on a cross-cultural basis.
- *Priming effects.* Compared to relatively unimportant traits, does early exposure to more important traits have a greater effect on the subsequent evaluation of trait-relevant information (Higgins, Rholes, & Jones, 1977)?
- *Causal attributions.* Personality traits are generally viewed as internal, uncontrollable, and stable causes of behavior. Do people perceive more important traits as being more internal, uncontrollable, and stable than less important traits (Betancourt & Weiner, 1982; Weiner, 1985)?
- *Intergroup stereotypes.* Do stereotypes containing more important adjectives have a greater impact on intergroup behavior than stereotypes containing less important adjectives?
- *Role of PI as a moderating or mediating variable.* Person perception studies have shown cultural differences in the relations between certain personality dimensions and certain behavioral intentions. Perhaps cultural differences in PI are mediating these relationships (Bond, 1983; Bond & Forgas, 1984).

METHODOLOGICAL APPLICATIONS

Having examined some substantive issues for future research, we turn now to some methodological considerations. The basic research method in the present project was the 300 item Adjective Check List, using translated versions as necessary. The main study involved the scaling of the individual items for psychological importance in 20 countries, employing 13 different languages. The secondary study involved the scaling of the items for favorability in 10 countries, employing eight different languages. The PI and favorability values for each of the 300 items in each country studied are shown in Appendix A and Appendix B.

Future researchers employing the ACL method in any of the countries studied may find the psychological importance and/or favorability values useful as control measures in the study of other variables. For example, one might conduct a study in which the ACL items were scaled relative to concept X in two countries with the between-country similarity assessed by a correlation coefficient computed across the 300 items. One could then ascertain whether the observed relationship was altered when item favorability and importance were controlled by partial correlation techniques. Alternatively, if one is selecting a set of person descriptors for use in a research study involving people from two or more countries, the psychological importance and favorability scores could be used to insure that the items chosen do not differ on these variables in the countries of interest.

In countries other than those studied, the PI and favorability scores might be used to provide *language-specific* values. For example, investigators in other Spanish-speaking countries might make use of the Spanish language PI ratings made in Argentina, Chile, and Venezuela, perhaps by averaging them.

The high degree of cross-cultural agreement in the favorability ratings suggests another research strategy. If culture- or language-specific favorability ratings are not available for certain countries, the investigator is on reasonably safe ground in using the English language favorability ratings obtained in the United States, or by using the 10-country mean for each item computed from the data in Appendix B. As noted earlier, one does not always wish to control for item favorability since many concepts have an intrinsic favorability component, as in the case of the scales of the Five Factor Model. However, in situations where favorability is viewed as an unfortunate confound, the data in Appendix B provide a useful control measure.

CROSS-CULTURAL AGREEMENT FOR DIFFERENT PSYCHOLOGICAL CONCEPTS

Prior to the present project, the ACL items had been used in two other cross-cultural projects in which the 300 items were scaled for certain psychological characteristics in a large number of countries. The first project concerned gender stereotypes, with the items scaled as to their degree of association with men or with women in 27 countries (Williams & Best, 1990a). The second project concerned age stereotypes with the 300 items scaled as to their degree of association with old adults and young adults in 19 countries (Williams, 1993). Table 9.1 lists the 36 countries and 17 languages in which the 300 ACL items have been scaled for one or more of four factors: psychological importance; favorability; gender stereotypes; and age stereotypes. It should be noted that trans-

TABLE 9.1. Countries Where the 300 ACL Items Have Been Scaled for Psychological Importance (PI), Favorability (FAV), Gender Stereotypes, and Age Stereotypes

Country	Language	PI[a]	FAV[b]	Gender[c]	Age[d]
Argentina	Spanish	X			
Australia	English	X		X	
Bolivia	Spanish			X	
Brazil	Portuguese			X	
Canada	English			X	X
Chile	Spanish	X	X		X
China	Chinese	X	X		
England	English			X	X
Finland	Finnish	X		X	X
France	French			X	
Germany	German	X		X	X
Hong Kong	Chinese	X			
Ireland	English			X	
India	English	X		X	X
Italy	Italian			X	
Israel	Hebrew			X	
Japan	Japanese	X		X	
Korea	Korean	X	X		X
Malaysia	Bahasha Malaysian			X	X
Nepal	English	X			
Netherlands	Dutch	X		X	
New Zealand	English			X	X
Nigeria	English	X	X	X	
Norway	Norwegian	X	X	X	X
Pakistan	Urdu	X	X	X	X
Peru	Spanish			X	X
Poland	Polish				X
Portugal	Portuguese	X	X	X	X
Scotland	English			X	
Singapore	English	X	X	X	
South Africa	English			X	X
Trinidad	English			X	
Turkey	Turkish	X	X		X
United States	English	X	X	X	X
Venezuela	Spanish	X		X	X
Zimbabwe	English			X	X

[a]Psychological Importance ratings from 20 countries in present study (Appendix A).
[b]Favorability ratings from 10 countries in present study (Appendix B).
[c]Gender stereotype ratings from 27 countries in Williams and Best (1990a).
[d]Age stereotype ratings from 19 countries in Williams (1993).

The fact that a similar, ACL-based method was used in all four studies enables one to compare the amount of cross-cultural agreement in the four concepts: psychological importance, favorability, gender stereotypes, and age stereotypes. In each study, a correlation coefficient was computed, across the 300 items, for each pair of countries. Each coefficient (r) was then expressed as percent common variance ($r^2 \times 100$), with the mean common variance computed across all pairs of countries. Thus, mean common variance provides an index of the overall agreement, across all countries, for a given concept. Bear in mind, however, that the countries composing the sample varied somewhat from study to study (see Table 9.1).

The mean common variance for each of the four concepts is shown in Figure 9.1. Here it can be seen that the percent agreement for the concepts was: favorability, 68 percent; age stereotypes, 46 percent; gender stereotypes, 42 percent; and psychological importance, 25 percent. Thus, the cross-country agreement was higher for favorability and lower for psychological importance than in the two stereotype studies. While there was evidence of cross-cultural agreement for all four concepts, the agreement on psychological importance was much less than the agreement on gender and age stereotypes—and all were much lower than the agreement on favorability.

The 68 percent agreement on favorability provides a useful "benchmark" for cross-cultural work employing the ACL indicating that it is possible to obtain such a high degree of cross-cultural agree-

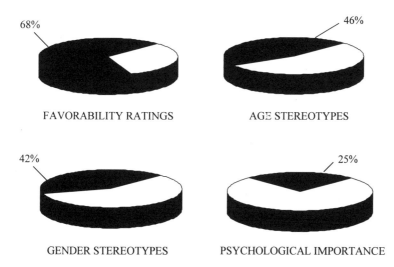

FIGURE 9.1. Mean percent common variance in various cross-cultural applications of the ACL methodology.

The 68 percent agreement on favorability provides a useful "benchmark" for cross-cultural work employing the ACL indicating that it is possible to obtain such a high degree of cross-cultural agreement despite the many possible sources of error (e.g., translation problems, etc.) in such research. As a final methodological point, it should be noted that in the present study the average *within*-country agreement was substantially higher for favorability than for importance—94 percent versus 77 percent—indicating that, in general, the importance ratings were relatively less reliable than the favorability ratings. This lesser reliability may be responsible, at least in part, for the lower between-country agreement. Relative to the conceptually clear nature of favorability, the concept of importance may have been a bit "fuzzy" both within and between countries. On the other hand, the reliability of the concept of importance was quite adequate for meaningful study.

THE VERSATILITY OF THE ACL METHOD

From the studies mentioned, it is obvious that the ACL item pool has a great variety of applications in research involving person characteristics. The ACL adjectives constitute a general set of person descriptors which can be employed in many different ways to describe real or hypothetical individuals or groups. The wide variety of research questions which can be addressed via the ACL item pool has been summarized elsewhere (Williams & Best, 1983, pp. 165–166):

- *Descriptions of individual persons.* A frequent application is one in which subjects are asked to describe self, significant others (spouse, parent, child, etc.), or persons whom the subjects have observed in particular settings (e.g., therapists describing clients; teachers describing pupils; supervisors describing employees, etc.). The method could be used, for example, to compare the manner in which well-known politicians are perceived by the public.
- *Descriptions of groups of persons.* Another common use is to ask subjects to consider groups of persons with whom they have had extensive experience and to indicate the traits which characterize them collectively (e.g., successful employees). A variation of this use is to compare two or more groups and to indicate the traits which are considered differentially characteristic (e.g., clinical type A versus clinical type B, etc.).
- *Social stereotypes.* Related to the foregoing are applications in which subjects are asked to describe their *beliefs* concerning the psychological characteristics of persons classified into broad

social groups: ethnic group A versus ethnic group B; men versus women; etc.

- *Historical figures.* The item pool can be used in psychobiographical studies in which subjects are asked to describe their impressions of historically important persons; e.g., Nehru, Stalin, Roosevelt, Churchill, etc.
- *Hypothetical persons.* The method may be employed to delineate the characteristics of various sorts of hypothetical persons. Illustrative here is the use of the item pool to characterize various ideal types such as ideal self, ideal mate, ideal physician, etc.
- *Personified concepts.* Subjects may be asked to use the item pool to characterize a variety of non-person concepts which, nevertheless, can be meaningfully personified. Illustrative here are the studies reported by Gough and Heilbrun (1980, p. 40) comparing the cities of Rome and Paris, and Fiat and Volkswagen automobiles. The ACL would appear to have many other such applications in the areas of environmental and advertising psychology.

In addition to its applicability in the assessment of a wide variety of concepts, the utility of the ACL is further enhanced by the availability of the four theoretically based scoring systems described in Chapters 1 and 2—affective meanings, ego states, Five Factor Model, and psychological needs—plus the scoring systems for psychological importance and favorability developed in the present project. The variety of concepts that can be studied and the different ways the results can be viewed combine to produce a highly versatile research procedure.

Illustrative of the more creative uses of the ACL are two studies from the area of psychology and religion. Daws (1980) used the ACL to identify the psychological characteristics which American university students associated with their concept of God and related these findings to differences in religious affiliations and practices. Saiz, Mella, Vargas, and Velasquez (1994) used the Spanish language version of the ACL to identify the traits that Chilean Catholic adults ascribed to God and reported that the findings revealed three social images, namely: *padre bueno* ("benevolent father"), *señor todopoderoso* ("powerful lord"), and *humilde* ("humble being"). The images were described in terms of affective meanings, ego states, and psychological needs. The authors note the correspondence between these three images and the three constituents of the Holy Trinity, as conceptualized in Roman Catholic theology.

The versatility of the ACL as a research procedure extends into the area of cross-cultural research via the existing translations of the item pool from English into 20+ additional languages. Thus, for example, one could study similarities and differences in the concept of God among adherents of different major religions in various countries around the world.

We conclude this discussion of the versatility of the ACL method by noting its application to two major topics of current interest in personality psychology: the Five Factor Model of personality; and the recently revived issue of "traitedness," which challenges the notion that the same set of personality traits are applicable in the description of all persons.

THE FIVE FACTOR MODEL OF PERSONALITY

The five factor system, described in detail in Chapter 2, employs the factors of Extraversion, Agreeableness, Conscientiousness, Emotional Stability, and Openness, which have been proposed by Western psychologists as the five basic dimensions of human personality. While this proposition already has been supported by some cross-cultural findings (e.g., McCrae & Costa, 1997), more research is needed to determine whether the Five Factor Model is adequate for the description of human personality on a pancultural basis. The ACL provides a valuable research tool for the further exploration of this topic via factor analyses in a wide variety of linguistic and cultural contexts.

THE CONCEPT OF TRAITEDNESS

Customarily, multidimensional personality assessment procedures carry the trait assumption that each of the dimensions employed is relevant to the description of every individual assessed, i.e., that every person can be meaningfully placed at some point along each trait dimension, whether low, medium, or high. Recently, this idea has been challenged by a number of authors (e.g., Baumeister & Tice, 1988; Britt, 1993), who contend that a given person's behavior in a given domain—say Conscientiousness—may be so variable that the trait notion is not meaningful and that it is best to consider this individual to be "untraited" on that dimension. Thus, different persons may be traited on different traits, e.g., one person might be traited on Conscientiousness but not on Extraversion while a second person might show the reverse pattern.

Whether an individual is considered relatively traited or relatively untraited is usually indexed by the standard deviation of the individual's responses to items scored for a given domain such as Conscientiousness: if the standard deviation is small, the person is considered relatively traited; if the standard deviation is large, the person is considered relatively untraited. Further support for this notion is found by the demonstration that persons who appear traited (or untraited) on a given dimension at a first administration of the instrument continue to appear traited (or untraited) at a later second administration.

Support for the traitedness concept among American university students has been found in a series of recent studies by the first author and his students (Satterwhite, Fogle, & Williams, in press). Employing both the NEO-FFI (see pp. 35–37) and a self-descriptive ACL, evidence of reliable individual differences in traitedness was found for each of the Big Five factors.

A phenomenon, later labeled supertraitedness, was also observed. When the individual's standard deviations for the five factors were averaged for the first administration of the procedure and again for the second administration, there was a substantial tendency for persons with small (large) mean standard deviations at administration one to also have small (large) mean standard deviations at administration two. Persons with small mean standard deviations were said to be "super-traited." If personality is conceptualized as behavioral consistency across situations and time, then highly supertraited persons might be described as having "more personality" than persons scoring low on the supertraitedness dimension.

Studies are underway exploring the concepts of traitedness and supertraitedness in a cross-cultural context. If one accepts the premise that behavior is more situationally determined in more collectivistic societies than in more individualistic societies (Matsumoto, 1996; Triandis, 1995), then one would expect less evidence of traitedness in persons from the former than from the latter. Thus, in a study now in progress, we expect to find higher average traitedness, and more supertraitedness, among persons from the more individualistic society of the United States than among persons from the more collectivistic society of India. This study is viewed as a pilot study for a possible large-scale, multi-country project examining the concept of traitedness in relationship to the dimension of individualism–collectivism.

One might also explore the possible relationship between the concepts of traitedness and psychological importance; for example, is traitedness equally evident when attention is directed to items either high or low in psychological importance, or are people more traited on relatively more important items? These and many other questions await the further application of the ACL methodology in the area of cross-cultural personality/social psychology.

IN CONCLUSION

The current project—like our previous cross-cultural efforts—has involved the voluntary participation of psychologists from many countries around the world. The listing of their names on the cooperating researchers page of this book is but a small token of our appreciation for their assistance. Organizing such research groups is not as difficult as one might suppose. There are well-trained psychologists in all countries, many with cross-cultural interests that lead them to participate in projects such as ours simply for the advancement of knowledge.

We believe that a key factor in assembling our international research teams has been the treatment of the cooperating persons as professional peers, reflected in our invitation to participate in the design of the research and by our policy of treating the data collected at a given research site as the property of the local cooperating researcher who is free to use them in whatever way he or she chooses—reading or publishing a paper, etc. All that we have asked is that the data be shared with us for cross-cultural analyses. In these ways, we have tried to develop truly cooperative endeavors and to avoid the "intellectual imperialism" which characterized some of the early work in cross-cultural psychology. Apart from the new knowledge developed, we believe that our several cross-cultural projects have provided an encouraging demonstration of international scientific cooperation which bodes well for our collective future in the global village.

APPENDIX A

TABLE A. Pooled Gender Means of Psychological Importance Ratings of 300 Adjectives in Each of 20 Countries with Grand Mean for All Countries[a,b,c]

Item #	ARG	AUS	CHL	CHN	FIN	GER	HK	IND	JAP	KOR	NEP	NET	NIG	NOR	PAK	POR	SIN	TUR	USA	VEN	Grand mean
001	301	251	273	238	209	225	222	296	244	272	269	230	194	267	210	243	271	251	274	281	251
002	381	304	358	347	353	363	392	364	366	356	376	358	321	304	350	378	321	364	316	360	351
003	399	333	375	393	358	342	437	336	342	377	335	317	303	325	406	360	349	322	350	241	350
004	323	328	307	304	286	279	351	318	263	285	334	335	283	295	389	305	322	269	322	368	317
005	307	292	329	321	342c	332	156	312	283	261	326	346	264	267	306	297	292	267	270	221	289
006	409	399	421	372	323	404	406	371	360	371	363	411	322	359	417	395	349	325	374	362	376
007	398	370	419	381	344	422	397	327	324	301	280	391	295	372	259	343	403	311	379	327	352
008	321	335	306	352	269	336	439	348	319	336	316	331	312	273	380	380	327	236	319	338	329
009	309	271	325	272	315	290	216	265	262	304	255	340	259	275	247	290	310	276	304	225	281
010	331	371	369	313	325	321	406	378	287	335	359	303	338	299	438	367	370	345	397	336	349
011	296	331	321	219	287	232	229	307	229	266	281	314	289	247	314	285	313	236	306	229	277
012	346	286	377	240	283	324	228	274	328	263c	247	300	257	322	198	289	291	326	336	209	286
013	416	359	351	250	217	382	407	325	287	388c	350	341	358	284	406	335	313	263	339	367	337
014	306	322	345	274	287	341	261	306	234	319	313	288	278	279	343	303	330	263	344	293	299
015	343	343	367	315	344	394	145	287	302	291	252	382	234	327	211	315	389	316	396	272	312
016	251	316	290	294	279	233	367	308	224	291	302	304	311	251	389c	324	318	331	281	291	298
017	297	343	312	300	289	270	191	303	351	346	297	341	247	285	308	293	377	274	353	349	306
018	289	334	285	327	283	283	401	329	378	255	342	330	289	270	401	333	324	243	294	368	318
019	345	272	393	305	300	354	166	309	307	340	262	301	245	257	210	292	320	305	269	263	291
020	286	248	289	274	201	222	156	242	277	245	246	287	218	204	158	225	285	215	233	208	236
021	351	290	363	273	280	241	154	259	216	340c	202	320	236	247	198	271	274	170	334	217	262
022	323	236	336	215	228	202	225	253	291	277	249	320	234	319c	197	293	230	188	222	223	253
023	330	304	335	267	305	315	184	294	330	272	245	338	251	332	192	281	346	280	334	288	291
024	345	318	353	312	307	369	140	308	230	325	276	346	268	339	250	307	353	271	367	272	303
025	352	335	340	362	335	360	396	322	373	317	329	369	297	332	386	348	373	347	332	333	347
026	408	345	388	352	297	312	453	372	354	361	372	334	332	329	419	384	398	369	355	348	364

027	325	279	324	261	232	318	196	288	295	289	265	322	256	250	224	258	322	289	325	283	280
028	338	309	320	264	245	273	361	319	316	359c	342	299	328	268	342	336	334	320	308	333	316
029	362	312	382	285	256	337	229	316	298	303	301	332	297	258	290	285	302	302	294	302	302
030	328	320	310	340	259	225	415	343	291	324	342	322	307	301	396	346	303	314	296	361	322
031	429	388	403	290	265	379	418	361	388	372	377	405	309	326	402	398	358	359	368	377	368
032	376	313	378	325	313	217	421	368	324	390c	381	364	336	267	431	385	273	313	309	333	341
033	384	325	348	337	331	318	444	363	359	408c	370	379	338	280	403	376	339	332	333	336	355
034	336	346	349	350	273	265	459	338	358	381c	373	318	348	290	280	361	339	351	330	334	339
035	290	264	283	295	290	252	198	281	248	334c	230	352	245	285	199	309	255	266	271	239	269
036	342	289	340	269	296	395	209	294	347	278	236	309	248	314	221	298	303	299	346	206	292
037	280	213	250	248	232	230	290	258	265	263	269	258	244	208	179	257	197	251	211	233	242
038	265	307	326	228	259	225	207	276	267	254	254	326	242	268	194	275	290	264	321	291	267
039	314	277	337	264	263	326	285	284	276	270	278	304	234	241	201	285	279	224	272	248	273
040	346	287	338	291	337	367	219	313	283	277	350	356	271	287	246	297	312	324	377	241	306
041	382	374	357	343	324	319	417	388	294	360	382	383	322	317	417	376	402	299	396	338	359
042	330	277	316	232	232	244	240	277	181	249	241	281	254	255	232	294	290	223	266	240	263
043	348	338	333	340	305	353	406	338	331	378	347	355	307	390	410	381	345	389	358	351	355
044	302	307	292	304	259	313	272	297	272	310	265	281	311	258	314	290	345	295	308	264	293
045	299	373	326	345	321	277	429	334	409	373	338	370	316	376	347	380	372	300	386	326	350
046	395	316	339	271	290	307	358	307	238	292	321	375	327	287	381	353	323	269	314	371	321
047	270	283	279	277	283	255	294	273	208	272	294	271	301	222	316	253	283	217	243	239	267
048	356	287	329	357	265	325	331	300	357	319	262	276	283	281	411c	306	281	345	251	277	310
049	409	359	379	321	360	314	407	377	343	379	393	346	315	355	409	383	353	328	355	323	360
050	390	332	341	352	318	276	425	383	341	354	386	337	330	265	455	367	342	365	332	348	352
051	336	281	314	280	242	290	204	292	307	340c	220	310	234	258	203	284	306	327	290	189	273
052	382	306	398	321	337	397	147	296	306	295	221	359	238	344	240	317	356	333	390	204	309
053	303	312	334	291	306	336	314	323	250	318	343	354	247	302	309	318	277	264	299	336	310
054	353	309	411c	295	308	328	248	293	314	309	219	322	231	330	199	304	317	341	326	284	298
055	335	301	326	321	279	241	232	312	212	311	335	323	264	282	434c	333	328	290	291	336	307
056	380	340	362	308	348	389	141	304	352	316	243	375	257	321	216	351	359		385	240	314

(continued)

TABLE A. (Continued)

Item #	ARG	AUS	CHL	CHN	FIN	GER	HK	IND	JAP	KOR	NEP	NET	NIG	NOR	PAK	POR	SIN	TUR	USA	VEN	Grand mean
057	311	298	306	272	238	283	281	307	234	287	351	310	316	250	383ᶜ	277	317	234	301	290	292
058	379	243	361	301	282	263	400	290	350	398ᶜ	330	321	288	292	436ᶜ	327	260	368	258	305	322
059	376	280	369	286	287	298	308	291	387	309	301	345	285	296	291	351	363	242	334	313	316
060	469	399	464	333	420ᶜ	447	429	311	426	324	264	437	290	401	429	446	396	330	439	384	392
061	354	307	341	281	269	305	223	284	271	275	244	329	276	281	228	316	342	299	339	213	289
062	345	275	304	241	286	239	183	283	183	265	214	309	264	263	226	292	263	260	267	214	259
063	421	347	387	332	347	356	405	369	206	372	358	358	308	311	441	388	378	352	356	376	358
064	295	342	275	259	230	218	395	343	288	343	370	311	292	224	439ᶜ	374	306	273	314	278	309
065	356	308	377	319	258	346	432	319	334	372ᶜ	249	347	266	238	322	307	277	388	266	302	319
066	314	261	307	234	255	259	182	264	309	265	225	263	240	202	211	251	256	232	241	279	252
067	323	245	295	206	251	309	210	268	255	245	253	332	238	216	200	273	263	222	250	231	254
068	296	272	296	193	249	255	213	281	210	240	220	281	231	208	202	241	240	268	221	267	244
069	352	353	353	269	300	325	215	290	219	297	236	363	238	281	205	292	363	327	397ᶜ	251	296
070	367	353	404	263	311	390	186	352	256	286	305	358	260	328	297	317	362	264	352	268	314
071	310	266	334	254	234	277	238	283	301	265	260	274	215	266	208	316	259	278	244	328	271
072	328	273	313	219	307	214	196	261	285	254	208	326	199	251	200	257	255	241	276	217	254
073	380	376ᶜ	349	318	245	292	430	286	322	297	298	292	269	209	246	273	331	269	342	358	309
074	323	289	350	266	255	258	268	306	249	273	204	260	282	218	251	271	294	273	267	192	268
075	413	329	369	329	330	303	447	348	341	342	365	307	344	328	422	392	355	204	315	331	345
076	336	319	366	327	344	428	130	345	380	319	253	348	322	322	257	318	355	332	382	239	321
077	340	351	380	310	340	395	223	353	369	333	304	372	318	339	308	354	365	290	353	345	337
078	380	326	358	342	346	335	406	341	297	328	369	365	368	322	368	368	322	291	357	358	347
079	420	353	408	380	328	323	409	342	195	356	325	371	362	306	396	355	326	368	313	355	350
080	401	360	386	359	339	365	448	355	223	331	357	411	280	341	398	347	349	261	365	349	351
081	320	286	323	224	256	254	239	275	200	252	198	301	270	287	191	300	261	245	276	235	260
082	300	318	302	257	272	320	245	282	288	267	314	280	277	246	365	311	272	279	294	333	291
083	432	364	425	336	325	224	426	341	300	356	368	409	313	390	406	379	293	338	328	355	355

084	336	261	353	254	275	381	205	292	266	281	258	294	275	311	213	356	310	283	328	286	291
085	308	287	301	246	259	268	203	270	272	284	238	282	254	250	220	266	267	266	257	222	261
086	326	312	346	265	264	265	256	287	304	263	243	310	263	273	203	306	292	289	273	199	277
087	333	258	342	268	356[c]	272	228	278	271	304	242	293	233	248	193	276	313	263	269	257	275
088	281	294	291	300	247	222	174	275	231	247	241	288	222	245	202	283	330	275	284	311	262
089	303	272	314	277	210	211	166	255	334[c]	240	201	280	227	251	208	287	274	255	278	203	252
090	324	265	342	298	265	260	430[c]	285	295	275	288	325	262	190	287	290	313	213	328	304	292
091	338	286	349	338	279	215	446	328	280	366[c]	348	310	312	252	406	309	355	301	276	353	322
092	292	257	279	255	232	276	231	263	308	271	241	279	277	236	232	250	299	204	266	252	260
093	304	386	322	307	301	296	403	318	370	372	330	377	307	261	408	257	347	305	391	242	330
094	290	251	252	276	245	255	261	273	217	276	325[c]	262	302	232	276	262	222	245	221	239	259
095	434	292	436	400	355	406	422	348	364	387	372	396	321	356	430	429	359	401	314	323	377
096	419	436	418	353	353	410	452	372	372	399	391	432	318	350	419	342	377	332	422	369	388
097	330	279	345	311	256	323	181	265	328	277	225	280	278	238	241	285	275	214	252	215	270
098	276	279	268	283	231	270	210	257	247	280	196	287	266	204	188	279	299	210	260	236	251
099	411	378	400	328	263	318	432	316	326	367	372	312	304	270	397	388	346	327	364	348	348
100	417	371	397	328	303	351	415	352	371	271	387	351	300	369	428	377	326	306	351	352	356
101	329	251	351	276	268	288	221	260	340	267	268	320	283	284	237	274	260	245	285	215	276
102	276	289	250	280	235	224	368	309	257	325	335	305	304	228	366	295	269	232	269	390[c]	290
103	313	392	297	314	307	350	416	382	373	378	371	378	300	280	431	328	360	319	391	309	350
104	338	297	343	310	307	375	165	267	266	321	215	340	246	317	231	287	337	271	361	296	294
105	264	286	258	288	220	237	410[c]	319	277	290	334	291	305	224	362	325	259	250	257	381[c]	292
106	320	258	324	278	319	345	183	293	349	329	270	345	283	271	222	307	311	334	322	313	299
107	338	303	347	311	299	386	224	301	355	297	246	309	267	293	248	304	338	262	343	254	301
108	299	237	310	268	232	197	197	267	308	307	258	260	279	219	224	300	252	267	247	288	261
109	288	301	315	262	258	332	183	329	237	307	283	334	286	293	235	277	319	315	333	238	286
110	350	329	277	343	251	196	416	305	317	324	356	333	306	264	368	336	262	331	297	385	317
111	397	366	355	366	292	390	447	360	198	361	389	398	304	364	397	373	365	271	356	353	355
112	328	273	292	253	269	345	205	293	270	329	215	326	287	274	247	277	295	271	308	363[c]	286
113	458	454	442	379	399	436	441	381	426	419	398	451	341	444	444	453	395	403	466	363	419

(continued)

TABLE A. (*Continued*)

Item #	ARG	AUS	CHL	CHN	FIN	GER	HK	IND	JAP	KOR	NEP	NET	NIG	NOR	PAK	POR	SIN	TUR	USA	VEN	Grand mean
114	358	309	367	274	341	369	172	321	369	297	244	360	271	362	295	325	353	251	363	243	312
115	392	386	346	358	262	377	393	331	365	369	325	393	293	356	362	388	357	303	369	383	355
116	305	242	308	206	231	215	287	252	262	272	280	279	276	262	237	289	248	258	229	288	261
117	326	318	381	226	241	339	307	325	240^c	364^c	343	339	304	290	325	318	332	272	313	329	311
118	341	344	363	333	300	361	359	325	320	290	294	367	300	297	301	370	319	320	332	339	329
119	356	340	367	264	277	325	202	269	249	227	240	340	270	284	202	303	348	227	360	242	285
120	321	284	317	221	249	320	210	278	313	292	241	315	257	272	211	252	344	362^c	336	257	282
121	336	280	355	242	310	357	198	282	280	299	270	341	272	326	246	288	341	304	331	337	300
122	371	333	381	355	311	325	381	366	345	344	363	369	284	356	340	345	397	341	390	384	354
123	347	267	312	291	310	314	202	294	305	281	289	324	276	311	215	296	294	245	286	251	285
124	336	360	361	293	328	348	231	330	286	306	287	337	297	306	332	311	376	313	371	285	320
125	429	283	408	369	275	278	437	308	317	366	341	289	325	308	421	401	339	369	311	376	347
126	328	251	326	271	255	279	196	277	331	284	217	312	254	277	215	293	266	237	294	257	271
127	292	247	263	297	334^c	266	351	281	222	249	247	278	270	264	206	263	225	235	234	357^c	269
128	373	274	358	345	289	308	409	281	208	282	307	278	304	275	355	321	293	323	313	380^c	314
129	314	281	318	318	284	317	244	276	222	249	271	300	276	263	219	298	273	227	285	218	273
130	410	336	378	265	325	333	386	334	315	359	311	364	329	335	386	378	342	304	319	385	345
131	346	298	348	361	318	331	433	311	286	300	333	313	328	330	418	321	331	348	319	347	336
132	406	399	434	379	354	373	451	385	292	372	376	374	329	353	459	429	355	339	393	368	381
133	337	290	299	260	290	326	222	275	230	247	229	316	263	312	278	283	260	195	300	210	271
134	373	339	353	316	304	347	376	340	281	284	342	372	289	359^c	380	366	269	255	324	363	335
135	345	294	364	250	339^c	285	192	270	227	284	247	348	242	355	221	306	322	266	339	282	289
136	374	294	393	360	297	307	422	312	256	358	340	339	281	327	402	322	280	354	304	377	331
137	393	337	400	274	314	434	154	280	383	296	236	356	217	320	216	320	419	327	375	269	316
138	338	313	353	221	276	340	226	283	371^c	284	226	325	237	301	198	287	348^c	278	323	273	290
139	342	312	344	291	328	331	401	347	374	344	311	314	257	308	420	301	293	303	300	363	329
140	402	409	385	305	272	309	446	355	407	358	361	404	297	332	422	376	360	355	389	330	364

141	304	318	360	277	258	286	184	254	300	270	201	301	241	285	199	288	342	302	306	245	275
142	288	290	276	318	221	226	332	267	265	229	245	369[c]	263[c]	237	249	272	241	229	257	267	269
143	340	355	295	349	305	266	416	357	260	383	340	361	301	282	256	326	321	337	303	289	322
144	303	302	274	231	246	239	266	271	277	238[c]	238	301	267	237	236	251	264	205	290	263	260
145	436	413	443	362	341	231	434	352	398	368	359	420	316	416	432	430	370	269	421	358	378
146	386	313	367	324	300	211	426	348	405[c]	356	342	333	352	319	423	313	268	360	308	311	338
147	380	278	359	376[c]	242	266	287	294	359	269	324	288	339	234	365	285	259	304	269	361	306
148	400	368	391	363	304	335	386	337	270	385	361	298	328	334	394	386	384	291	398	297	351
149	336	268	299	280	215	288	312	274	278	329[c]	285	266	312	220	301	294	278	245	264	301	283
150	300	265	304	293	283	212	397	297	350	316	321	265	318	215	386[c]	329	256	292	246	293	296
151	302	263	280	285	236	286	380	285	358[c]	342[c]	273	297	241	238	405[c]	400[c]	233	281	231	238	296
152	288	269	285	261	242	253	236	272	277	271	246	302	304	355[c]	308	295	293	220	286	348[c]	277
153	313	262	294	292	248	226	384[c]	287	279	331[c]	301	272	292	205	358	311	245	255	238	283	284
154	347	314	320	339	259	308	416	322	214	383[c]	327	343	242	268	337	349	309	362	311	297	321
155	336	326	310	296	251	364	209	309	193	281	275	344	236	297	261	306	297	274	334	293	290
156	326	298	316	233	269	331	206	272	237	288	222	324	284	295	215	266	295	256	312	258	273
157	382	350	387	300	349	393	372	340	334	385	347	355	241	368	278	351	283	276	304	358	340
158	332	313	326	216	269	298	232	282	354[c]	287	239	315	245	292	213	298	280	296	286	259	281
159	281	280	256	216	245	248	224	255	314	246	211	289	280	291	209	253	274	211	269	327[c]	257
160	290	297	265	319	309	268	437	340	327	378[c]	302	267	255	319	320	262	311	324	266	343	311
161	362	300	348	291	309	328	155	280	292	260	208	314	295	297	194	299	333	247	374[c]	302	287
162	334	340	334	287	278	355	190	315	235	303	325	320	305	272	211	287	322	343	369	310	300
163	372	308	396	333	296	358	277	326	215	317	272	315	327	273	257	320	323	309	329	274	309
164	424	377	428	351	343	381	415	354	359	374	336	394	332	353	378	373	375	323	384	369	368
165	401	330	378	340	279	264	421	356	198	354	346	305	330	259	401	359	358	271	308	260	326
166	376	348	372	371	314	311	417	353	316	352	356	360	320	275	396	374	308	337	324	360	347
167	359	372	364	338	383[c]	292	343	330	350	361	276	327	343	361	333	347	345	307	379	359	342
168	365	344	367	306	337	277	363	319	343	420[c]	264	315	338	281	423	389	361	258	339	372	339
169	378	225	355	352	269	285	410	313	299	334	293	276	337	272	426[c]	328	263	292	253	279	312
170	370	339	347	322	313	331	427	309	376	354	292	373		325	431	362	370	347	363	268	348

(continued)

TABLE A. (*Continued*)

Item #	ARG	AUS	CHL	CHN	FIN	GER	HK	IND	JAP	KOR	NEP	NET	NIG	NOR	PAK	POR	SIN	TUR	USA	VEN	Grand mean
171	367	332	349	300	306	341	389	312	372	371	347	354	348	298	417	350	305	277	324	298	338
172	302	246	312	300	256	257	225	301	333	263	285	293	300	245	333	299	270	298	254	329	285
173	418	285	395	358	272	277	438	309	343	308	329	322	321	279	426	327	337	364	309	343	338
174	379	319	375	374	268	312	434	297	349	290	303	295	290	294	314	357	359	276	329	343	328
175	360	295	383	295	291	375	196	276	304	282	237	348	275	338	333	296	357	291	353	225	305
176	365	262	340	348	285	260	401	315	226	351	340	315	289	269	391	278	280	354	249	306	311
177	383	375	374	314	311	317	424	339	362	340	363	362	308	325	361	372	336	305	340	337	347
178	364	322	320	270	262	272	224	307	237	280	323	307	267	292	261	265	274	282	296	258	284
179	390	272	398	339	339	373	387	266	248	390[c]	262	345	283	308	361	361	249	282	281	315	322
180	266	265	277	366[c]	256	229	426[c]	278	293	337[c]	290	281	299	233	410[c]	269	223	299	252	258	290
181	365	331	335	322	290	283	300	376[c]	227	361	367	328	293	282	411	362	344	272	310	337	325
182	278	304	264	281	233	209	351	306	263	251	317	296	288	299	352	264	241	279	284	293	283
183	334	273	300	280	295	296	368	312	245	356[c]	301	305	299	312	297	321	283	310	267	346	305
184	324	339	377	264	307	340	212	293	290	300	260	366	250	318	268	311	356	289	393[c]	233	304
185	301	268	336	289	252	249	368	263	229	271	280	295	251	229	225	302	232	328	255	318	277
186	374	298	367	328	280	248	380	349	284	326	373	325	312	242	416	328	270	336	266	350	323
187	309	275	298	254	231	259	202	274	212	348[c]	299	284	246	258	314	290	262	246	264	279	270
188	331	274	323	248	298	334	192	284	233	301	216	331	229	294	211	276	327	262	336	293	280
189	275	271	325	268	265	228	212	267	267	258	226	286	248	233	209	262	267	211	271	201	252
190	317	288	253	312	241	214	401[c]	300	376[c]	292	331	276	276	226	277	275	266	226	229	329	285
191	281	280	293	314	256	310	369	315	336	248	323	325	285	239	310	241	300	280	284	295	294
192	342	261	346	278	228	314	301	274	307	305	227	322	281	332	211	283	268	237	314	248	284
193	355	349	346	343	313	306	413	329	292	380	324	340	318	328	288	362	338	340	333	286	334
194	332	225	366	303	290	268	184	287	233	271	231	300	302	255	190	289	250	241	237	206	263
195	385	352	382	340	324	378	286	368	294	394	354	353	335	300	427	361	371	303	336	308	347
196	397	355	372	367	281	371	412	364	333	346	366	381	321	260	410	330	368	354	352	319	353
197	325	304	385	331	301	335	200	296	292	288	247	325	247	277	249	308	362	288	340	350	303

198	361	297	366	268	270	256	188	265	305	253	231	304	249	259	217	259	342	263	333	231	276
199	376	321	384	300	254	323	324	305	238	309	312	327	289	269	368	320	312	313	288	298	311
200	302	327	330	271	263	264	338	292	334	320	299	355	299	295	239	316	263	196	293	274	293
201	441	407	431	373	401	397	419	374	386	426	365	442	335	196	450	454	395	358	421	354	391
202	346	291	359	282	265	361	187	282	317	256	262	360	297	185	224	294	305	255	316	262	285
203	330	273	326	306	255	310	277	311	327	377[c]	289	287	315	215	246	291	287	298	276	261	293
204	363	305	350	348	303	211	418	310	270	366[c]	335	310	339	279	367	355	342	260	310	325	323
205	428	400	404	370	342	374	451	359	327	382	395	402	346	392	446	421	431	405	418	303	390
206	293	276	297	229	259	253	245	275	363[c]	283	268	285	272	283	233	260	267	267	239	281	271
207	286	224	309	255	259	267	269	234	272	294	249	295	271	262	288	266	211	254	203	238	260
208	303	241	308	279	252	265	200	289	297	288	282	290	258	294	253	274	302	280	258	250	273
209	224	223	195	329	296	255	373[c]	285	221	344[c]	289	257	293	270	254	250	264	261	243	262	269
210	328	329	329	310	306	315	216	271	294	299	215	295	246	235	230	253	350	285	381[c]	227	286
211	322	342	341	294	309	325	155	295	309	285	249	344	212	288	191	276	356	262	339	245	289
212	354	334	384	312	345	380	194	314	350	301	312	365	268	353	213	284	387	318	408	263	322
213	399	366	418	363	342	412	377	384	328	398	390	369	312	348	386	393	371	326	413	373	373
214	356	365	375	234	282	317	364	369	324	391[c]	373	351	326	301	427	350	350	314	366	348	344
215	343	291	362	345	252	326	405	288	231	261	254	331	270	278	241	316	299	343	296	327	303
216	314	284	326	390[c]	265	368	245	275	314	249	273	337	254	293	242	261	294	239	331	289	292
217	298	287	346	301	256	306	275	294	205	258	252	308	238	292	265	258	287	245	309	236	276
218	311	293	345	322	317	355	163	301	352	289	256	335	261	339	278	310	307	310	328	264	305
219	375	328	403	371	347	392	142	290	338	324	234	379	249	296	221	322	378	329	403	247	318
220	361	401	411	378	311	384	253	342	310	284	358	379	293	373	347	397	388	286	392	367	351
221	330	311	370	349	307	223	251	340	285	329	361	337	271	284	370	372	335	284	318	333	318
222	309	342	318	271	265	311	395	330	379	358	322	364	289	283	375	368	331	266	343	250	323
223	318	249	312	310	245	280	288	266	338	265	270	338	242	264	256	306	261	249	274	219	277
224	297	314	280	217	264	279	301	302	263	272	266	304	222	219	255	354	269	285	282	377[c]	281
225	345	277	347	236	281	383[c]	214	260	214	255	229	330	226	279	253	298	313	223	358	222	277
226	280	325	295	245	320	295	406	287	242	315	313	336	251	227	422[c]	364	318	290	290	331	307
227	328	236	351	272	247	232	205	266	241	264	282	289	244	206	213	303	220	264	241	213	258

(continued)

TABLE A. (Continued)

Item #	ARG	AUS	CHL	CHN	FIN	GER	HK	IND	JAP	KOR	NEP	NET	NIG	NOR	PAK	POR	SIN	TUR	USA	VEN	Grand mean
228	311	293	278	313	231	342	180	290	227	289	230	270	259	209	220	288	319	270	323	283	271
229	325	251	321	291	269	296	370	315	256	323	273	304	284	254	344	389c	337	288	295	288	304
230	279	286	300	298	289	290	272	285	343	269	259	319	283	242	249	278	311	250	322	230	283
231	269	255	285	326	252	286	287	308	335	284	313	305	266	234	196	261	260	252	272	217	273
232	332	246	330	304	287	228	322	329	350	325	349	296	285	228	388	336	283	259	257	209	297
233	447	378	435	271	345	394	417	376	358	238	377	410	293	370	430	428	394	332	396	367	373
234	331	235	313	270	261	256	326	288	300	260	230	265	254	213	172	262	269	250	223	247	261
235	301	234	263	213	237	214	255	241	285	249	225	279	240	211	253	227	260	217	221	217	242
236	288	296	268	265	272	311	143	272	327	322	204	323	272	322	226	325	335	298	285	258	281
237	333	255	340	311	301	316	186	279	281	249	245	332	251	309	201	303	280	239	279	263	278
238	306	295	323	361	262	314	160	281	217	276	260	318	254	275	247	292	335	259	377c	350	288
239	399	387	393	350	328	333	307	342	358	311	364	403	334	317	418	386	365	350	368	365	359
240	438c	340	402	257	292	302	301	354	410c	348	348	289	340	255	426	390	324	355	339	342	342
241	279	301	277	261	279	262	300	320	272	392c	308	321	305	231	409c	291	288	225	282	318	296
242	311	231	298	284	240	289	178	260	262	277	241	284	290	243	246	267	290	254	236	288	263
243	300	270	302	339c	318	213	154	254	269	276	231	299	255	331c	231	262	307	301	315	212	272
244	361	318	395	287	348	349	377	330	342	276	330	398	251	344	267	362	319	340	324	373	332
245	321	245	337	321	299	289	428	307	387c	301c	297	315	240	283	261	302	251	302	298	362	307
246	374	327	385	333	283	302	366	335	306	390c	323	355	273	307	403	352	322	298	327	296	333
247	382	300	382	347	285	320	346	325	322	299	315	322	277	270	414	340	322	344	305	336	328
248	330	261	324	293	274	296	289	283	291	276	243	309	256	255	199	287	292	303	280	237	279
249	340	223	349	267	251	348	196	272	219	293	222	335	255	289	217	288	312	300	302	214	275
250	324	212	312	245	231	359c	231	278	270	275	216	275	264	189	219	276	248	224	252	253	258
251	317	331	310	226	262	291	417	344	235	337	338	297	306	240	393	305	311	327	320	378	314
252	310	278	339	262	285	291	208	298	255	315	239	297	263	301	225	289	355	284	354	283	287
253	305	269	338	290	275	357	307	297	250	323	276	313	288	295	414c	282	332	250	310	207	299
254	289	283	309	341	258	382	230	297	219	292	336	354	281	309	338	289	263	213	266	228	289

255	253	232	241	225	248	275	195	274	251	281	223	275	217	270	223	239	224	230	338	261	338ᶜ
256	241	244	204	209	285	252	205	224	265	255	259	222	244	257	199	192	202	336ᶜ	257	241	263
257	288	293	286	299	301	263	297	283	276	327	275	290	328	283	205	268	283	302	302	285	314
258	347	273	363	329	326	392	410	352	329	357	350	373	293	338	411	354	338	339	341	322	364
259	336	369	346	289	358	296	351	251	321	368	342	345	367	337	421	342	300	268	370	354	322
260	295	216	340	296	342	270	418	282	260	334	249	276	271	258	253	352	276	275	347	287	298
261	306	303	298	259	303	301	260	298	249	331	291	358ᶜ	333	292	400	275	289	354	304	321	305
262	303	315	323	293	345	308	206	334	271	329	277	316	286	292	225	359	311	317	340	295	320
263	266	259	282	242	274	264	221	255	244	311	254	242	215	278	242	285	268	348ᶜ	284	275	274
264	275	197	313	265	287	280	244	283	234	338	246	297	269	271	140	313	269	277	327	282	366
265	309	260	298	323	323	271	436ᶜ	287	279	291	296	336	327	299	377	275	268	318	316	286	305
266	345	310	373	396	378	300	404	285	297	320	359	362	431ᶜ	354	418	321	276	287	335	356	342
267	286	283	252	313	307	259	388ᶜ	301	267	274	222	326	228	280	394ᶜ	243	252	289	281	234	332
268	275	233	272	292	286	284	209	267	236	278	231	307	341	264	224	314	275	318	326	259	281
269	340	277	333	358	358	350	343	370	307	382	330	379	341	324	381	250	328	303	378	346	368
270	283	258	306	234	305	297	238	310	284	318	280	260	265	312	212	339	272	269	304	281	317
271	297	262	281	325	294	275	266	293	290	290	282	313	320	308	365	276	269	300	324	296	304
272	258	310	404	362	367	380	434	361	325	362	328	354	321	362	372	389	303	284	369	390	386
273	307	313	257	225	278	275	360	301	261	301	284	341	344	278	389	353	244	332	399	232	375
274	275	182	311	276	264	284	212	262	241	286	244	246	251	260	345	307	275	280	343	276	355
275	295	297	255	285	292	283	351	253	257	301	223	340	253	268	382	281	283	240	374	267	414ᶜ
276	288	353	271	273	309	269	229	282	246	290	267	271	323	284	308	317	270	330	286	267	305
277	312	188	379	263	335	322	240	355	267	394	292	274	366	305	191	399	356	257	385	285	378
278	373	337	410	357	403	399	416	383	339	377	381	394	350	370	402	301	325	318	400	398	413
279	297	230	322	299	297	315	271	361ᶜ	226	346	265	272	276	272	295	303	321	234	384	295	365
280	273	228	284	267	248	255	350	294	233	294	240	246	201	271	290	271	278	205	372	284	349
281	292	229	383ᶜ	265	333	289	207	342	226	365	214	289	374ᶜ	300	191	381	310	192	327	329	319
282	297	370ᶜ	307	261	279	341	317	283	244	309	243	324	223	282	303	328	310	268	343	311	303
283	269	203	315	243	257	294	221	283	209	305	225	279	242	258	190	312	304	263	322	332	328
284	283	198	366	290	318	292	192	320	210	346	211	276	345	269	211	244	306	253	336	326	357

(continued)

TABLE A. (*Continued*)

Item #	ARG	AUS	CHL	CHN	FIN	GER	HK	IND	JAP	KOR	NEP	NET	NIG	NOR	PAK	POR	SIN	TUR	USA	VEN	Grand mean
285	328	281	339	217	285	338	197	273	288	292	221	314	217	269	246	262	316	251	301	224	273
286	348	289	351	319	335	413[c]	177	285	249	299	216	357	250	317	251	313	366	281	306	239	298
287	312	375	319	266	304	383	396	331	233	371	309	337	282	267	366	294	338	286	389	363	326
288	336	317	358	328	242	315	223	266	312	286	246	308	263	309	233	282	315	264	311	202	286
289	376	310	377	327	311	364	172	309	337	300	244	341	281	309	244	321	307	255	350	221	303
290	334	323	327	310	311	333	440	341	287	383[c]	318	355	330	297	305	328	309	335	321	308	330
291	382	394	383	341	310	379	407	346	398	377	325	388	296	330	364	343	352	341	363	307	356
292	359	257	350	378[c]	250	297	373	296	295	307	223	327	261	278	382	303	274	337	251	366	308
293	292	296	303	358[c]	265	233	217	258	319	256	217	290	240	228	208	257	265	247	262	203	261
294	305	257	278	224	277	269	242	284	250	252	219	288	243	225	233	244	234	251	301	199	254
295	411	322	388	256	290	319	397	310	307	369[c]	296	281	299	288	399	292	283	317	304	363	324
296	415	349	393	331	323	326	438	361	334	336	364	357	339	289	434	333	371	344	361	320	356
297	304	289	284	254	276	334	188	288	308	291	267	320	281	248	221	292	301	229	301	254	276
298	339	339	316	245	242	319	398	320	309	308	349	368	286	305	355	317	327	349	317	383	324
299	337	290	328	265	231	260	222	281	243	271	265	348	263	270	232	270	291	252	284	312	276
300	309	282	314	268	228	195	340	269	258	246	239	267	257	257	257	273	252	314	258	298	269

[a] Two decimal places omitted.
[b] See Appendix D for item names.
[c] Items found to be atypically high in psychological importance in the indicated countries. See Chapter 5 for a description of this analysis.

APPENDIX B

TABLE B. Pooled Gender Means of Favorability Ratings in
Each of 10 Countries with Grand Mean for All Countries[a,b]

Item #	CHL	CHN	KOR	NIG	NOR	PAK	POR	SIN	TUR	USA	Grand mean
001	207	254	200	171	177	171	203	209	243	186	202
002	433	366	419	450	411	438	424	408	429	441	422
003	439	428	430	390	456	421	438	440	400	447	429
004	393	386	368	369	383	419	380	414	320	426	386
005	174	134	238	315	169	252	196	238	168	253	214
006	455	406	455	409	442	433	402	413	443	422	428
007	174	409	190	201	171	304	164	215	168	306	230
008	413	425	288	380	279	460	429	432	315	443	386
009	218	214	374	287	259	276	214	191	348	216	260
010	259	373	361	413	285	452	337	355	349	409	359
011	266	264	270	347	237	300	244	225	255	250	266
012	155	246	233	273	142	188	155	237	162	161	195
013	433	357	382	414	386	438	402	441	440	429	412
014	315	289	246	308	378	409	402	262	290	238	314
015	167	194	143	206	143	142	136	139	141	168	158
016	401	394	136	435	413	433	398	427	375	424	383
017	357	219	401	296	221	330	350	345	407	346	327
018	370	394	270	399	414	447	402	423	343	432	389
019	204	160	144	157	180	207	273	213	286	277	210
020	177	185	240	201	186	145	202	220	208	188	195
021	127	146	225	183	155	138	139	168	159	143	158
022	164	223	197	209	138	128	209	230	167	220	189
023	166	183	166	234	146	135	137	144	165	161	164
024	183	143	151	236	134	197	162	142	305	173	183
025	337	405	443	313	367	435	367	413	359	408	385
026	461	427	441	365	456	461	445	457	416	438	437
027	206	238	205	230	204	186	195	197	190	172	202
028	391	301	389	337	327	421	398	368	404	357	369
029	209	197	192	335	261	192	295	297	252	325	255
030	400	406	426	398	438	445	419	418	405	421	418
031	463	434	432	425	465	445	459	454	429	454	446
032	467	425	421	439	383	483	443	405	444	406	432
033	448	439	430	431	444	464	437	443	408	449	439
034	438	451	439	450	446	269	443	437	447	435	425
035	213	185	197	220	146	202	181	208	139	192	188
036	194	214	224	240	171	200	169	188	197	156	195
037	293	306	203	238	301	304	253	270	257	246	267
038	272	222	168	233	165	200	191	183	183	150	197
039	215	281	238	232	262	211	221	272	233	285	245
040	141	192	192	255	148	202	153	174	155	143	175
041	416	415	376	378	388	451	418	442	402	411	410
042	194	224	213	226	246	226	219	226	250	222	225
043	366	420	438	321	445	459	415	423	428	427	414
044	297	238	239	316	262	323	282	285	195	307	274

TABLE B. (*Continued*)

Item #	CHL	CHN	KOR	NIG	NOR	PAK	POR	SIN	TUR	USA	Grand mean
045	381	407	384	382	458	388	431	442	437	449	416
046	441	289	408	392	395	409	432	385	339	391	388
047	313	225	231	359	288	340	288	293	303	296	293
048	381	400	404	341	186	433	377	364	346	340	357
049	439	408	410	403	449	464	433	428	393	424	425
050	418	427	427	430	411	478	423	446	427	419	431
051	204	223	206	197	167	161	152	165	162	180	182
052	130	156	131	169	107	119	122	132	135	126	133
053	352	348	375	247	319	228	334	348	305	380	323
054	125	331	176	216	145	207	129	234	247	197	201
055	339	385	396	248	325	426	362	379	356	353	357
056	154	155	165	210	112	114	113	145	146	137	145
057	301	273	253	299	261	411	301	260	346	237	294
058	410	402	420	293	398	461	371	260	425	323	376
059	372	335	217	271	286	328	343	219	284	251	290
060	483	419	395	276	480	476	469	407	354	462	422
061	237	256	199	256	229	204	234	232	224	262	233
062	181	192	190	292	231	171	193	232	184	213	208
063	432	394	416	391	428	461	421	424	450	413	423
064	341	331	352	380	389	471	449	416	412	388	393
065	409	413	440	261	393	278	389	356	410	367	372
066	221	194	181	174	196	147	194	210	192	190	190
067	194	237	193	189	211	195	264	218	168	208	208
068	224	229	188	209	219	209	195	229	223	233	216
069	253	209	151	199	180	161	214	161	226	149	190
070	215	203	209	271	189	311	211	239	326	261	243
071	344	255	399	236	320	228	354	264	257	284	294
072	181	209	188	201	192	152	232	193	157	171	188
073	422	386	255	343	316	242	283	410	279	414	335
074	164	284	192	314	178	288	225	233	307	235	242
075	458	433	325	411	429	454	437	440	394	431	421
076	186	151	165	330	153	207	190	200	135	182	190
077	372	301	389	354	364	252	354	285	356	311	334
078	365	432	401	443	402	409	420	405	397	427	410
079	461	438	447	456	402	440	419	415	389	414	428
080	462	430	297	370	426	402	421	437	387	443	408
081	207	208	177	302	200	185	278	233	230	218	224
082	319	276	221	359	311	169	317	310	256	331	287
083	467	416	403	359	481	440	470	401	418	420	427
084	209	226	132	224	134	150	381	181	167	171	197
085	213	207	220	253	194	197	260	223	191	216	217
086	278	192	354	275	351	216	294	330	359	334	298
087	229	195	173	211	214	185	251	183	197	206	204
088	294	130	149	186	302	147	306	185	285	234	222
089	159	159	180	174	156	166	171	182	139	176	166

(*continued*)

TABLE B. (*Continued*)

Item #	CHL	CHN	KOR	NIG	NOR	PAK	POR	SIN	TUR	USA	Grand mean
090	251	379	321	264	311	311	382	234	202	275	293
091	406	407	420	390	400	440	385	421	425	408	410
092	212	227	227	270	213	221	200	208	228	200	221
093	325	385	407	392	302	438	252	438	431	445	381
094	318	259	210	384	264	295	284	294	277	285	287
095	461	394	438	427	408	461	448	386	424	406	425
096	467	419	423	434	463	485	409	457	442	463	446
097	188	134	178	270	172	219	209	221	250	243	208
098	183	332	198	273	203	154	281	195	153	195	217
099	453	415	412	396	413	438	434	431	434	448	427
100	465	417	395	398	463	469	447	413	371	448	429
101	197	254	203	299	187	250	217	196	161	165	213
102	369	333	403	403	390	433	392	397	410	420	395
103	385	392	429	395	384	464	399	448	441	468	420
104	197	148	144	216	127	119	314	156	152	132	170
105	372	386	389	362	423	416	386	391	390	416	393
106	215	165	339	233	326	204	228	250	381	207	255
107	188	156	172	232	180	185	175	163	158	164	177
108	217	196	210	266	259	204	189	214	340	203	230
109	225	222	212	262	230	192	214	262	225	248	229
110	437	439	423	417	435	430	448	430	419	436	431
111	433	435	382	420	463	461	440	455	419	449	436
112	367	215	178	319	192	226	271	245	186	236	243
113	474	429	449	431	481	473	468	446	448	476	457
114	178	170	167	213	140	142	178	156	143	146	163
115	424	455	390	312	456	400	438	424	419	431	415
116	282	298	223	291	210	211	256	245	250	234	250
117	366	297	326	372	374	352	346	327	406	346	351
118	422	388	413	362	421	376	416	403	324	382	391
119	209	260	229	237	200	204	184	186	286	159	215
120	232	212	405	219	214	178	206	184	212	178	224
121	236	231	212	237	390	290	252	188	168	270	247
122	412	418	401	341	446	335	386	422	370	423	395
123	214	339	201	296	172	204	222	257	232	202	234
124	229	217	207	342	337	319	188	288	187	420	273
125	455	419	437	406	418	452	450	415	430	436	432
126	230	274	178	245	249	233	204	221	250	173	226
127	318	322	309	256	343	273	293	329	250	358	305
128	440	412	440	307	394	416	402	418	173	416	382
129	243	386	167	268	194	271	241	233	212	210	243
130	454	249	365	406	443	433	421	432	404	416	402
131	413	431	449	404	436	438	355	428	319	419	409
132	476	447	419	440	467	461	452	460	434	443	450
133	202	209	232	278	166	323	221	226	222	195	227
134	436	418	373	349	441	361	421	385	381	431	399

TABLE B. (*Continued*)

Item #	CHL	CHN	KOR	NIG	NOR	PAK	POR	SIN	TUR	USA	Grand mean
135	169	177	208	241	152	202	153	180	154	167	180
136	451	425	442	373	426	426	408	406	426	404	419
137	135	153	158	200	150	161	145	130	169	146	155
138	172	185	202	194	158	135	153	160	237	148	174
139	427	423	438	317	397	452	368	407	390	424	404
140	452	406	441	405	416	464	435	454	410	459	434
141	166	178	168	196	179	192	191	185	166	164	178
142	294	411	307	286	255	259	219	344	249	333	296
143	384	431	395	343	355	347	368	383	432	409	385
144	188	195	267	287	193	266	216	241	183	224	226
145	475	419	361	408	440	457	465	452	423	443	434
146	443	412	441	415	422	445	410	400	424	400	421
147	431	432	387	381	343	347	339	358	360	384	376
148	428	401	400	420	385	447	422	433	445	435	421
149	336	204	333	370	217	347	319	287	363	247	302
150	369	387	382	376	319	419	363	340	372	319	364
151	343	399	371	377	371	440	441	306	404	286	374
152	326	338	164	215	113	297	202	273	223	263	241
153	346	361	352	326	309	416	368	316	387	319	350
154	380	389	432	347	299	445	372	396	427	377	386
155	216	200	164	234	174	290	242	215	201	202	214
156	186	192	160	215	132	188	169	164	150	134	169
157	416	399	412	335	417	340	414	402	427	420	398
158	206	219	147	234	217	221	217	215	200	203	208
159	205	199	167	236	164	197	190	202	390	193	214
160	336	409	411	308	409	419	258	320	426	344	364
161	134	158	139	255	111	138	127	165	151	126	150
162	181	189	311	324	249	159	219	258	170	269	233
163	169	359	142	351	270	185	154	312	181	340	246
164	460	422	383	400	427	416	411	429	419	433	420
165	445	410	352	428	376	461	429	432	422	423	418
166	446	431	416	422	380	407	446	430	404	442	422
167	383	376	342	393	420	345	415	415	383	439	391
168	389	374	164	397	348	447	418	369	462	321	369
169	430	411	403	375	347	461	377	324	397	334	386
170	392	415	429	377	422	442	413	433	410	442	418
171	387	444	424	387	413	454	418	428	465	432	425
172	359	219	379	340	308	364	326	267	300	240	310
173	455	419	429	357	403	452	366	442	379	388	409
174	422	434	263	305	399	457	365	353	224	351	357
175	149	217	185	278	178	261	173	195	173	175	198
176	384	394	415	380	329	404	331	380	396	377	379
177	438	421	418	384	408	433	425	434	418	431	421
178	282	273	233	334	198	242	266	293	225	366	271
179	431	400	401	315	394	407	411	360	416	404	394

(*continued*)

TABLE B. (*Continued*)

Item #	CHL	CHN	KOR	NIG	NOR	PAK	POR	SIN	TUR	USA	Grand mean
180	348	430	408	374	264	450	343	374	431	378	380
181	417	374	335	399	400	467	407	389	413	404	400
182	332	346	409	393	422	357	276	365	298	388	359
183	398	346	399	354	435	371	381	386	420	375	386
184	186	238	180	255	139	154	179	177	167	169	184
185	354	395	419	303	308	250	273	251	277	223	305
186	426	394	406	389	350	445	370	395	397	383	395
187	320	209	185	240	147	290	243	261	293	196	239
188	198	193	176	183	125	150	161	149	158	151	164
189	214	211	296	200	281	180	191	238	236	148	219
190	353	408	301	315	363	276	355	377	365	375	349
191	271	411	339	334	315	311	266	314	263	348	317
192	187	201	185	270	127	157	215	176	130	149	180
193	389	405	394	358	414	359	382	404	413	400	392
194	141	179	173	340	158	157	181	227	166	175	190
195	398	376	307	406	402	459	398	385	411	411	395
196	415	413	400	402	370	459	386	418	409	425	410
197	241	332	203	202	285	235	241	215	229	229	241
198	184	213	186	200	205	200	243	185	180	175	197
199	398	377	392	304	364	414	376	395	376	374	377
200	354	367	236	357	387	235	387	382	322	414	344
201	450	409	412	414	314	445	468	455	454	461	428
202	168	191	251	339	208	295	230	184	212	165	224
203	323	347	217	374	284	342	280	268	399	314	315
204	419	427	263	411	374	350	402	428	423	422	392
205	461	426	432	418	447	454	454	466	412	454	442
206	246	226	201	242	255	235	227	252	199	246	233
207	231	244	270	248	268	273	222	254	251	250	251
208	219	218	274	238	238	202	205	199	187	210	219
209	340	394	361	258	372	283	336	367	407	366	348
210	153	171	166	151	221	178	185	137	155	131	165
211	166	157	159	223	203	164	193	156	183	199	180
212	158	188	182	307	153	204	180	148	144	143	181
213	422	412	397	413	333	416	392	357	416	405	396
214	413	387	375	417	394	435	376	407	419	418	404
215	395	359	412	268	205	214	335	268	222	296	297
216	220	232	276	251	166	221	190	167	207	164	209
217	179	234	260	227	176	238	209	183	155	188	205
218	229	172	178	254	157	345	132	250	139	263	212
219	144	158	153	223	159	159	132	141	142	143	155
220	384	301	307	342	389	338	413	377	305	401	356
221	329	281	325	339	280	378	373	372	364	370	341
222	332	311	257	338	311	407	386	363	376	359	344
223	238	270	182	285	245	147	207	238	229	213	225
224	393	314	351	269	378	226	401	348	355	404	344

TABLE B. (*Continued*)

Item #	CHL	CHN	KOR	NIG	NOR	PAK	POR	SIN	TUR	USA	Grand mean
225	172	173	222	232	185	138	215	168	215	184	190
226	305	399	407	249	343	435	409	407	360	400	371
227	166	229	167	224	197	209	190	258	194	188	202
228	199	201	168	219	221	173	228	155	185	177	193
229	379	392	193	221	370	116	422	278	387	300	306
230	214	296	274	242	232	316	233	277	234	274	259
231	276	294	280	311	243	240	279	278	274	263	274
232	314	349	252	361	290	416	380	326	350	280	332
233	450	403	392	416	422	464	460	453	418	442	432
234	187	195	201	268	170	197	194	192	208	216	203
235	228	238	234	271	232	280	219	231	226	213	235
236	255	178	155	241	172	142	385	171	252	247	220
237	174	178	192	226	308	138	174	183	211	194	198
238	290	135	147	198	179	135	187	141	143	142	170
239	434	354	397	383	374	435	432	420	352	409	399
240	441	406	430	365	271	438	416	352	419	274	391
241	328	370	146	360	309	373	359	366	446	355	341
242	210	183	186	246	195	197	330	208	170	242	217
243	208	129	165	224	153	200	182	148	175	168	175
244	426	308	415	275	392	314	400	413	300	359	360
245	386	387	352	283	411	207	395	332	195	387	333
246	408	413	401	355	402	447	397	408	416	394	404
247	430	416	428	353	364	440	372	415	372	408	400
248	279	209	348	240	242	197	239	270	240	254	252
249	152	138	300	189	143	161	162	169	193	166	177
250	305	297	194	238	227	161	207	286	181	248	234
251	383	408	404	363	380	419	378	401	390	411	394
252	217	204	264	217	282	214	244	212	241	217	231
253	196	252	178	294	163	392	193	245	355	245	251
254	191	242	249	322	177	319	274	304	342	293	271
255	166	232	183	235	136	257	155	183	180	179	191
256	202	187	213	248	232	173	213	191	201	226	209
257	343	197	193	267	213	169	185	192	208	218	218
258	377	393	417	376	434	423	438	388	420	413	408
259	423	411	335	374	331	342	360	433	402	416	383
260	168	324	327	211	170	214	191	165	155	171	209
261	344	387	204	204	307	230	297	253	336	315	288
262	276	272	187	270	308	195	263	226	243	221	246
263	192	236	281	255	193	214	213	223	224	206	224
264	148	140	132	221	132	142	154	164	128	165	152
265	361	391	324	328	394	428	286	384	390	385	367
266	400	418	446	352	376	438	342	445	366	439	402
267	381	380	400	253	383	440	273	382	388	368	365
268	218	236	208	241	200	180	230	218	259	242	223
269	374	400	438	366	428	407	383	412	441	408	406

(*continued*)

TABLE B. (*Continued*)

Item #	CHL	CHN	KOR	NIG	NOR	PAK	POR	SIN	TUR	USA	Grand mean
270	218	205	236	318	226	302	289	212	195	196	240
271	214	308	391	356	351	195	223	370	358	324	309
272	317	368	460	385	430	445	398	407	369	432	401
273	395	381	212	280	350	395	240	318	394	278	324
274	144	306	168	210	314	221	191	244	243	181	222
275	366	341	377	238	269	402	314	339	386	279	331
276	310	349	365	255	315	328	287	337	267	310	312
277	158	192	198	297	133	171	167	194	202	153	186
278	435	408	425	447	433	452	452	456	431	451	439
279	157	291	219	242	157	335	144	231	224	213	221
280	160	298	324	214	198	354	195	238	262	212	246
281	164	188	187	182	134	223	175	154	154	139	170
282	330	185	343	220	258	350	392	319	343	358	310
283	163	314	207	173	168	150	214	193	182	188	195
284	162	246	173	182	122	185	141	154	162	139	166
285	195	231	226	196	191	183	190	201	179	178	197
286	165	206	161	219	165	135	127	199	147	181	170
287	324	353	365	369	253	361	201	413	414	434	349
288	182	206	203	232	182	185	206	193	189	178	195
289	145	192	196	273	123	161	125	209	150	193	177
290	344	410	436	380	392	442	349	407	426	433	402
291	419	436	429	351	442	421	403	432	411	453	420
292	410	352	412	280	370	419	361	272	296	249	342
293	199	199	237	228	207	216	206	186	211	186	208
294	177	232	176	240	141	202	183	182	169	152	185
295	446	141	417	324	433	407	375	391	413	402	402
296	445	410	433	409	441	454	395	448	414	442	429
297	217	231	204	286	257	216	223	210	237	196	226
298	398	438	425	258	404	371	352	416	319	418	380
299	182	246	179	212	263	195	237	204	205	186	211
300	249	343	376	245	165	269	226	321	156	329	268

[a]Two decimal places omitted.
[b]See Appendix D for item names.

APPENDIX C

TABLE C1. Cultural Comparison Variables: Indices Available in Sets of Countries[a]

Hofstede values (N = 16)[b]
1. Power Distance (PDI)
2. Uncertainty Avoidance (UAI)
3. Individualism (IDV)
4. Masculinity (MAS)

Schwartz values (N = 14)[c]
5. Harmony (HARM)
6. Conservatism (CONS)
7. Hierarchy (HIER)
8. Mastery (MAST)
9. Affective Autonomy (AFAU)
10. Intellectual Autonomy (INAU)
11. Egalitarian Commitment (EGCO)

Demographics (N = 18–20)[d]
12. Economic/Social Development-Rank (ESR)
13. Cultural Homogeneity (HOM)
14. Percentage Christian (CHR)
15. Population Density (DEN)
16. Percentage Urban (URB)

	Hofstede				Schwartz							Demographics				
	1	2	3	4	5	6	7	8	9	10	11	12	13	14	15	16
	PDI	UAI	IDV	MAS	HARM	CONS	HIER	MAST	AFAU	INAU	EGCO	ESR	HOM	CHR	DEN	URB
ARG	49	86	46	56	—	—	—	—	—	—	—	46	69	96	154	82
AUS	36	51	90	61	3.93	3.94	2.24	3.96	3.37	4.00	4.85	16	68	84	181	89
CHL	63	86	23	28	—	—	—	—	—	—	—	57	86	92	147	80
CHN	—	—	—	—	3.59	3.85	3.57	4.59	3.20	4.15	4.37	86	88	1	98	13
FIN	33	59	63	26	4.40	3.72	1.90	3.50	3.37	4.49	5.14	5	84	94	148	62
GER	35	65	67	66	4.29	3.29	2.15	3.95	3.90	4.62	5.25	14	97	93	26	85
HK	68	29	25	57	3.21	3.92	2.69	4.05	2.97	3.94	4.73	—	98	18	4	90
IND	77	40	48	56	3.83	3.94	3.43	4.34	3.51	3.84	4.38	103	—	4	32	22
JAP	54	92	46	95	3.94	3.74	2.73	4.14	3.41	4.55	4.57	7	99	3	20	78
KOR	—	—	—	—	—	—	—	—	—	—	—	41	100	31	15	55
NEP	—	—	—	—	4.03	4.31	3.24	4.27	2.95	3.86	4.70	131	30	1	97	5
NET	38	53	80	14	3.85	3.56	2.13	3.85	3.38	4.31	5.27	9	90	86	17	76
NIG	—	—	—	—	—	—	—	—	—	—	—	124	—	49	81	20
NOR	31	50	69	8	—	—	—	—	—	—	—	3	96	98	152	53
PAK	55	70	14	50	—	—	—	—	—	—	—	112	36	2	99	28
POR	63	104	27	31	4.16	3.63	1.95	4.12	3.40	3.99	5.50	26	99	95	59	31
SIN	74	8	20	48	3.60	4.25	2.63	3.80	2.91	3.56	4.67	31	58	9	5	100

TUR	66	85	37	45	4.13	4.14	3.16	3.77	3.12	3.99	5.00	78	75	1	86	47
USA	40	46	91	62	3.56	3.77	2.25	4.21	3.51	4.07	4.70	9	50	88	128	77
VEN	81	76	12	72	3.80	3.98	2.27	4.01	2.92	4.12	4.99	51	89	96	145	83

[a]For variable 12, lower numbers indicate higher development. For variable 15, lower numbers indicate higher density.
[b]From Hofstede (1980).
[c]The country scores for the seven values were provided by Professor Schwartz.
[d]Variable 12 from Sivard (1993); others from Kurian (1993).

TABLE C2. Correlation Matrix for 16 Cultural Comparison Variables[a]

	UAI 2	IDV 3	MAS 4	HARM 5	CONS 6	HIER 7	MAST 8	AFAU 9	INAU 10	EGCO 11	ESR 12	HOM 13	CHR 14	DEN 15	URB 16
PDI 1	-01	-81	28	-41	65	61	33	-65	-64	-37	64	-02	-52	-33	-13
UAI 2	—	-20	11	61	-37	-22	06	26	50	50	10	27	24	29	-31
IDV 3		—	-11	20	-46	-32	-02	67	39	05	-61	01	42	21	16
MAS 4			—	-18	09	30	50	08	16	-56	11	-12	-35	-16	27
HARM 5				—	-32	-32	-43	45	49	57	-14	08	35	26	-22
CONS 6					—	57	08	-82	-78	-51	63	-66	-62	17	-22
HIER 7						—	61	-33	-41	-78	83	-30	-90	-19	-59
MAST 8							—	02	-20	-59	53	-10	-39	-07	-56
AFAU 9								—	62	26	-45	33	43	-07	05
INAU 10									—	34	-51	56	41	05	17
EGCO 11										—	-48	36	73	05	21
ESR 12											—	-59	-61	-02	-75
HOM 13												—	31	28	28
CHR 14													—	50	43
DEN 15														—	-02

[a]Decimals omitted.

APPENDIX D

TABLE D. Five Factor and Ego State Scores
for the 300 Items of the Adjective Check List

Adjective	Five factor scores[a]					Ego state scores[b]				
	EXT	AGR	CON	EMS	OPN	CP	NP	A	FC	AC
1. absent-minded	2.32	2.27	1.37	2.56	2.72	0.5	0.3	0.4	1.3	3.4
2. active	4.77	3.65	4.19	3.12	4.29	2.4	2.3	2.5	3.7	2.3
3. adaptable	4.19	4.14	4.08	4.17	4.43	0.1	1.8	2.4	1.1	3.3
4. adventurous	4.76	3.49	3.49	3.40	4.78	0.1	0.7	1.3	4.0	0.6
5. affected	3.04	3.37	3.14	2.18	3.06	1.8	1.4	0.3	0.7	3.6
6. affectionate	4.24	4.48	3.19	3.74	3.36	0.1	3.9	0.3	3.9	1.7
7. aggressive	3.91	2.50	3.90	2.17	3.86	3.4	0.8	0.8	3.2	2.8
8. alert	4.10	3.61	4.32	3.07	3.93	1.9	2.0	3.7	3.3	1.9
9. aloof	2.19	2.21	2.40	2.65	2.50	3.0	0.2	1.7	0.3	2.8
10. ambitious	4.35	3.39	4.79	3.35	4.11	2.2	1.2	1.7	2.0	3.1
11. anxious	2.98	2.62	3.38	1.37	3.14	1.8	0.9	0.1	0.5	4.0
12. apathetic	1.93	2.19	2.21	3.04	2.15	0.7	0.1	0.3	0.2	4.0
13. appreciative	3.85	4.38	3.56	3.62	3.76	0.3	3.2	0.9	2.1	2.4
14. argumentative	2.75	1.80	3.22	1.84	2.87	3.3	0.2	1.1	1.5	3.7
15. arrogant	2.47	1.50	2.76	2.68	2.44	3.3	0.2	0.1	0.8	3.7
16. artistic	3.43	3.19	3.26	3.14	4.26	0.0	0.6	1.5	4.0	0.9
17. assertive	4.53	3.26	4.44	3.21	3.78	2.9	1.7	2.3	3.5	1.7
18. attractive	3.57	3.21	3.07	3.17	3.23	0.4	1.8	1.3	3.6	1.6
19. autocratic	3.04	2.69	3.49	2.86	2.97	3.9	0.5	0.3	1.2	1.5
20. awkward	2.00	2.45	2.36	2.25	2.50	0.7	0.0	0.3	1.3	3.7
21. bitter	1.42	1.47	2.33	1.61	2.09	2.4	0.1	0.0	0.1	3.9
22. blustery	2.60	2.38	2.58	2.45	2.76	2.7	0.3	0.0	1.6	3.1
23. boastful	2.73	1.59	2.78	3.04	2.79	1.5	0.5	0.0	2.4	3.0
24. bossy	2.87	1.65	3.09	2.58	2.51	3.8	1.2	0.1	1.7	2.7
25. calm	3.02	4.00	3.65	4.27	3.10	0.2	2.7	3.4	0.9	0.9
26. capable	3.93	4.01	4.64	3.39	3.89	2.2	2.5	3.8	1.6	0.9
27. careless	2.39	1.88	1.40	2.47	2.77	0.6	0.1	0.0	2.5	3.5
28. cautious	2.57	3.43	3.99	3.24	2.33	2.3	1.7	2.1	0.7	3.4
29. changeable	3.55	3.49	3.10	3.07	4.19	1.3	0.9	1.5	3.5	2.1
30. charming	4.11	3.98	3.21	3.68	3.39	0.2	2.0	0.4	3.7	2.3
31. cheerful	4.67	4.21	3.32	4.33	3.64	0.0	2.3	0.4	3.5	1.5
32. civilized	3.76	3.88	3.96	3.42	3.18	2.4	2.4	2.7	0.7	2.9
33. clear-thinking	3.72	4.11	4.68	4.13	3.66	0.8	1.1	4.0	1.3	0.5
34. clever	3.93	3.60	4.28	3.28	3.93	0.8	0.7	2.5	3.3	2.3
35. coarse	2.09	2.03	2.69	2.24	2.56	2.5	0.2	0.2	1.8	2.5
36. cold	1.35	1.40	2.55	2.22	2.17	3.3	0.0	2.5	0.0	3.0
37. commonplace	2.25	2.83	2.73	3.06	1.82	1.0	1.1	1.5	0.5	2.8
38. complaining	1.71	1.71	2.35	1.82	2.04	3.0	0.3	0.1	1.6	3.9
39. complicated	2.59	2.59	3.15	2.14	3.06	1.4	0.9	2.9	1.2	2.9
40. conceited	2.36	1.41	2.61	2.89	2.40	2.3	0.5	0.2	1.4	3.5
41. confident	4.47	3.82	4.44	4.17	4.26	2.7	2.7	2.3	2.8	1.3
42. confused	2.17	2.39	1.94	1.99	2.37	0.6	0.2	0.3	0.5	3.7
43. conscientious	3.61	4.00	4.37	2.99	3.21	2.7	2.4	2.1	0.3	2.7
44. conservative	2.50	3.31	3.51	3.20	1.68	3.5	2.0	1.7	0.0	2.1

TABLE D. (*Continued*)

Adjective	Five factor scores[a]					Ego state scores[b]				
	EXT	AGR	CON	EMS	OPN	CP	NP	A	FC	AC
45. considerate	4.04	4.72	3.56	3.72	3.41	0.6	3.8	1.5	0.9	2.1
46. contented	3.55	3.81	3.31	4.27	2.72	0.1	2.4	1.2	2.5	1.2
47. conventional	2.72	3.19	3.41	3.51	1.90	3.4	1.9	1.6	0.2	3.0
48. cool	3.41	3.14	3.26	3.53	3.22	1.7	0.2	2.9	0.2	1.6
49. cooperative	3.87	4.43	4.14	3.79	3.75	0.6	2.5	2.7	1.1	2.5
50. courageous	4.18	3.59	3.88	3.63	4.43	1.4	1.7	1.3	2.9	0.0
51. cowardly	1.67	2.33	2.13	2.40	1.49	0.9	0.5	0.2	0.8	3.3
52. cruel	1.52	1.20	2.37	2.40	2.34	3.2	0.1	0.0	1.5	2.9
53. curious	4.17	3.61	3.88	3.02	4.72	0.0	0.7	2.8	3.6	0.6
54. cynical	1.86	1.90	2.68	1.82	2.17	3.3	0.0	0.1	0.1	2.7
55. daring	4.24	3.15	3.41	3.20	4.61	0.1	0.4	0.8	3.7	0.9
56. deceitful	1.87	1.32	2.18	2.47	2.56	1.3	0.1	0.1	0.7	3.5
57. defensive	2.26	2.20	2.94	1.63	2.27	2.3	0.4	0.1	0.8	3.7
58. deliberate	3.21	3.03	4.09	2.96	2.93	2.4	1.5	3.5	0.5	1.8
59. demanding	2.99	2.18	3.78	2.29	3.05	3.6	0.9	0.4	2.5	3.3
60. dependable	3.89	4.59	4.70	3.81	3.15	1.8	2.7	3.1	0.5	2.0
61. dependent	2.48	2.53	2.31	2.14	2.31	0.5	0.2	0.2	1.7	4.8
62. despondent	2.17	2.39	2.50	2.28	2.55	0.9	0.1	0.0	1.1	3.6
63. determined	4.35	3.71	4.70	3.35	4.02	3.1	1.9	2.1	2.5	2.1
64. dignified	3.65	3.57	3.82	3.67	3.25	2.5	1.5	1.6	0.1	1.8
65. discreet	2.67	3.42	3.15	3.58	2.63	0.7	1.2	1.9	0.1	2.1
66. disorderly	2.41	2.30	1.23	2.27	2.92	0.3	0.1	0.0	3.1	2.7
67. dissatisfied	2.21	2.16	2.45	1.71	3.21	2.9	0.7	0.5	1.8	3.0
68. distractible	2.60	2.34	1.95	2.13	3.05	0.4	0.3	0.5	3.3	2.6
69. distrustful	1.91	1.34	2.03	2.18	2.30	3.1	0.4	0.7	1.1	3.3
70. dominant	3.84	2.26	3.73	3.08	3.04	3.7	1.5	0.7	1.4	1.9
71. dreamy	3.36	3.12	2.65	2.78	4.00	0.0	0.4	0.0	3.2	2.5
72. dull	1.57	2.44	2.59	3.00	1.74	1.2	0.7	1.8	0.0	2.9
73. easy-going	4.01	4.09	3.06	4.16	3.86	0.0	2.0	1.2	2.3	1.5
74. effeminate	2.75	3.14	2.90	3.11	2.90	0.4	1.3	0.2	1.0	2.5
75. efficient	3.73	3.75	4.73	3.63	3.20	1.9	1.4	3.6	0.7	1.5
76. egotistical	2.66	1.65	2.93	2.84	2.70	2.5	0.5	0.3	1.7	2.6
77. emotional	3.67	3.70	2.88	1.66	3.45	2.1	2.2	0.1	3.7	3.1
78. energetic	4.77	3.87	4.09	3.28	4.40	1.3	1.3	1.4	3.8	1.5
79. enterprising	4.24	3.60	4.39	3.55	4.38	1.0	0.9	2.6	2.9	1.5
80. enthusiastic	4.77	4.13	4.14	3.80	4.42	0.5	1.4	0.7	3.9	1.7
81. evasive	2.22	2.13	2.55	2.73	2.44	1.5	0.4	0.1	0.8	3.6
82. excitable	4.41	3.53	3.51	2.54	4.11	2.0	0.9	0.2	3.8	2.7
83. fair-minded	3.56	4.02	3.68	3.75	3.56	1.1	2.0	3.6	0.7	0.9
84. fault-finding	2.19	1.62	2.97	1.91	2.09	3.9	0.5	0.4	0.7	2.7
85. fearful	1.93	2.36	2.48	1.91	1.78	1.2	0.6	0.2	1.8	3.8
86. feminine	2.81	3.25	2.81	3.07	2.92	0.6	2.0	0.8	1.9	1.9
87. fickle	2.48	2.28	2.48	2.29	2.58	1.1	0.1	0.0	2.3	2.5
88. flirtatious	3.73	2.97	2.78	3.23	3.44	0.0	0.3	0.1	3.7	2.7
89. foolish	2.57	2.21	1.97	2.61	2.95	0.8	0.1	0.0	1.9	3.5

(*continued*)

TABLE D. (*Continued*)

	Five factor scores[a]					Ego state scores[b]				
Adjective	EXT	AGR	CON	EMS	OPN	CP	NP	A	FC	AC
90. forceful	3.16	2.15	3.51	2.95	3.15	3.6	1.5	1.5	2.1	1.9
91. foresighted	3.30	3.43	4.14	3.58	3.28	1.5	1.9	3.5	0.7	1.0
92. forgetful	2.42	2.17	1.47	2.61	2.65	0.8	0.3	0.1	1.8	3.3
93. forgiving	3.83	4.50	3.42	3.83	3.50	0.3	3.5	0.6	1.9	1.1
94. formal	2.87	2.97	3.51	3.32	2.50	3.0	0.9	2.0	0.0	1.9
95. frank	3.62	3.88	3.72	2.83	3.43	1.7	1.6	2.1	3.2	0.7
96. friendly	4.72	4.58	3.62	3.81	3.77	0.1	3.1	0.8	3.7	1.8
97. frivolous	3.08	2.45	2.15	2.89	3.36	0.0	0.3	0.0	3.2	2.5
98. fussy	2.13	1.96	2.86	1.99	2.25	2.7	0.6	0.1	0.9	3.3
99. generous	4.06	4.38	3.45	3.68	3.65	0.4	3.5	0.4	2.3	1.2
100. gentle	3.69	4.46	3.19	3.83	3.35	0.3	3.9	0.5	1.7	1.2
101. gloomy	1.30	1.95	2.32	1.65	1.98	2.2	0.3	0.0	0.6	3.4
102. good-looking	3.31	3.11	3.03	3.29	3.15	0.8	1.1	0.8	2.6	1.4
103. good-natured	4.33	4.34	3.67	3.92	3.88	0.2	3.1	0.6	2.9	1.9
104. greedy	2.02	1.59	2.73	2.61	2.49	1.2	0.3	0.1	2.5	3.4
105. handsome	3.30	3.08	3.03	3.29	3.17	0.7	1.1	0.7	2.5	1.5
106. hard-headed	2.55	1.97	3.11	2.30	2.07	3.4	0.5	0.9	0.9	2.5
107. hard-hearted	1.85	1.50	2.89	2.27	2.36	3.5	0.1	0.5	0.3	2.6
108. hasty	2.81	2.28	2.18	2.21	3.03	1.7	0.3	0.2	2.6	2.9
109. headstrong	3.65	2.64	3.90	2.83	3.04	2.3	0.3	0.5	2.5	2.7
110. healthy	3.85	3.44	3.60	2.67	3.57	0.6	2.1	1.6	3.3	0.9
111. helpful	4.25	4.59	4.03	2.78	3.60	0.7	3.5	1.6	1.4	2.0
112. high-strung	3.33	2.38	3.16	1.90	3.22	1.5	0.2	0.1	1.6	3.3
113. honest	3.82	4.79	3.96	3.43	3.49	1.2	2.0	2.9	2.4	1.0
114. hostile	1.85	1.43	2.46	1.54	2.35	3.3	0.1	0.1	0.8	3.1
115. humorous	4.21	3.68	3.21	3.75	3.68	0.3	1.1	0.7	3.8	1.6
116. hurried	2.94	2.47	2.65	2.18	2.71	1.9	0.2	0.1	1.0	3.7
117. idealistic	3.60	3.41	3.65	3.23	3.46	1.5	2.2	0.8	2.0	1.7
118. imaginative	4.14	3.61	3.69	3.11	4.62	0.1	0.7	1.5	3.9	0.6
119. immature	2.52	2.08	1.89	2.26	2.66	0.9	0.1	0.1	2.7	3.6
120. impatient	2.71	1.58	2.42	1.74	2.63	2.6	0.5	0.1	2.8	3.1
121. impulsive	3.88	2.60	2.32	1.62	4.23	1.2	0.1	0.1	3.3	2.3
122. independent	4.03	3.23	4.30	3.66	4.39	1.5	1.3	3.2	2.7	0.6
123. indifferent	2.20	1.86	2.34	3.13	2.44	1.3	0.1	1.7	1.1	2.3
124. individualistic	3.81	3.08	3.90	3.19	4.22	0.6	0.9	2.1	3.1	1.1
125. industrious	3.92	3.50	4.68	3.52	3.86	1.5	1.2	2.9	1.6	2.1
126. infantile	2.34	2.27	2.04	2.27	2.48	0.5	0.1	0.1	2.3	3.2
127. informal	3.25	3.05	2.63	3.01	3.43	0.1	1.6	0.8	2.9	1.1
128. ingenious	3.52	3.36	3.87	2.43	3.83	0.1	0.4	2.4	3.6	1.9
129. inhibited	1.82	2.37	2.64	2.45	1.76	2.3	0.6	0.5	0.3	3.9
130. initiative	4.40	3.79	4.59	3.62	4.29	1.4	1.6	1.9	2.8	1.1
131. insightful	3.87	3.94	4.29	3.51	4.03	0.4	1.0	3.1	3.1	1.1
132. intelligent	3.71	3.74	4.44	3.10	3.87	0.9	1.1	3.5	2.3	1.3
133. interests narrow	1.66	2.09	2.52	2.41	1.32	2.8	1.2	0.5	0.7	3.0
134. interests wide	4.47	3.96	3.69	3.59	4.79	0.3	1.1	3.1	3.3	0.7

TABLE D. (*Continued*)

Adjective	Five factor scores[a]					Ego state scores[b]				
	EXT	AGR	CON	EMS	OPN	CP	NP	A	FC	AC
135. intolerant	1.99	1.44	2.65	1.94	1.72	3.8	0.5	0.2	0.9	2.6
136. inventive	4.00	3.53	4.02	3.39	4.25	0.5	0.9	3.0	3.5	1.0
137. irresponsible	2.21	1.79	1.30	2.30	2.78	0.1	0.1	0.1	2.7	3.2
138. irritable	1.86	1.57	2.43	1.46	2.38	3.0	0.1	0.1	1.5	3.2
139. jolly	4.36	4.06	3.27	4.26	3.62	0.1	2.1	0.2	3.1	0.8
140. kind	4.39	4.65	3.35	3.79	3.45	0.3	3.8	0.5	1.8	1.3
141. lazy	1.76	2.27	1.38	2.62	2.01	0.1	0.3	0.1	1.6	2.9
142. leisurely	3.00	3.17	2.16	3.40	3.05	0.1	1.9	1.0	2.4	0.9
143. logical	3.34	3.60	4.38	3.70	3.15	0.7	0.6	4.0	0.3	0.7
144. loud	3.64	2.54	2.94	2.60	3.19	2.1	0.4	0.1	3.3	2.4
145. loyal	3.87	4.64	3.79	3.46	2.95	1.6	2.7	1.2	1.4	2.3
146. mannerly	3.49	3.78	3.89	3.67	2.89	1.7	1.5	1.0	0.3	3.1
147. masculine	3.07	2.93	3.12	3.05	3.07	1.7	0.9	0.9	1.5	1.7
148. mature	3.49	4.01	4.27	3.88	3.47	2.3	2.5	2.7	0.9	0.8
149. meek	1.91	2.98	2.62	2.92	2.30	0.1	0.3	0.0	0.3	3.4
150. methodical	2.88	3.18	4.37	3.27	2.46	1.5	0.8	3.8	0.1	1.5
151. mild	2.42	3.36	2.97	3.70	2.72	0.4	2.3	1.3	0.7	1.7
152. mischievous	3.35	2.25	2.34	2.54	3.63	0.1	0.1	0.1	3.5	2.6
153. moderate	2.74	3.35	3.24	3.52	2.84	1.1	1.7	2.1	0.4	1.7
154. modest	2.76	4.21	3.27	3.36	2.61	0.6	1.0	0.6	0.3	3.0
155. moody	2.21	2.06	2.61	1.35	2.73	1.2	0.4	0.0	1.6	3.7
156. nagging	1.92	1.74	2.64	1.96	2.40	3.6	1.0	0.1	0.5	2.8
157. natural	3.81	3.74	3.27	3.50	3.72	0.1	1.4	1.3	3.9	0.1
158. nervous	2.11	2.44	2.70	1.72	2.22	1.6	0.5	0.1	0.5	3.8
159. noisy	3.41	2.40	2.71	2.52	3.09	1.3	0.3	0.2	3.7	2.7
160. obliging	3.37	3.88	3.40	3.33	3.20	0.6	1.8	0.6	0.3	3.3
161. obnoxious	2.63	1.68	2.32	2.17	2.71	2.2	0.3	0.1	1.6	3.1
162. opinionated	3.51	2.44	3.48	2.12	2.96	3.9	1.1	0.3	0.8	2.1
163. opportunistic	4.04	3.09	4.22	3.09	4.12	1.0	0.3	1.4	2.6	2.3
164. optimistic	4.53	4.22	4.14	4.32	4.19	0.3	2.5	1.2	2.8	1.1
165. organized	3.61	3.75	4.87	3.64	3.14	1.7	1.6	3.7	0.3	1.3
166. original	4.07	3.62	3.92	3.38	4.35	0.2	0.7	2.1	3.7	0.5
167. outgoing	4.87	4.19	3.89	3.93	4.37	0.9	1.4	1.0	3.7	1.1
168. outspoken	4.32	3.03	3.67	3.09	3.68	2.9	1.0	1.3	3.3	1.6
169. painstaking	2.77	2.93	3.53	2.85	2.76	2.1	1.2	2.3	0.1	2.5
170. patient	3.18	4.42	3.82	4.25	3.44	0.5	3.1	2.1	0.3	1.9
171. peaceable	3.55	4.39	3.63	4.13	3.47	0.4	3.0	1.7	1.1	1.8
172. peculiar	2.89	2.81	2.97	2.25	3.60	1.2	0.3	0.1	1.4	2.7
173. persevering	3.76	3.65	4.49	3.37	3.61	2.7	2.2	2.2	1.2	2.1
174. persistent	4.11	3.42	4.70	3.12	3.64	2.4	1.9	2.2	1.9	2.7
175. pessimistic	1.60	1.67	2.03	1.58	1.80	2.5	0.5	0.4	0.2	3.3
176. planful	3.44	3.57	4.59	3.62	2.85	1.2	1.3	3.6	0.3	1.1
177. pleasant	4.17	4.33	3.45	4.10	3.55	0.3	3.0	1.3	2.3	1.3
178. pleasure-seeking	4.73	3.56	3.05	3.24	4.30	0.1	0.8	0.7	3.9	1.4
179. poised	3.65	3.52	3.85	3.70	3.22	1.3	1.5	2.1	0.7	1.7

(*continued*)

TABLE D. (*Continued*)

Adjective		EXT	AGR	CON	EMS	OPN	CP	NP	A	FC	AC
		Five factor scores[a]					Ego state scores[b]				
180.	polished	3.54	3.38	3.89	3.89	3.07	1.3	1.2	2.3	0.5	1.8
181.	practical	3.25	3.72	4.40	3.71	2.74	1.7	1.3	3.5	0.3	1.0
182.	praising	3.85	4.22	3.36	3.95	3.38	0.3	3.9	0.6	0.8	1.2
183.	precise	3.25	3.37	4.46	3.49	2.88	1.7	0.6	3.9	0.1	1.0
184.	prejudiced	2.04	1.64	2.42	2.45	1.71	3.8	0.9	0.1	0.4	2.3
185.	preoccupied	2.56	2.16	2.67	2.01	2.19	1.6	1.1	0.5	0.7	2.8
186.	progressive	3.78	3.34	36.73	3.36	4.22	0.5	1.8	2.7	1.6	0.7
187.	prudish	2.05	2.48	2.88	2.81	1.93	3.3	0.7	0.1	0.5	3.1
188.	quarrelsome	1.95	1.34	2.46	1.75	2.37	2.3	0.2	0.3	1.3	3.4
189.	queer	2.15	2.27	2.58	2.59	2.99	1.0	0.2	0.0	1.0	2.5
190.	quick	3.78	3.19	3.59	3.01	3.50	1.3	1.1	1.9	3.0	1.1
191.	quiet	1.69	3.06	2.90	3.36	2.47	0.4	1.3	1.7	0.7	2.5
192.	quitting	1.54	1.83	1.24	2.34	1.90	0.7	0.1	0.3	0.8	3.1
193.	rational	3.44	3.71	4.34	4.11	3.02	0.5	0.5	4.0	0.6	0.4
194.	rattlebrained	2.39	2.17	1.65	2.09	2.66	0.3	0.2	0.0	1.1	3.0
195.	realistic	3.22	3.66	4.21	3.87	2.90	0.8	1.1	3.9	0.8	0.7
196.	reasonable	3.70	4.05	4.26	4.08	3.34	0.7	1.6	3.9	0.6	0.9
197.	rebellious	3.26	2.06	2.19	2.11	3.79	0.5	0.1	0.1	1.9	3.6
198.	reckless	3.05	1.91	1.68	2.11	3.60	0.5	0.1	0.0	2.6	2.6
199.	reflective	3.13	3.70	3.74	3.34	3.32	0.4	1.3	3.2	0.5	0.5
200.	relaxed	3.36	3.84	3.18	4.40	3.58	0.2	1.9	1.4	1.9	0.7
201.	reliable	3.78	4.52	4.77	3.96	3.16	1.7	2.5	3.2	0.6	1.4
202.	resentful	1.66	1.55	2.24	1.81	2.24	2.1	0.1	0.1	0.5	3.6
203.	reserved	1.67	2.96	3.00	3.18	1.80	1.1	0.8	1.7	0.3	2.4
204.	resourceful	4.14	3.58	4.58	3.59	4.02	0.7	1.5	3.0	3.0	1.4
205.	responsible	3.83	4.30	4.89	3.71	3.32	2.5	2.7	3.1	0.3	1.1
206.	restless	3.55	2.45	2.68	1.88	3.77	0.7	0.2	0.1	2.4	2.7
207.	retiring	1.65	2.64	2.34	3.24	2.19	0.3	0.8	0.8	0.1	2.1
208.	rigid	1.87	1.90	3.13	2.57	1.61	3.9	0.8	0.4	0.1	2.1
209.	robust	3.45	2.96	3.06	3.16	3.42	1.1	1.0	0.9	3.2	0.5
210.	rude	1.82	1.25	2.38	2.11	2.60	2.3	0.2	0.0	2.0	2.5
211.	sarcastic	2.28	1.64	2.60	1.90	2.62	2.7	0.2	0.0	1.2	2.8
212.	self-centered	2.36	1.35	2.69	2.20	2.42	1.4	0.1	0.3	2.7	2.9
213.	self-confident	4.42	3.78	4.32	4.03	4.22	1.6	1.9	2.4	2.7	1.3
214.	self-controlled	3.63	3.88	4.46	3.98	3.47	1.9	1.5	2.3	0.5	2.4
215.	self-denying	2.52	2.93	2.77	2.74	2.16	1.5	1.9	0.4	0.1	2.8
216.	self-pitying	1.75	1.89	2.09	1.83	2.02	1.1	0.5	0.1	0.3	3.3
217.	self-punishing	1.83	2.18	2.79	2.05	2.24	1.9	0.3	0.0	0.2	3.5
218.	self-seeking	3.12	2.59	3.41	2.75	3.91	1.3	0.5	1.1	2.4	2.4
219.	selfish	2.17	1.37	2.37	2.26	2.57	1.4	0.4	0.1	2.0	3.0
220.	sensitive	3.87	4.63	3.38	2.87	3.50	0.7	2.8	0.9	2.3	2.3
221.	sentimental	3.56	4.07	3.05	3.12	3.10	0.5	2.4	0.1	1.3	2.3
222.	serious	2.72	3.49	4.33	2.54	2.76	2.7	1.3	3.3	0.5	2.7
223.	severe	2.03	2.19	3.03	2.17	2.47	3.6	0.5	0.3	0.1	1.8
224.	sexy	3.44	3.06	2.94	3.32	3.38	0.1	0.5	0.2	3.9	1.1

TABLE D. (*Continued*)

	Adjective	EXT	AGR	CON	EMS	OPN	CP	NP	A	FC	AC
		\multicolumn{5}{c}{Five factor scores[a]}						
225.	shallow	2.31	1.75	2.42	2.65	1.85	1.0	0.3	0.0	0.4	3.1
226.	sharp-witted	3.82	3.43	3.90	3.17	3.80	1.1	0.6	2.3	3.3	1.1
227.	shiftless	2.59	2.34	2.63	2.75	2.61	0.2	0.1	0.0	1.4	2.7
228.	show-off	3.44	1.81	2.70	3.13	3.33	0.8	0.3	0.1	3.4	2.5
229.	shrewd	2.65	2.74	3.55	2.81	3.03	1.1	0.4	2.1	3.1	2.1
230.	shy	1.40	2.69	2.51	2.53	1.84	0.1	0.3	0.0	0.9	3.2
231.	silent	1.42	2.48	2.47	2.84	2.15	0.3	0.5	0.5	0.3	2.2
232.	simple	2.48	3.18	2.85	3.39	2.42	0.4	0.7	0.3	0.8	1.2
233.	sincere	3.84	4.60	3.75	3.48	3.43	1.1	2.8	2.5	2.0	1.1
234.	slipshod	2.53	2.40	2.34	2.74	2.80	0.3	0.1	0.0	1.3	2.6
235.	slow	2.01	2.72	2.03	3.03	2.37	0.3	0.5	0.5	0.5	2.6
236.	sly	2.97	2.17	2.93	2.70	3.25	1.0	0.0	0.3	1.9	3.0
237.	smug	2.33	1.93	2.70	2.71	2.55	2.3	0.3	0.1	1.4	2.4
238.	snobbish	2.13	1.42	2.55	2.78	2.06	3.0	0.3	0.0	0.5	3.0
239.	sociable	4.85	4.20	3.54	3.99	4.23	0.6	2.0	1.4	2.7	1.9
240.	soft-hearted	3.88	4.52	3.12	3.58	3.40	0.1	3.3	0.0	1.4	2.1
241.	sophisticated	3.41	3.36	3.70	3.49	3.47	1.1	0.4	2.3	0.6	2.1
242.	spendthrift	2.91	2.75	2.93	2.92	3.00	0.6	0.7	0.3	2.3	2.5
243.	spineless	1.90	1.94	2.09	2.53	1.84	1.1	0.2	0.1	0.7	3.1
244.	spontaneous	4.50	3.38	2.89	2.68	4.63	0.2	1.0	1.2	3.9	0.5
245.	spunky	4.49	3.45	3.15	3.40	4.27	0.3	0.7	0.4	3.7	0.9
246.	stable	3.47	3.94	4.28	4.61	2.86	2.1	2.3	3.5	1.0	1.2
247.	steady	3.40	3.95	4.30	4.47	2.74	1.9	2.3	3.5	0.7	1.1
248.	stern	2.41	2.56	3.48	2.82	2.41	3.8	0.3	0.3	0.1	1.2
249.	stingy	1.91	1.80	2.74	2.70	2.17	2.5	0.3	0.2	0.3	3.1
250.	stolid	2.46	2.70	3.03	3.15	2.62	2.5	1.1	0.7	0.2	1.3
251.	strong	3.84	3.67	3.95	3.62	3.59	2.5	2.4	2.4	1.9	1.6
252.	stubborn	2.70	2.21	3.43	2.37	2.08	2.2	0.5	0.2	1.1	3.3
253.	submissive	1.90	2.81	2.18	2.86	2.55	0.3	0.6	0.3	0.4	3.4
254.	suggestible	3.37	3.35	3.21	2.87	3.51	0.1	0.5	0.3	1.6	3.3
255.	sulky	1.84	2.07	2.52	1.81	2.33	1.2	0.0	0.0	0.7	3.7
256.	superstitious	2.73	2.58	2.63	2.40	2.55	1.3	0.6	0.0	1.7	3.3
257.	suspicious	2.34	2.07	2.87	1.93	2.37	2.8	0.3	0.1	1.1	3.3
258.	sympathetic	3.83	4.59	3.20	3.52	3.42	0.4	3.5	0.7	1.2	1.7
259.	tactful	3.71	4.07	4.09	3.58	3.38	0.7	2.7	1.7	0.5	1.9
260.	tactless	2.13	1.75	1.91	2.46	2.61	2.3	0.2	0.3	2.4	2.5
261.	talkative	4.58	3.57	3.32	3.12	3.70	2.0	1.9	1.3	2.5	2.7
262.	temperamental	2.84	2.34	2.65	1.69	2.83	1.4	0.4	0.0	1.7	3.3
263.	tense	2.11	2.30	3.11	1.69	2.24	2.0	0.3	0.1	0.3	3.6
264.	thankless	2.07	1.72	2.30	2.52	2.42	1.2	0.1	0.1	1.1	2.7
265.	thorough	3.50	3.62	4.74	3.33	3.34	2.4	2.0	3.6	0.5	1.6
266.	thoughtful	4.14	4.66	3.93	3.65	3.65	0.5	2.5	2.7	0.9	1.0
267.	thrifty	3.04	2.97	3.66	3.07	3.05	2.1	1.4	1.9	0.3	1.9
268.	timid	1.47	2.65	2.38	2.69	1.85	0.2	0.5	0.1	0.6	3.3
269.	tolerant	3.70	4.28	3.50	3.95	3.85	0.1	3.5	1.9	0.9	1.1

(*continued*)

TABLE D. (*Continued*)

	Five factor scores[a]					Ego state scores[b]				
Adjective	EXT	AGR	CON	EMS	OPN	CP	NP	A	FC	AC
270. touchy	2.39	2.33	2.65	1.71	2.37	2.1	0.1	0.0	0.9	3.5
271. tough	3.28	2.90	3.74	3.19	3.35	2.7	1.3	1.1	1.8	2.2
272. trusting	3.97	4.52	3.73	3.81	3.77	0.2	2.8	1.2	2.7	1.3
273. unaffected	2.63	2.55	2.98	3.96	3.00	0.9	0.8	1.5	2.1	1.0
274. unambitious	1.61	2.35	1.31	2.80	1.75	0.5	0.7	0.7	1.2	2.1
275. unassuming	2.61	2.99	2.55	3.50	2.85	0.3	1.1	1.7	1.9	1.7
276. unconventional	3.16	2.79	2.60	2.82	3.97	0.6	0.5	1.3	3.3	0.9
277. undependable	2.01	1.48	1.17	2.32	2.69	0.9	0.1	0.0	2.2	2.7
278. understanding	4.13	4.71	3.80	3.67	3.74	0.5	3.5	2.1	1.1	0.9
279. unemotional	1.72	1.94	2.91	4.20	2.42	0.9	0.3	3.6	0.1	1.0
280. unexcitable	1.49	2.19	2.64	3.94	1.76	1.1	1.2	3.5	0.0	0.9
281. unfriendly	1.27	1.38	2.45	3.57	2.18	2.8	0.3	0.9	0.2	2.7
282. uninhibited	3.55	3.04	2.76	3.27	4.04	0.5	0.7	1.3	3.9	0.4
283. unintelligent	2.13	2.34	1.54	3.12	2.45	1.1	0.4	0.0	0.3	1.9
284. unkind	1.61	1.30	2.41	2.57	2.38	3.1	0.0	0.3	0.5	2.2
285. unrealistic	2.56	2.45	1.87	2.37	3.18	1.9	0.9	0.0	2.2	2.7
286. unscrupulous	2.39	2.20	2.40	2.85	2.87	1.9	0.3	0.1	1.2	2.7
287. unselfish	3.65	4.31	3.27	3.65	3.55	0.6	3.5	1.1	1.3	0.9
288. unstable	2.21	2.15	1.69	1.48	2.99	1.3	0.1	0.0	1.9	2.4
289. vindictive	1.90	1.51	2.48	2.08	2.62	2.9	0.2	0.1	0.8	3.1
290. versatile	4.13	3.82	4.04	3.52	4.54	0.3	1.3	3.5	3.3	0.7
291. warm	4.56	4.51	3.38	3.83	3.57	0.4	3.8	0.6	2.9	0.9
292. wary	2.25	2.44	3.03	2.19	2.25	2.3	0.7	1.0	0.9	2.9
293. weak	1.75	2.47	1.99	2.43	2.17	0.7	0.1	0.1	0.5	2.9
294. whiny	1.73	1.73	2.13	1.88	2.01	0.5	0.1	0.0	1.1	3.7
295. wholesome	3.60	3.90	3.55	3.53	3.07	0.7	2.3	2.3	2.5	0.8
296. wise	3.45	3.89	4.40	3.47	3.73	1.4	2.5	3.3	1.1	0.5
297. withdrawn	1.36	2.19	2.46	2.07	1.84	0.5	0.1	0.1	0.7	3.3
298. witty	4.06	3.58	3.61	3.36	3.61	0.1	0.5	1.4	3.2	0.7
299. worrying	2.03	2.49	2.94	1.61	1.96	1.8	1.4	0.2	0.3	3.4
300. zany	4.20	3.18	2.87	3.24	4.00	0.2	0.1	0.3	3.4	1.0

[a]The five scores for each item are the mean ratings on a five-point scale, for Extraversion (EXT), Agreeableness (AGR), Conscientiousness (CON), Neuroticism (NEU), and Openness (OPN) from FormyDuval (1993). In analyses reported in this book the Neuroticism scores are reversed to obtain Emotional Stability (EMS) scores, i.e., EMS = 6 − NEU.
[b]The five scores for each item indicate its mean rating, on a 0 to 4 scale, for Critical Parent (CP), Nurturing Parent (NP), Adult (A), Free Child (FC), and Adapted Child (AC) from Williams (1978). In the ego state analyses reported in this book, the ego state scores for a given set of items are obtained by summing the points for each ego state and expressing this sum as a proportion of the total points accumulated across all five ego states.

REFERENCES

Allport, G. W. (1937). *Personality: A psychological interpretation*. New York: Holt.

Allport, G. W., & Odbert, H. S. (1936). Trait names: A psycho-lexical study. *Psychological Monographs, 47* (1, Whole No. 211).

Anderson, N. H. (1981). *Foundations of information integration theory.* New York: Academic Press.

Asch, S. E. (1946). Forming impressions of personality. *Journal of Abnormal and Social Psychology, 41,* 258–290.

Bartlett, F. C. (1932). *Remembering.* Cambridge: Cambridge University Press.

Baumeister, R. F., & Tice, D. M. (1988). Metatraits. *Journal of Personality, 56,* 571–598.

Berne, E. (1961). *Transactional analysis in psychotherapy.* New York: Grove Press.

Berne, E. (1966). *Principles of group treatment.* New York: Oxford University Press.

Berry, J. W. (1969). On cross-cultural comparability. *International Journal of Psychology, 4,* 119–128.

Berry, J. W. (1980). Introduction to methodology. In H. C. Triandis & J. W. Berry (Eds.), *Handbook of cross-cultural psychology* (Vol. 2, pp. 1–28). Boston: Allyn & Bacon.

Berry, J. W., Poortinga, Y. H., Segall, M., & Dasen, P. (1992). *Cross-cultural psychology: Research and applications.* Cambridge and New York: Cambridge University Press.

Berry, J. W., Poortinga, Y. H., & Pandey, J. (Eds.). (1997). *Handbook of cross-cultural psychology* (2nd ed., Vol. 2). Boston: Allyn & Bacon.

Best, D. L., & Williams, J. E. (1996). Anticipations of aging: A cross-cultural examination of young adults' views of growing old. In J. Pandey, D. Sinha, & D. P. S. Bhawuk (Eds.), *Asian contributions to cross-cultural psychology.* New Delhi: Sage.

Best, D. L., Williams, J. E., & Briggs, S. R. (1980). A further analysis of the affective meanings associated with male and female sex-trait stereotypes. *Sex Roles, 6,* 735–746.

Betancourt, H., & Weiner, B. (1982). Attributions for achievement-related events, expectancy, and sentiments: A study of success and failure in Chile and the United States. *Journal of Cross-Cultural Psychology, 13,* 362–374.

Bochner, S. (1994). Cross-cultural differences in the self concept: A test of Hofstede's individualism/collectivism distinction. *Journal of Cross-Cultural Psychology, 25,* 273–283.

Bond, M. H. (1983). Linking person perception dimension to behavioral intention dimension: The Chinese connection. *Journal of Personality and Social Psychology, 14,* 41–63.

182   REFERENCES

Bond, M. H., & Forgas, J. P. (1984). Linking person perception to behavioral intention across cultures: The role of cultural collectivism. *Journal of Cross-Cultural Psychology, 15,* 337–352.

Bond, M. H., Nakazato, H., & Shiraishi, D. (1975). Universality and distinctiveness in dimensions of Japanese person perception. *Journal of Cross-Cultural Psychology, 6*(3), 346–356.

Brislin, R. W. (1980). Translation and content analysis of oral and written materials. In H. C. Triandis & J. W. Berry (Eds.), *Handbook of cross-cultural psychology* (Vol. 2, pp. 389–444). Boston: Allyn & Bacon.

Brislin, R. W. (1983). Cross-cultural research in psychology. *Annual Review of Psychology, 34,* 363–400.

Brislin, R. W. (1993). *Understanding culture's influence on behavior.* Orlando, FL: Harcourt Brace Jovanovich.

Britt, T. W. (1993). Metatraits: Evidence relevant to the validity of the construct and its implications. *Journal of Personality and Social Psychology, 65,* 554–562.

Buss, D. M. (1989). Sex differences in human mate preferences: Evolutionary hypotheses tested in 37 cultures. *Behavioral and Brain Sciences, 12,* 1–49.

Campbell, D. T., & Stanley, J. C. (1966). *Experimental and quasi-experimental designs for research.* Chicago: Rand McNally.

Cattell, R. B. (1943). The description of personality: Basic traits resolved into clusters. *Journal of Abnormal and Social Psychology, 38,* 476–507.

Cattell, R. B. (1946). *Description and measurement of personality.* Yonkers-on-Hudson, NY: World Book Company.

Cattell, R. B. (1947). Confirmation and clarification of primary personality factors. *Psychometrika, 12,* 197–220.

Cattell, R. B. (1965). *The scientific analysis of personality.* Baltimore: Penguin Books.

Cattell, R. B., Eber, H. W., & Tatsuoka, M. M. (1970). *Handbook for the Sixteen Personality Factor Questionnaire.* Champaign, IL: Institute of Personality Ability Testing.

Cook, T. D., & Campbell, D. T. (1979). *Quasi-experimentation: Design and analysis issues for field settings.* Chicago: Rand McNally.

Costa, P. T., & McCrae, R. R. (1992). *The Revised NEO Personality Inventory manual.* Odessa, FL: Psychological Assessment Resources.

Daws, J. T. (1980). Adjective Check List descriptions of God and their relation to religious orientation. Master's thesis, Wake Forest University.

Diaz-Guerrero, R. (1992). La psicologia de la personalidad en el siglo XXI [The psychology of personality in the 21st century]. *Revista Interamericana de Psicologia, 26*(1), 37–52.

Diener, E., Diener, M., & Diener, C. (1995). Factors predicting the subjective well-being of nations. *Journal of Personality and Social Psychology, 69,* 851–864.

Ebbinghaus, H. (1908). *Abriss der Psychologie.* Leipzig: Veit.

Edwards, A. L. (1959). *Edwards Personal Preference Schedule manual.* New York: The Psychological Corporation.

Eysenck, H. J. (1947). *Dimensions of personality.* London: Routledge & Kegan Paul.

Eysenck, H. J. (1990). Biological dimensions of personality. In L. A. Pervin (Ed.), *Handbook of personality theory and research* (pp. 244–276). New York: Guilford.

Fiske, S. T. (1995). Social cognition. In A. Tesser (Ed.), *Advanced social psychology* (pp. 149–193). New York: McGraw-Hill.

FormyDuval, D. L. (1993). *Scaling the Adjective Check List for the Five-Factor Model of Personality.* Unpublished Master's thesis, Wake Forest University.

FormyDuval, D. L., Williams, J. E., Patterson, D. J., & Fogle, E. E. (1995). A "Big Five" scoring system for item pool of the Adjective Check List. *Journal of Personality Assessment, 65,* 59–76.

Franzoi, S. L. (1996). *Social psychology.* Dubuque, IA: Brown and Benchmark.

Gabrenya, W. K., Jr., Wang, Y., & Latané, B. (1985). Social loafing on an optimising task: Cross-cultural differences among Chinese and Americans. *Journal of Cross-Cultural Psychology, 16,* 223–242.

Goldberg, L. R. (1981). Language and individual differences: The search for universals in personality lexicons. In L. Wheeler (Ed.), *Review of personality and social psychology* (Vol. 2, pp. 141–165). Beverly Hills, CA: Sage.

Goodman, R. C., & Williams, J. E. (1996). *Social desirability: Favorability gradients in the Five Factor Model of personality.* Paper presented at the meeting of the Southeastern Psychological Association, Norfolk, VA.

Gough, H. G. (1987). *California Psychological Inventory administrator's guide.* Palo Alto, CA: Consulting Psychologists Press.

Gough, H. G., & Heilbrun, A. B., Jr. (1965). *Adjective Check List manual.* Palo Alto, CA: Consulting Psychologists Press.

Gough, H. G., & Heilbrun, A. B., Jr. (1980). *The Adjective Check List manual.* Palo Alto, CA: Consulting Psychologists Press.

Gudykunst, W. B. (1993). *Communication in Japan and the United States.* Albany: State University of New York Press.

Gudykunst, W. B., Gao, G., Schmidt, K. L., Nishida, T., Bond, M. H., Leung, K., Wang, G., & Barraclough, R. A. (1992). The influence of individualism-collectivism, self-monitoring, and predicted outcome value on communication in ingroup and outgroup relationships. *Journal of Cross-Cultural Psychology, 23,* 196–213.

Higgins, E. T., Rholes, W. S., & Jones, C. R. (1977). Category accessibility and impression formation. *Journal of Experimental Social Psychology, 13,* 141–154.

Hofstede, G. (1979). Value systems in forty countries: Interpretation, validation and consequences for theory. In L. Eckensberger, W. Lonner, & Y. H. Poortinga (Eds.), *Cross-cultural contributions to psychology* (pp. 389–407). Lisse, The Netherlands: Swets & Zeitlinger.

Hofstede, G. (1980). *Culture's consequences: International differences in work-related values.* Beverly Hills, CA: Sage.

Ibrahim, F. A., & Kahn, H. (1987). Assessments of world views. *Psychological Reports, 60,* 163–176.

Isaka, H. (1990). Factor analyses of trait names in everyday Japanese language. *Personality and Individual Differences, 11,* 115–124.

John, O. P. (1989). Towards a taxonomy of personality descriptors. In D. M. Buss & N. Cantor (Eds.), *Personality psychology: Recent trends and emerging directions* (pp. 261–271). New York: Springer-Verlag.

John, O. P., Goldberg, L. R., & Angleitner, A. (1984). Better than the alphabet: Taxonomies of personality-descriptive terms in English, Dutch, and German. In H. Bonarius, G. van Heck, N. Smid (Eds.), *Personality psychology in Europe: Theoretical and empirical developments.* Berwyn, PA: Swets North America.

John, O. P., Angleitner, A., & Ostendorf, F. (1988). The lexical approach to personality: A history review of trait taxonomic research. *European Journal of Personality, 2,* 171–203.

John, O. P., Hampson, S. E., & Goldberg, L. R. (1991). The basic level in personality trait hierarchies: Studies in trait use and accessibility. *Journal of Personality and Social Psychology, 60,* 348–361.

Kelly, G. A. (1955). *The psychology of personal constructs.* New York: Norton.

Kim, U., Triandis, H. C., Kagitcibasi, C., Choi, S. C., & Yoon, G. (Eds.). (1994). *Individualism and collectivism: Theory, method, and applications.* Newbury Park, CA: Sage.

Kluckhohn, F. R. (1968). Variations in value orientations as a factor in educational planning. In E. M. Bower & W. G. Hallister (Eds.), *Behavioral science frontiers in education*. Evanston, IL: Row and Peterson.

Kurian, G. T. (1993). *The new book of world rankings*. New York: Facts on File.

Latané, B., Williams, K., & Harkins, S. (1979). Many hands make light the work: The causes and consequences of social loafing. *Journal of Personality and Social Psychology, 37*, 322–332.

Lonner, W. J., & Berry, J. W. (1986). Sampling and surveying. In W. J. Lonner & J. W. Berry (Eds.), *Field methods in cross-cultural research* (pp. 85–110). Beverly Hills, CA: Sage.

Lonner, W. J., & Malpass, R. S. (1994). *Psychology and culture*. Needham Heights, MA: Allyn and Bacon.

Malpass, R. S., & Poortinga, Y. H. (1986). Strategies for design and analysis. In W. J. Lonner & J. W. Berry (Eds.), *Field methods in cross-cultural research* (pp. 47–86). Beverly Hills, CA: Sage.

Markus, H., & Kitayama, S. (1991). Culture and the self: Implications for cognition, emotion, and motivation. *Psychological Review, 90*, 224–253.

Matsumoto, D. (1996). *Culture and psychology*. New York: Brooks Cole.

McCrae, R. R., & Costa, P. T. (1987). Validation of the Five-Factor Model of Personality across instruments and observers. *Journal of Personality and Social Psychology, 52*(1), 81–90.

McCrae, R. R., & Costa, P. T. (1989). The structure of interpersonal traits: Wiggins' circumplex and the five-factor model. *Journal of Personality and Social Psychology, 56*, 586–595.

McCrae, R. R., & Costa, P. T. (1990). *Personality in adulthood*. New York: Guilford Press.

McCrae, R. R., & Costa, P. T. (1997). Personality trait structure as a human universal. *American Psychologist, 52*, 509–516.

McCrae, R. R., Costa, P. T., & Piedmont, R. L. (1993). Folk concepts, natural language, and psychological constructs: The California Psychological Inventory and the Five-Factor Model. *Journal of Personality, 61*, 1–26.

Moghaddam, F. M. (1998). *Social psychology: Exploring universals across cultures*. New York: W. H. Freeman.

Moghaddam, F. M., Taylor, D. M., & Wright, S. C. (1993). *Social psychology in cross-cultural perspective*. New York: W. H. Freeman.

Munroe, R. L., & Munroe, R. H. (1980). Perspectives suggested by anthropological data. In H. C. Triandis & W. W. Lambert (Eds.), *Handbook of cross-cultural psychology* (Vol. 1, pp. 253–318). Boston: Allyn & Bacon.

Murray, H. A. (1938). *Explorations in personality*. New York: Oxford University Press.

Myers, D. G. (1996). *Social psychology*. New York: McGraw-Hill.

Norman, W. T. (1963). Toward an adequate taxonomy of personality attributes: Replicated factor structure in peer nomination personality ratings. *Journal of Abnormal and Social Psychology, 66*(6), 574–583.

Oerter, R., Oerter, R., Agostiani, H., Kim, H., & Wibowo, S. (1996). The concept of human nature in East Asia: Etic and emic characteristics. *Culture and Psychology, 2*, 9–51.

Osgood, C. E., May, W. H., & Miron, M. S. (1975). *Cross-cultural universals of affective meaning*. Urbana: University of Illinois Press.

Osgood, C. E., Suci, G. J., & Tannenbaum, P. H. (1957). *The measurement of meaning*. Urbana: University of Illinois.

Paunonen, S. V., Jackson, D. N., Trzebinski, J., & Forsterling, F. (1992). Personality structure across cultures: A multimethod evaluation. *Journal of Personality and Social Psychology, 62*(3), 447–456.

Piedmont, R. L., McCrae, R. R., & Costa, P. T. (1991). Adjective Check List scales and the Five-Factor Model. *Journal of Personality and Social Psychology, 60*(4), 630–637.

Poortinga, Y. H. (1992). Towards a conceptualization of culture for psychology. In S. Iwawaki, Y. Kashima, & K. Leung (Eds.), *Innovations in cross-cultural psychology.* Amsterdam: Swets and Zeitlinger.

Rivers, W. H. R. (1905). Observations on the senses of the Todas. *British Journal of Psychology, 1,* 321–396.

Saiz, J. L., Mella, C., Vargas, G., & Velasquez, M. E. (1994). Representaciones sociales de Dios [Social representations of God]. *Persona y Sociedad, 8*(4), 123–133.

Saiz, J. L., & Williams, J. E. (1992). Estereotipos del indigena mapuche: Una verificacion empirica de proposiciones y hallazgos previos [Stereotypes of Mapuche Indians: An empirical verification of propositions and previous findings]. In Y. Kumarochi & P. de la Pena (Eds.), *Sobre culturas indigenas: Lenguaje e identidad.* Temuco, Chile: Conicyt, Universidad Catolica de Temuco, y Universidad de La Frontera.

Satterwhite, R. C., Fogle, E. E., & Williams, J. E. (in press). Revisiting the stability of variability: Traitedness and supertraitedness on the ACL and NEO-FFI. *Social Behavior and Personality.*

Schwartz, S. H. (1990). Individualism-collectivism: Critique and proposed refinements. *Journal of Cross-Cultural Psychology, 21,* 139–157.

Schwartz, S. H. (1992). Universals in the content and structure of values: Theoretical advances and empirical tests in 20 countries. In M. P. Zanna (Ed.), *Advances in Experimental Social Psychology,* (Vol. 25, pp. 1–65). New York: Academic Press.

Schwartz, S. H. (1994). Beyond individualism/collectivism: New cultural dimensions of values. In U. Kim, H. C. Triandis, C. Kagitcibasi, S. Choi, & G. Yoon (Eds.), *Individualism and collectivism: Theory, method, and applications.* Thousand Oaks, CA: Sage.

Schwartz, S. H., & Bilsky, W. (1987). Toward a psychological structure of human values. *Journal of Personality and Social Psychology, 53,* 550–562.

Schwartz, S. H., & Bilsky, W. (1990). Toward a theory of the universal content and structure of values: Extensions and cross-cultural replications. *Journal of Personality and Social Psychology, 58,* 878–891.

Schwartz, S. H., & Roa, M. (1995). Values in the West: A theoretical and empirical challenge to the individualism-collectivism cultural dimension. *World Psychology, 1,* 91–122.

Segall, M. H. (1986). Culture and behavior: Psychology in global perspective. *Annual Review of Psychology, 37,* 523–564.

Segall, M. H., Dasen, D. R., Berry, J. W., & Poortinga, Y. H. (1990). *Human behavior in global perspective: An introduction to cross-cultural psychology.* Elmsford, NY: Pergamon.

Shirikasi, S. (1985). Social loafing of Japanese students. *Hiroshima Forum for Psychology, 10,* 35–40.

Sivard, R. L. (1993). *World military and social expenses.* Washington, DC: World Priorities.

Smith, P. B., & Bond, M. H. (1994). *Social psychology across cultures.* Needham Heights, MA: Allyn and Bacon.

Sodowsky, G. R., Maguire, K., Johnson, P., Ngumba, W., & Kohles, R. (1994). World views of white American, mainland Chinese, Taiwanese, and African students. *Journal of Cross-Cultural Psychology, 25,* 309–324.

Thomas, A. (1993). *Kulturvergleichende Psychologie: Eine Einfuhrung* [Cultural psychology: An introduction]. Gottingen, Bern, Toronto, Seattle: Hogrefe.

Triandis, H. C. (1994). *Culture and social behavior.* New York: McGraw-Hill.

Triandis, H. C. (1995). *Individualism and collectivism.* San Francisco: Westview Press.

Triandis, H. C., & Berry, J. W. (Eds.). (1980). *Handbook of cross-cultural psychology.* Boston: Allyn & Bacon.

186

REFERENCES

Triandis, H. C., Marin, G., Lisansky, J., & Betancourt, H. (1984). Simpatia as a cultural script of Hispanics. *Journal of Personality and Social Psychology, 47*, 1363–1375.

Triandis, H. C., Bontempo, R., Leung, K., & Hui, C. H. (1990). A method for determining cultural, demographic, and personal constructs. *Journal of Cross-Cultural Psychology, 21*, 302–318.

Tupes, E. C., & Christal, R. E. (1961). Recurrent personality factors based on trait ratings. *USAF ASD Tech. Rep.*, No. 61–97. (Reprinted, 1992).

Weiner, B. (1985). An attributional theory of achievement motivation and emotion. *Psychological Review, 92*, 548–573.

Whiting, B. (1976). The problem of the packaged variable. In K. F. Riegel & J. A. Meacham (Eds.), *The developing individual in a changing world*. The Hague, The Netherlands: Mouton.

Williams, J. E. (1993). Young adults' view of aging: A 19 nation study. In M. I. Winkler (Ed.), *Documentos: Conferencias del XXIV Congreso Interamericano de Psicologia* (pp. 101–123). Santiago, Chile: Sociedad Interamericana de Psicologia.

Williams, J. E., & Best, D. L. (1977). Sex stereotypes and trait favorability on the Adjective Check List. *Educational and Psychological Measurement, 37*, 101–110.

Williams, J. E., & Best, D. L. (1983). The Gough-Heilbrun Adjective Check List as a cross-cultural research tool. In J. B. Deregowski, S. Dziurawiec, & R. C. Annis (Eds.), *Expiscations in cross-cultural psychology*. Lisse, Netherlands: Swets & Zeitlinger.

Williams, J. E., & Best, D. L. (1990a). *Measuring sex stereotypes: A multination study* (revised ed.). Beverly Hills, CA: Sage Publications.

Williams, J. E., & Best, D. L. (1990b). *Sex and psyche: Gender and self-concepts viewed cross-culturally*. Newbury Park, CA: Sage Publications.

Williams, J. E., Munick, M. L., Saiz, J. L., & FormyDuval, D. L. (1995). Psychological importance of the "Big Five": Impression formation and context effects. *Personality and Social Psychology Bulletin, 21*, 818–826.

Williams, J. E., Saiz, J. L., FormyDuval, D. L., Munick, M. L., Fogle, E. E., Adom, A., Haque, A., Neto, F., & Yu, J. (1995). Cross-cultural variation in the importance of psychological characteristics: A seven-country study. *International Journal of Personality, 30*, 529–550.

Williams, K. B. (1978). *An empirical procedure for the assessment of ego states illustrated by ego-grams as described in Transactional Analysis theory*. Unpublished doctoral dissertation, Fielding Institute, Santa Barbara, California.

Williams, K. B., & Williams, J. E. (1980). The assessment of Transactional Analysis ego states via the Adjective Check List. *Journal of Personality Assessment, 40*(2), 120–129.

Woolams, S., & Brown, M. (1978). *Transactional analysis*. Dexter, MI: Huron Valley Press.

Worchel, S., & Cooper, J. (1983). *Understanding social psychology*, 3rd ed. Homewood, IL: The Dorsey Press.

Yamaguchi, S., Kuhlman, D. M., & Sugimori, S. (1995). Personality correlates of allocentric tendencies in individualist and collectivist cultures. *Journal of Cross-Cultural Psychology, 26*, 658–672.

Yamaguchi, S., Okamoto, K., & Oka, T. (1985). Effects of coactor's presence: Social loafing and social facilitation. *Japanese Psychological Research, 27*, 215–222.

AUTHOR INDEX

187

SUBJECT INDEX